MW00388677

Landscaping for Wildlife

Landscaping
for *Wildlife*

A GUIDE TO THE
SOUTHERN GREAT PLAINS

Jeremy D. Garrett

ILLUSTRATED BY
Coral McCallister

University of Oklahoma Press
NORMAN

This book is published with the generous assistance of The Kerr Foundation, Inc.

LIBRARY OF CONGRESS CATALOGING-IN-PUBLICATION DATA

Garrett, Jeremy D., 1970–
  Landscaping for wildlife : a guide to the southern Great Plains / Jeremy D. Garrett ;
illustrated by Coral McCallister.
      p.   cm.
    ISBN 0–8061–3489–5 (pbk.)
    1. Gardening to attract wildlife—Great Plains. 2. Gardening to attract wildlife.
  I. Title.

QL59 .G377 2003
639.9'2'0978—dc21   2002026700

The paper in this book meets the guidelines for permanence and durability of the Committee on Production Guidelines for Book Longevity of the Council on Library Resources. ♾

Copyright © 2003 by the University of Oklahoma Press, Norman, Publishing Division of the University. All rights reserved. Manufactured in China.
                    1   2   3   4   5   6   7   8   9   10

Contents

Landscaping for Wildlife

Introduction

There is nothing in which the birds differ more from man than the way in which they can build and yet leave a landscape as it was before.

ROBERT LYND

People want to attract wildlife to their yards for a variety of reasons, but probably foremost among these is that birds and other animals bring us pleasure. The exuberant songs of cardinals and mockingbirds, the playful antics of young squirrels at feeders, and the sight of colorful butterflies dancing above wildflower patches provide us with both daily and lasting joy.

To be sure, some wildlife can assist humans by controlling insects, rodents, and other pests. Birds in particular give us flashes of natural beauty, such as when a painted bunting or cardinal is washing itself at a birdbath. But probably even more important to us is our growing need and desire to live close to the natural world—we need to experience the complex diversity of nature firsthand. What parent hasn't pointed out the first robin of spring to a child or explained the crazed antics of a chipmunk busily stuffing its cheek pouches full of seeds?

In an increasingly urbanized environment, where bulldozers and backhoes eliminate the living spaces of many wild creatures, it becomes especially critical to preserve native wildlife and plants in our cities and suburbs. We need to maintain that essential bond between people and nature to remember the sense of stewardship we once had for the land beyond city limits. Unfortunately, with more than 75 percent of the nation's population now living in urban areas, the fastest growing habitat is concrete and asphalt.

It is simple to attract wildlife to your yard if you provide four basic requirements: food, water, cover, and space. Plants play an important role in providing these requirements because a well-planned landscape can create the habitat that wild creatures need to eat, rest, raise young, and find protection. A diverse landscape with many plant species supports an abundance of wildlife. Many more wildlife species will visit a small or average-sized yard with high habitat diversity than will visit a yard with a large expanse of manicured lawn.

Moreover, managing yards for wildlife benefits humans in a multitude of ways. Diverse landscapes are less vulnerable to insect and rodent pests. By encouraging insect-eating predators, you can cut down costs associated with insecticide use and extermination services. Yards offering a wide range of plant species have fewer disease problems and need little maintenance because less lawn is set aside to be mown and watered. Native plants are a big plus to a yard because they are already suited to the local climate and need little attention. Also, adding plants to an area will help control erosion and stabilize the environment while providing food and shelter for the wildlife that visit. This process of landscaping with the habitat needs of wildlife in mind is called *wildscaping.*

The National Wildlife Federation found that landscaping with wildlife considerations increased home and property values. The real estate value of your home could increase as much as 10 percent if you add only $200 in plants to your property. According to a recent survey of realtors in 10 states, more than half of the respondents thought that wildscaped homes had a positive impact on potential buyers' impressions of both the home and the neighborhood. Eighty-four percent felt that a wildscaped home would be as much as 20 percent more salable than a home that wasn't landscaped for wildlife needs.

A small investment also can result in energy savings. Conifers planted on the north and west sides of your home can block winter winds and prevent snow accumulation, which can reduce your heating bills. Hardwoods planted on the south and west sides of your house can reduce your cooling bills by providing summer shade. These arrangements not only lower your energy costs but also provide year-round habitat for wildlife.

FIGURE I-1. Oklahoma City skyline. Native wildlife and plants in our cities and suburbs will help retain a bond to the sense of stewardship we once had for the land beyond the city limits.

As the human population increases, more green space is consumed for our needs, squeezing wildlife out of the habitat they need for survival. This situation creates an even greater need to manage land for wildlife not only in existing forests and large private holdings but also in developed areas—in our cities and suburbs. A quarter-acre suburban lot, a five-acre townhouse development, the small city park, and even our highway roadsides can all be managed with wildlife in mind. If we begin with the simple yet pleasant task of bringing wildlife closer to home, we will set a precedent to manage for wildlife on a larger scale. No matter where you live, you can make habitat improvements that will benefit your wildlife neighbors.

This book is intended to be applicable to the southern Great Plains states, with emphasis on Oklahoma. Property owners in Arkansas, Colorado, Kansas, Louisiana, Missouri, Nebraska, New Mexico, and Texas also should benefit from the concepts, recommended plantings, and common backyard wildlife discussed in this guide. For a list of the particular wildlife and plant species in your state, contact the state sources listed in appendix I.

Natural Communities

Urban and rural landowners alike should have some knowledge of the natural community in which their properties occur. For the urban property owner planning a wildscape, learning about the plants and wildlife that naturally occur in the surrounding area will help determine realistically the wildlife species that might visit the wildscape. Although wildscaping is aimed primarily at enhancing areas within towns and cities for wildlife, rural landowners can apply similar concepts to their homes and acreages. In general, it is always best to imitate the local habitat in any planting regime, simply because those plants are already adapted to local rainfall and temperature conditions. Likewise, native plants will best suit the habitat needs of the local wildlife.

Managing natural communities is complex because the species and community structure differ greatly from east to west. By managing natural communities that characterize their region, landowners will help retain their distinctive local features and species. Though on a smaller scale, the urban backyard can help retain the character of the surrounding natural area and can serve as a way to inspire and share with neighbors, family, and friends.

Diverse natural communities provide a number of benefits for the landowner. Diverse natural grasslands provide more reliable forage for livestock and wildlife than do improved pastures, especially during drought conditions. Natural communities also provide opportunities for a wide range of outdoor recreation, such as wildlife watching, hiking, hunting, and fishing. Finally, by managing our diverse natural communities, we will ensure that future generations can enjoy the wildlife and plants—such as "horny toads" and Indian blanket—that make our region unique.

All natural communities are vital to maintaining a wealth of living resources, and the integrity of each area should be addressed. Therefore, land managers should concentrate on the landscape that defines their locale rather than attempting to establish communities that normally do not occur there. For example, establishing woodlots in areas normally dominated by prairies has caused significant impacts to prairie communities and has threatened some wildlife and plant species. Similarly, establishing pine trees in an urban lot that is located in a prairie community would have little if any habitat value for the wildlife that are dependent on prairie plantings and that would have no interest in pine seeds. The natural communities of the southern Great Plains define a transition from extensive forests in the east to prairies that are progressively shorter in the west (fig. I-2). As you move west, forests gradually become more open and are eventually restricted to narrow fingers extending westward along streams and ravines.

In any management scheme, special features should be identified and should receive individual attention. Wetlands, caves, springs, rock outcrops, hibernation areas, and prairie dog towns are examples of special or sensitive habitat types. Landowners can obtain information from their state wildlife agency, county extension office, and Conservation District office on how to manage these areas to maintain their species and ecological functions.

Fire, grazing, and floods are important in maintaining many of our natural communities. Fire is especially important for preventing red cedar invasion into prairies (fig. I-3). Although some landowners are unable to use these tools, alternate methods are available. Rotational cattle grazing can simulate the effects of grazing bison herds, while low mowing or light discing can mimic fire and grazing impacts. Whether fire, grazing, or substitute practices are used, landowners should conduct

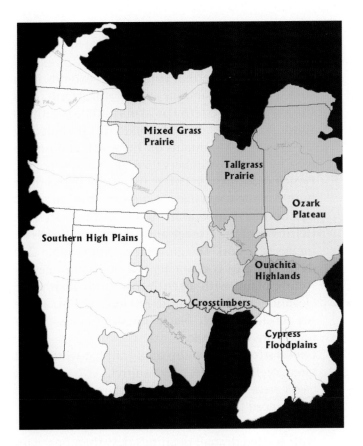

FIGURE I-2. Map showing transition from forests to prairies across the southern Great Plains.

FIGURE I-3. Fire prevents red cedar invasion of the prairie.

disturbances on a rotational basis. The resulting mosaic will satisfy the needs of the full spectrum of species inhabiting the ecoregion.

Landowners with large-scale farming operations should consider protecting any ground-nesting birds that use their property. Many species of birds, including killdeer, common nighthawk, mountain plover and horned lark, will actually nest on tilled ground. In addition, meadowlarks, quail, turkey, and lark and grasshopper sparrows build nests both in fallow fields with grasses and weeds and in hay meadows.

To avoid killing the adults and young, delay mowing or plowing these areas until after July 15, when the young are able to leave the nest. To allow ground-nesting birds the best chance of escaping from the nest, provide some warning by mowing or plowing from the center of the field outward to the edge. Don't mow or plow these fields in early morning or late at night—and definitely not during the night—or you will lose both adult birds and young.

The following descriptions provide very generalized views of seven dominant natural communities in various parts of the southern Great Plains. The recommendations are general and should be tailored to meet the goals of the landowner and the needs of special features. The descriptions were adapted from a map based on "Ecoregions of the Conterminous United States" by J. M. Omernick (1987) and from *Oklahoma's Biodiversity Plan* published by the Oklahoma Department of Wildlife Conservation (1996). For urban landowners, wildscaping will be serving the needs of the wildlife of the surrounding natural community and should therefore focus on the local components. Though small, the wildscape will have conservation value.

CYPRESS FLOODPLAINS

DESCRIPTION: Moist upland forests are dominated by sweetgum, black gum, American holly, and various oaks; vines such as grape, poison ivy, and greenbriar often reach into upper levels of the canopy. Swampy areas with bald cypress, willow oak, water oak, and white oak occur in low-lying depressions and along rivers and streams. Drier upland sites are dominated by scattered bluejack oak with very open understories, while blueberry bushes form a thick, low ground cover in concert with a variety of wildflowers. Tallgrass prairie communities occur in scattered openings, where you'll find big and little bluestem, Indian grass, and a host of wildflowers. Larger wetlands are dominated by water lily, lotus, rush, and cattail.

DISTRIBUTION: This natural community extends from southeastern Oklahoma and northeastern Texas through northwestern Louisiana and the southern third of Arkansas. In Oklahoma, it is bounded by the Ouachita Mountains on the north and on the west by the Crosstimbers natural community.

PHYSICAL CHARACTERISTICS: This is the warmest and most humid of the seven natural communities. The average annual temperature is 66° Fahrenheit (18° Celsius) and the average annual precipitation is 45 inches (115 cm). The growing season is about 240 days. The area is characterized by level to gently rolling plains with a gentle dip to the southeast; elevation averages around 400 feet (122 m) above sea level. The rich black limestone soils in the region are very fertile.

COMMON SPECIES: Yellow-throated warbler, white-eyed vireo, orchard oriole, gray squirrel.

UNIQUE SPECIES: Pygmy sunfish, Swainson's warbler, bird-voiced treefrog, alligator.

MANAGEMENT: Maintain large tracts of mature forest with scattered small openings (less than one acre) to provide multiple successional stages.

OUACHITA HIGHLANDS

DESCRIPTION: Southern slopes of the Ouachita Mountains support savannas of shortleaf pine with an open understory of grassland species. North-facing slopes often support a moist forest dominated by hickory, maples, sweetgum, and white, northern red, and chinquapin oaks. Tall bottomland forests dominated by water and willow oaks, hickory, sweetgum, black gum, and basswood occur along streams and other bodies of water in the Ouachitas, with an understory consisting of flowering dogwood, ironwood, beech, spicebush, and buttonbush. Within the broad valley that occurs to the south of the Ouachita Mountains, dry forests of post oak, blackjack oak, and scattered hickory with a significant cover of tallgrass prairie dominate the rugged areas and extend west toward the plains. Lush forests of oaks, elms, and hackberries occur along streams and rivers that drain into the

FIGURE I-4. The Cypress Floodplains natural community extends from southeastern Oklahoma and northeastern Texas through northwestern Louisiana and the southern third of Arkansas.

valley, usually with an understory of trees and dense mats of leaves and other litter. Grape, poison ivy, and greenbriar vines are common.

DISTRIBUTION: This natural community ranges from eastern Oklahoma to central Arkansas. Its broad valley and mountain range separate the rugged Ozark Plateau to the north from the Cypress Floodplains to the south. The Crosstimbers natural community forms the western border.

PHYSICAL CHARACTERISTICS: This region's climate is mild and receives the most precipitation. The average temperature is about 63° Fahrenheit (17° Celsius) and yearly rainfall averages 47 inches (119 cm). The growing season is about 216 days. Sandstone ridges separated by broad valleys dominate the mountainous region, while flat lowlands with poor natural drainage characterize the valley formed by the Arkansas and Canadian rivers.

COMMON SPECIES: Smallmouth bass, pine warbler, Kentucky warbler, summer tanager, chipmunk, gray squirrel, lowbush blueberry, beautyberry.

UNIQUE SPECIES: Mussels, darters, Rich Mountain salamander, red-cockaded woodpecker, brown-headed nuthatch, Bachman's sparrow, black bear, Ouachita goldenrod.

MANAGEMENT: Maintain large tracts of mature forest with scattered small openings (less than one acre) to provide multiple successional stages.

OZARK PLATEAU

DESCRIPTION: A relatively open canopy of blackjack oak, post oak, white oak, black hickory, and winged elm occurs on well-drained soils of slopes, hills, and plains, with coralberry, huckleberry, and sassafras representative of the understory. In riparian areas, a closed canopy of sugar maple, white oaks, chinquapin oak, and hickory tower over redbud, flowering dogwood, pawpaw, spicebush, sassafras, coralberry and shade-tolerant floor plants (mayapple, dogtooth violet, bloodroot, mosses, ferns, and liverworts). Bottomland hardwood forests have tall overstories of oaks, sycamore, cottonwood, and elms, with a forest floor often covered with gravel, sand, or a thick layer of humus and grasses.

DISTRIBUTION: The Ozark Plateau extends from northeastern Oklahoma through southern Missouri and into the northern third of Arkansas. The Tallgrass Prairie natural community forms the western boundary, while the Ouachita Highlands border

FIGURE I-5. The Ouachita Highlands natural community runs from eastern Oklahoma to central Arkansas.

FAMILY ACTIVITIES

Make bark and leaf rubbings

Children can make a permanent record of the tree species on their property by making rubbings with old crayons and plain white paper. Hold the paper over the tree bark and rub with the long side of the crayon, causing the bark texture to come through on the paper.

Use leaves you pick up from the ground rather than ones you pluck from a tree. Sandwich the leaf or leaflets between two pieces of paper before rubbing the crayon over the top piece.

For older children, show them how to make leaf paintings. Put a leaf on a clean piece of newspaper. Carefully paint over the leaf with acrylic paint. Next, set a clean piece of paper over the top of the painted leaf and press firmly, beginning at the center. This procedure transfers the paint from the leaf to the new piece of paper. Gently pick up the top paper to see the imprint. Rubbings and leaf paintings can be made into unique stationery or wrapping paper.

the Ozark Plateau on the south.

PHYSICAL CHARACTERISTICS: The average annual temperature is 60° Fahrenheit (16° Celsius) and annual rainfall averages 42 inches (107 cm). The growing season averages 209 days. The topography consists of rugged hills and low mountains, sloping toward the southwest. Soils are fertile but quite stony. Extensive underground drainage results in a large number of springs.

COMMON SPECIES: Smallmouth bass, red-eyed vireo, indigo bunting, scarlet tanager, whip-poor-will, chipmunk, gray squirrel, flowering dogwood, bird's-foot violet, mayapple.

UNIQUE SPECIES: Ozark big-eared bat, Ozark cavefish, cave crayfish, grotto salamander, Oklahoma salamander, Ozark spiderwort.

MANAGEMENT: Maintain large tracts of mature forest with scattered small openings (less than one acre) to provide multiple successional stages.

CROSSTIMBERS

DESCRIPTION: In level portions of the region, prairie communities cover most of the landscape, with woodlands occurring on some slopes, in draws, and along riparian areas. Open upland forests of post oak, blackjack oak, and hickory have rounded canopies that extend to the ground and provide shrub cover for wildlife. Grasslands in this region are primarily tallgrass prairies composed of bluestems, Indian grass, and switchgrass in deep, moist soils. Hackberry, river birch, willows, and cottonwood are common along streams in this ecore-

FIGURE I-6. The Ozark Plateau natural community extends from northeastern Oklahoma through southern Missouri and into the northern third of Arkansas.

gion, as are sedges and rushes. A few scattered sandstone caves support sporadic populations of bats during summer months.

DISTRIBUTION: The Crosstimbers begin in north-central Oklahoma and extend into central Texas, with the portion in Oklahoma becoming wider in the southern half. The Mixed Grass Prairie natural community forms the entire western border, the Tallgrass Prairie surrounds the northern edge, and the east is bordered by the Ouachita Highlands and Cypress Floodplains.

PHYSICAL CHARACTERISTICS: The average annual temperature

FIGURE I-7. The Crosstimbers natural community reaches from north-central Oklahoma into central Texas.

is 61° Fahrenheit (16° Celsius) and rainfall averages 40 inches (102 cm). The growing season is about 220 days but varies from north to south. This region's elevation slopes from 1,200 feet (366 m) in the northwestern portion to 600 feet (183 m) in the southern half. Topography is rolling or rough with pronounced hills and escarpments, and soils are deep and fertile. In general, this region's rivers and their tributaries are sluggish, muddy, and braided, divided into several channels by sandbars.

COMMON SPECIES: Redbud, sumac, bigflower coreopsis, Maximilian sunflower, American plum, pokeberry, five-lined skink, painted bunting, scissor-tailed fly-catcher, eastern bluebird, Bewick's wren, fox squirrel, largemouth bass.

UNIQUE SPECIES: Oklahoma penstemon, black-capped vireo.

MANAGEMENT: Burn uplands every three to five years to restore or maintain an open savanna community of scattered trees with shrubs and grasses on the ground. Some tree thinning may be necessary to open the canopy. Allow riparian areas to develop into rich, multilayered forests.

TALLGRASS PRAIRIE

DESCRIPTION: Tall grasses up to 8 feet (2.5 m) in height dominate the prairie plant community, growing in distinct bunches. Bluestems, Indian grass, and switchgrass are the primary grass species, joined by

sunflowers, Indian blanket, blazing star, and other wildflowers. Grasslands are relatively free of shrubs except at borders with woodlands or clumps of persimmon trees in drainages. Dry upland forests occur in draws and ravines and are dominated by post oak, blackjack oak, and black hickory. Broad floodplains support forests of elms, oaks, hackberry, cottonwood, and sycamore. In poorly drained sites, sedges and buttonbush form thickets, while willows occur along edges of floodplain wetlands.

DISTRIBUTION: This region occurs in northeastern Oklahoma and extends into Kansas, Missouri, and Iowa. The Ozark Plateau forms the eastern border, the Ouachita Highlands border it to the south, and the Crosstimbers form the western border.

PHYSICAL CHARACTERISTICS: The average annual temperature is 60° Fahrenheit (16° Celsius) and average rainfall is

FIGURE I-8. The Tallgrass Prairie natural community extends from northeastern Oklahoma into Kansas, Missouri, and Iowa.

40 inches (102 cm). The growing season is approximately 209 days. Low rolling hills dominate the landscape. Soils are relatively deep and fertile except on limestone outcrops. The Arkansas, Grand, and Verdigris rivers drain the region. Tributaries are sluggish and vary from muddy streams that form broad floodplains to clear streams that flow through narrow floodplains.

COMMON SPECIES: Big bluestem, Indian grass, switchgrass, purple coneflower, butterfly milkweed, compass plant, leadplant, largeflower penstemon, green sunfish, field sparrow, eastern kingbird, dickcissel.

UNIQUE SPECIES: Regal fritillary butterfly, prairie skink,

FIGURE I-9. The Mixed Grass Prairie natural community extends from Nebraska to central Texas, including the western half of Oklahoma.

upland sandpiper, greater prairie chicken, Henslow's sparrow.

MANAGEMENT: Burns are highly recommended for grassland areas. Burn uplands in a rotational pattern about every three to five years to maintain a variety of vegetation conditions ranging from old grasses and scattered shrubs to seedling growth. Before burning, however, first determine whether you have a high percentage of invasive woody species (i.e., red cedar, salt cedar, and Siberian elm). If you do not, wait at least another year before burning; otherwise, you may instead open up the area to these invasive species once you conduct the burn.

MIXED GRASS PRAIRIE

DESCRIPTION: Grasslands cover most of this region, with woodlands scattered in ravines and along streams. Fingers of the Crosstimbers natural community reach into the prairie from the east and form a heavily dissected eastern boundary, while mesquite and shinnery oak woodlands extend from the west. Dominated by little bluestem, the Mixed Grass Prairie region is a transition zone from tall grasses in the east to short grasses (such as buffalo grass and grama grass) in the west and consists of mixtures of species from both communities. Forests occurring along rivers and streams are dominated by cottonwood and willows. Sandy areas support plum and sumac thickets.

DISTRIBUTION: This region extends from Nebraska to

FIGURE I-10. Rotational burning and grazing will provide a mosaic of disturbed and undisturbed areas in a healthy prairie.

central Texas, passing through the western half of Oklahoma. The Tallgrass Prairie and Crosstimbers communities share the eastern border and the Southern High Plains form the western border.

PHYSICAL CHARACTERISTICS: Average temperature is 60° Fahrenheit (16° Celsius) and average rainfall is 27 inches (69 cm). The growing season is about 213 days. Rolling hills and plains are characteristic landforms, sloping from west to southeast. Caves are common in gypsum hills. Soils usually are deep and fertile except on stone outcrops. Rivers and tributaries are sluggish and muddy.

COMMON SPECIES: Sideoats grama, little bluestem, sand dropseed, Engelmann's daisy, pitcher sage, dotted blazing star, Great Plains toad, collared lizard, grasshopper sparrow, lark sparrow, dickcissel, Ord's kangaroo rat.

UNIQUE SPECIES: Texas horned lizard, grasshopper mouse, Red River pupfish, Arkansas shiner.

MANAGEMENT: Manage for large prairie tracts of native plant species with scattered trees along streams and some slopes. Western parts of this region should contain fewer trees than eastern sites. Burning every three to five years and rotational grazing are excellent tools for maintaining healthy prairies. Remember, burn a grassland area only if you develop a high percentage of invasive woody species. Otherwise, you will instead open up the area to these invasive species once you conduct a burn. Rotational burning and grazing should be managed to provide a mosaic of disturbed and undisturbed areas so that all stages are present (fig.

I-10). Riparian areas may be burned in alternate cycles to maintain an open riparian habitat with few scattered trees.

SOUTHERN HIGH PLAINS

DESCRIPTION: Short grasses of 3 to 5 inches—primarily grama grass and buffalo grass—form dense sods or patches separated by bare soil. Prickly pear, cholla, and other cacti are scattered throughout the region, occasionally forming extensive clumps. Cottonwood and shrubby willows are present along some streams, while woody shrubs such as wild plum and sumac form scattered thickets throughout bottomlands. Shallow, circular playa lakes used by waterfowl and shorebirds fill with water during wet periods.

DISTRIBUTION: This region extends from southern South Dakota into the Texas panhandle, including the Oklahoma panhandle, the eastern third of Colorado and New Mexico, and the western third of Nebraska and Kansas.

PHYSICAL CHARACTERISTICS: This region has an average annual temperature of 57° Fahrenheit (14° Celsius) and receives about 20 inches (51 cm) of precipitation annually. The growing season is about 190 days. This region slopes from west to east and includes the highest point in Oklahoma—Black Mesa—at 4,973 feet (1,516 m). Topography contains flat plains with sluggish, muddy streams in the east and sandstone mesas that rise 400 feet (122 m) above valley floors in the west.

COMMON SPECIES: Shinnery oak, spectacle-pod, stink-

weed, fragrant sumac, big bluestem, little bluestem, buffalo grass, soapweed yucca, sandreed, blue grama, sagebrush, ornate box turtle, blue grosbeak, lark bunting, loggerhead shrike, Ord's kangaroo rat, prairie dog, pronghorn antelope.

UNIQUE SPECIES: Earless lizard, mountain plover, lesser prairie chicken, scaled quail, swift fox, mule deer, Texas longnose snake, Cassin's sparrow.

MANAGEMENT: Maintain large tracts of shortgrass prairies with only a few isolated trees along streams. Prairie dog towns are a vital component of this region since an entire animal community is associated with them. A combination of rotational grazing and prairie dogs can create a mixture of heavily grazed and ungrazed patches that will support an array of wildlife and plant species and is likewise beneficial to livestock weight gains. Burning areas

FIGURE I-11. The Southern High Plains natural community is a sprawling region reaching from southern South Dakota to the Texas panhandle, the Oklahoma panhandle, the eastern third of Colorado and New Mexico, and the western third of Nebraska and Kansas.

of shinnery oaks every two to four years is important to maintain a desirable mixture of oak groves and grassland.

Whether wildscaping an urban backyard or managing several acres, learn as much as you can about the plants and animals native to your natural community. By incorporating native vegetation in your wildscape, you will ensure that your efforts to attract wildlife will be rewarded and your enjoyment enhanced.

CHAPTER 1
Establishing a Successful Wildscape

Creating a successful wildscape is comparable to baking a chocolate cake—you may be able to bake what appears to be an appetizing treat, but without all the right ingredients, it just won't taste the same. Successful wildscapes likewise involve certain necessary ingredients: they need habitat elements such as food, water, cover, and space appropriate for the target species you are trying to attract. You may have wildlife visiting your yard, but unless you meet their unique requirements, they won't live in your wildscape.

As you go through this guide, select which features you would like to adopt for your yard, keeping in mind the features that would be most compatible for your location. For example, you may wish to attract bats to your backyard to provide natural insect control. However, if you don't have any water sources located nearby, you may not be able to attract bats, even if you follow all of the suggestions in this guide.

For the best overall results, use the Wildscape Plans found in this chapter to develop a model for your own wildscape. Select native plants for your area and place other features (feeders, houses, water sources, etc.) at appropriate locations around the yard, depending upon what wildlife you wish to attract. Remember, your planned wildscape is different from anyone else's. Everyone has unique tastes and needs when it comes to planting flowers and trees. And bear in mind that the kinds of wildlife visiting your wildscape will depend upon its size, location in the state, and native vegetation.

No matter where you live, as long as you provide food, water, cover, and space, you can be assured that wildlife will visit your wildscape and perhaps even live there to raise their young.

FIGURE 1-1. Wildscaping has become a popular concept in landscaping since it was introduced several years ago. Today homeowners can receive Wildscape certification through many state Wildlife Diversity or Nongame Wildlife programs. This curved bed of wildlife-friendly plants is in Oklahoma Certified Wildscape #0077 in Tulsa.

Providing Wildlife Necessities

All wildlife have unique requirements for food, water, cover, and space, and they can only live where these needs will be satisfied. Together, these required elements make up an animal's *habitat,* or the place where it lives. The key to attracting wildlife to your property is to provide any or all of the four basic components of their habitat. The most successful wildscape plans include all of these components in some degree.

The best wildscapes supply all of these requirements during all four seasons. Food, water, cover, and space can be combined in many ways to achieve different habitat types. Within each habitat can be variations of plant species and habitat structures, such as rock and brush piles, nest boxes, bird feeders, thick vines, dense shrubs, and dead cavity trees. To attract the widest variety of wildlife, use native plants to simulate small areas of nearby habitat types. You may wish to visit the undeveloped areas closest to your neighborhood to note the types of plants and how they are arranged.

TARGET WILDLIFE SPECIES

Most states are home to more than 700 species of wildlife, not including invertebrates such as insects, snails, and clams. The numbers and kinds of animals that may visit your yard depend upon how suitable a habitat you create for them. The more closely your property mimics the natural conditions where these animals are found, the better your chances of attracting them. Each wildlife species has specific requirements that may change seasonally and over its life cycle. The more you know about the food, water, space, and cover requirements of the species you favor, the greater the likelihood of successfully persuading them into your yard.

Some animals, such as raccoon, opossum, and mockingbird, occur widely and adapt well to urban environments, but others are much more regional in occurrence. The summer tanager can be seen in the southeast portion of the Great Plains, while western kingbirds will be found only in the western half. Use the tables throughout this guide to

learn where you'll find the most common species of wildlife.

Animals can be drawn to your yard through various means. The following chapters give more specific guidelines on attracting birds, mammals, amphibians, reptiles, and insects. The information includes detail on preferred natural foods and whether you can offer supplemental feedings, the need for water sources, where animals are found, whether they will use artificial nesting and roosting sites, and what you can plant for their use.

Before you begin the process of making your property more attractive to wildlife, consult with your neighbors regarding their feelings toward wildlife in general. Some people may object to having wild animals in such close proximity to their own yards. City ordinances may also restrict what you can do to your yard. For example, your city may require you to cut your front lawn every three weeks, so you wouldn't be able to create a prairie meadow there.

You might also consider asking neighbors if they would like to work together with you to create a larger habitat for wildlife. The larger a tract

FIGURE 1-2. A good example of three habitat elements needed in a wildscape: food, shelter, and water. Multilayering the vegetation creates a variety of foraging areas and shelter for songbirds. Wildflowers provide a nectar source for butterflies and hummingbirds. Birds, squirrels, and other animals will use birdbaths for water.

that is planted to a natural habitat, the better the chances of attracting even more species of wildlife (see the "Neighborhood Wildscapes" section later in this chapter).

FOOD

Food should be provided by natural vegetation year-round. Animals and birds that eat plants or seeds will be attracted to your yard, but their food requirements vary seasonally due to different energy demands. Breeding, migration, and inclement weather are taxing on wildlife and can change their food needs. The ideal wildscape plan uses natural vegetation to supply food all year—from the earliest summer berries to fruits that persist through winter and spring. Supplemental feeding during the year is

FIGURE 1-3. Chickadee on sunflower.

another alternative, although it is probably more important for humans because it brings wild visitors closer, where they can be viewed more easily.

Watching wildlife is a popular activity for Americans of all ages. A recent U.S. Fish and Wildlife Service survey indicated that more than 60 million Americans like to feed, observe, or photograph wildlife on their own property. Backyard naturalists realize that feeding stations are often the key to attracting wildlife up close. Variety is the rule for adding feeding stations to your wildscape. By placing different types of feeders in various locales, you'll see a wider diversity of birds and other wildlife visiting your wildscape. You'll also notice that some species strongly prefer certain foods over others. However, the only way to increase your local wildlife populations permanently is to provide a habitat rich in diversity.

Not all wild creatures are *herbivores* (fruit or seed eaters). *Carnivores* (meat eaters) such as snakes eat insects, rodents, and bird eggs, while *omnivores*

(fruit and meat eaters) like raccoons will feast on whatever food is available—even tipping over your trash can to get at the scraps they smell inside. It is important to remember that all species serve important roles in the food chain as either prey or predator, and some that can make us uncomfortable, such as snakes and bats, can control many pest species, thus benefiting humans.

WATER

Fresh water is essential to all wildlife. Most animals need water to drink and bathe, but fish and amphibians such as frogs and salamanders need water to complete their life cycle. Migratory birds also are attracted to water as they rest during their long flights in fall and spring. Lack of fresh water is the factor most often limiting the wildlife that will visit yards.

Hence one of the best ways to bring birds and other wildlife to your wildscape is by providing a clean, dependable water source year-round. Water sources could include a natural stream, birdbath, small pond, or recirculating stream. Clean water in

Figure 1.4. The tiger salamander is the largest and most widespread of the salamanders in this region. Salamanders need easily accessible water in which to lay their eggs and moist soil areas such as under rotting logs, stones, and thick leaf litter for shelter.

close proximity to protective cover will make your yard even more attractive to animals. In fact, especially during spring and fall migrations and the hot summer months, a predator-safe birdbath will attract bird species that seldom visit feeders. For example, many migrant songbirds, including warblers, vireos, and gnatcatchers, normally dwell and consume insects in forest canopy. In the wild, these and other backyard residents—notably catbirds, thrashers, wrens, towhees, and thrushes—drink and bathe in water droplets among leafy branches.

Another way to provide water is to construct a circulating stream with small holding ponds. Besides attracting birds and mammals, such a backyard stream and its accompanying ponds would also provide a habitat for amphibians and fish. More specific information on creating water sources is found in chapter 3.

COVER

Wild animals need cover, or shelter, to protect them from predators and adverse weather. Traveling, resting, feeding, and breeding make individuals vulnerable, so they will stay clear of a yard that does not provide them with protective cover for these activi-

ties. Many trees and plants do double duty, providing both cover and food for wildlife.

Obviously, planting trees, shrubs, vines, and flowers will create sources of cover and shelter. In developing your planting strategy, keep several concepts in mind. *Vertical layering* of plants will stretch from ground cover to shrubs to medium trees to an upper canopy, providing different layers where wildlife can live. *Horizontal layering* involves planting several overlapping rows of trees and shrubs, providing a greenbelt within which wildlife can travel safely from one area to another (fig. 1-5). Finally, implement *curving edges* into your wildscape to mimic natural habitats more closely; nowhere in nature will you find a straight line that separates one habitat type from another (fig. 1-6).

Unfortunately, even the best wildscape design takes time to develop. While waiting for your trees and shrubs to grow taller and expand, you can create other cover sources. These sources are especially

left, FIGURE 1-5. Dense vegetation, such as a hedge, provides horizontal layering that helps wildlife move safely from one area to another.

below, FIGURE 1-6. This wildscape replicates nature by incorporating layers of vegetation and curves into the design. (Oklahoma Certified Wildscape #0103, Oklahoma City)

important in the beginning wildscape, when trees are small and ground cover hasn't been established.

The beginning wildscape can include a *brush pile* to provide safety from predators and the weather for all species of ground-feeding birds and for a variety of mammals and reptiles (fig. 1-7). Build a brush pile where vegetation is scarce by laying four logs on the ground parallel to one another and about 8 to 12 inches apart. Then place four similar logs perpendicular across the first four, which will keep tunnels open under the pile. Next, add large limbs and then smaller branches until you have created a structure 4 to 6 feet in height and diameter. Sticks and branches can then be added to the top as the pile rots at the bottom, which provides food for earthworms and grubs, further enriching the soil. If you want a brush pile for birds to use, but not rabbits, pile brush one or two feet off the ground on cement blocks. It will no longer shelter rabbits. To make the pile more attractive, plant native honeysuckle or climbing roses around the base.

Another thing that can be attempted in your wildscape is the construction of *rock walls* or *rock piles*. These provide shelter for chipmunks, rabbits, and other small mammals to raise their young. Lizards and frogs use them for cover and sunbathing spots, especially if such rock features are created along the edges of ponds. Butterflies use scattered, light-colored stones as morning basking sites.

Rock walls can be created by stacking field stone about 3 feet high; make sure that it has plenty of spaces and cavities where wildlife can hide and perch (fig. 1-8). Towhees, wrens, sparrows, and other ground-feeding birds can be attracted to rock mounds with sharp changes of slopes. Use cement in several places to give the wall additional stability. To build a rock pile, lay a number of large, rounded rocks in a spoke-wheel pattern to form a base. Use pieces of chimney tile or PVC pipe to create tunnels, and then add flattened rocks on top to create sheltered spots.

After your wildscape has grown for several years, you might be able to provide *snags, stumps* or *fallen logs*. These habitat elements provide excellent cover, nesting areas, food, storage, and places to perch, rest, and hibernate. Where it is safe to do so, leave large dead trees standing or shorten them to create stumps.

Snags are simply dead trees and can be produced by girdling old or deformed trees (fig. 1-9). If they have cavities, they will provide nesting places for wood ducks, flying squirrels, screech-owls and other cavity-nesting birds. Skinks also lay their eggs in tree cavities.

Stumps and snags without cavities provide a place for woodpeckers to excavate cavities for nesting, which in turn are used by other cavity nesters. Stumps and snags also provide both food for insectivores and perches that hawks and other predatory birds use to look for prey. Place snags or stumps in your wildscape by burying a large section of a dead tree or branch into the ground.

Fallen logs provide areas for squirrels and deer mice to cache food for winter. Old, rotten logs also absorb and retain water as they decay, creating a moist habitat where salamanders can burrow; lizards will bask on the tops of the logs.

By leaving some deep *leaf litter* under your shrubs and trees, you create a ground cover that contains insects eaten by wrens, lizards, salamanders, toads, and frogs. The gray treefrog hibernates in deep leaf litter.

SPACE

Finally, animals require a certain amount of space to mate and rear their young. Some species, such as bluebirds and woodpeckers, are territorial and require more space than others. Obviously, landowners with several acres will be able to attract more wildlife than will someone with a smaller lot, which may only be able to support one or two pairs of breeding animals. However, wildlife may require less space where food, water, and shelter are close together.

The types of wildlife present will depend on the structure and vertical distribution of the vegetation. Humans think of space on a horizontal scale, but birds also divide habitat into vertical layers, each species feeding in a different way at a different height. The greater the vertical distribution of vegetation, the more species can be accommodated. Maintaining woods at different stages of succession is the primary means of providing vertical diversity, but this may not be possible if your woodlot is a small one.

top, FIGURE 1-7. A brush pile provides safety from predators and the weather for all species of ground-feeding birds.

bottom, FIGURE 1-8. Rock gardens can provide shelter, food, and basking areas for lizards and butterflies. (Sunshine Nursery, Clinton, Oklahoma)

FIGURE 1-9. Snags can provide excellent cover, nesting areas, food, storage, and places to perch, rest, and hibernate.

Creating a Wildscape Plan

After determining which wildlife species you want to attract to your wildscape and researching their habitat requirements, you'll have to design a plan that is compatible with the needs of your home and property.

The first step in designing your wildscape should be an initial evaluation of your property. What wildlife and plant species do you already have present? What do you want to add? If you're starting with a bare lot, you'll have to invest more time, money, and energy in your design than if you simply want to modify an existing landscape. More likely you can design your whole wildscape around existing trees or structures. Then there is the question of how you will maintain your wildscape in the future. Complete the "Checklist to Design a Wildscape" in appendix A to determine what your wildscape currently provides and to see what you may wish to add.

EVALUATING YOUR WILDSCAPE

After you have evaluated your yard, you should design a wildscape that will require minimal mowing and pruning, although over the years you may need to remove some plants to make room for new growth. You should expect to complete your landscape over a reasonable time period, but it may take several years before the wildscape resembles your original plan. Also, be considerate of your neighbors. Make sure your developing wildscape does not interfere with their yard. Or, better yet, see if they would also like to wildscape their property, providing expanded habitat for wildlife needs.

STEP 1: Begin by taking an inventory of your property. Use a base map to note your property's dimensions and all structures above and below ground, including house, garage, fences, water pipes, septic tank, and other items. This step can prevent costly problems later, such as roots tangling in underground plumbing or wiring, or limbs interfering with power lines or buildings.

FIGURE 1-10. The first step in designing a landscape is to evaluate your property. Use the "Checklist to Design a Wildscape" (appendix A) to take inventory and determine the basic needs of the wildlife you wish to attract.

STEP 2: Look for sunny and shady areas in your wildscape and notice how they change during the day or over the seasons. Sketch these areas on a plastic overlay for your base map. Also examine your soil. Is it primarily fill dirt, sand, clay, sandy loam, topsoil, or some other type of soil? Ideally, it should not have a loose or lumpy texture but should be dark and moist. If your soil has these qualities, your plants will mostly care for themselves. Healthy soil and plants produce good food and cover for wildlife.

STEP 3: In evaluating your wildscape, consider your space requirements for work, entertainment, security, and comfort. If your lifestyle includes outside dogs or cats, you should expect less wildlife to visit your wildscape. Decide realistically how much and what type of space you will need for each activity, and sketch these areas onto another overlay for your base map.

STEP 4: List the trees, shrubs, vines, and herbaceous plants that are already growing in your wildscape. Also note their size, age, health, whether they are exotic or native to your area, and what energy conservation value or maintenance requirement they may have. How does your vegetation interact with

the physical characteristics of your yard to form habitats? These characteristics will influence the options you have for developing your wildscape.

STEP 5: Finally, list the wildlife currently visiting your wildscape. Notice how well your property provides cover, water, and space for visiting wildlife. Check for plants that produce food. Look for areas where habitat can be improved. Does your present landscape provide adequate cover and safe travel corridors for small animals and birds? Mammals especially require connected shrubs and hedgerows or larger wooded areas to move about.

Now that you've inventoried your property, it's time to prepare a master plan to guide your wildscaping efforts in the coming years. You may wish to use an already designed plan; however, try to customize your wildscape by choosing native plants that thrive in your natural community. Remember, with a wildscape, you are working with nature and watching natural processes take their course. Don't plan a clipped, artificial garden that will enslave you. Your primary jobs will include pruning and pulling out some plants from time to time to give the garden more room to grow. Now, prepare to bring wildlife closer to home.

FAMILY ACTIVITIES

Take a family field trip to view wildscaped areas

Visit places that are landscaped for wildlife or have examples of protected native plants. As listed in this chapter, Oklahoma has a number of regional wildscape demonstration areas that successfully showcase planting designs and provide homes for wildlife. While visiting these areas, try to identify plants to add to your wildscape. Watch for wildlife and look for signs left by animals as they carry out their daily activities.

STARTING FROM SCRATCH OR PLANNING MAJOR ALTERATIONS

The following steps serve as useful guidelines if your property has no current landscaping or if you wish to make significant changes in what your wildscape offers.

STEP 1: Plant overlapping tall native evergreen and deciduous trees along the perimeter of your wildscape; use as many food-producing varieties as possible. These will simulate the forest canopy and provide food, nest sites, and protective cover for wildlife. They also will screen your property from streets and other properties. Plant deciduous trees on the west and south sides of your house for summer shade, and plant evergreen trees on the west and north sides to block cold winter winds. Consider how wide the crowns of these trees will be when mature, and don't plant them too close together.

STEP 2: Plant smaller native flowering trees in curving clusters, not rows, near the tall trees to begin an understory; curving borders are more wildlife-friendly by mimicking natural habitats and are aesthetically pleasing to us. Mix several species of varying shape, height, and density to create an abundant selection of nest sites. Select trees that fruit at different times of the year to stagger food production for year-round feeding opportunities.

STEP 3: Plant native food-producing shrubs and ground cover around the smaller trees. These will provide shelter areas for ground-feeding birds and mammals.

STEP 4: Although you may wish to retain some lawn for recreation use, large sprawling lawns are labor and energy intensive. Consider letting unneeded lawn areas develop into wildflower meadows. Consult your county Cooperative Extension Service for recommendations on appropriate native prairie grasses for your area; buffalo grass is highly recommended in sunny lawns because it grows 4–6 inches in height and doesn't require costly fertilizers or weekly mowings. Remember to consult local mowing ordinances and your neighbors regarding grass and wildflower heights.

MODIFYING AN EXISTING LANDSCAPE

If you simply wish to add wildscaping features to your property, the following guidelines will provide information on how to modify your existing wildscape.

STEP 1: Begin by planting overlapping trees and shrubs around the edges of your wildscape. Remember not to plant in rows and to use curving, irregular borders to create more wildlife edge. Be sure solitary trees are surrounded by small shrubs to create ground cover.

STEP 2: Mulch by spreading dried leaves and lawn clippings about three inches deep between plants and around their bases (but not directly against tree or shrub trunks, to reduce damage caused by rodents and decay). This keeps soil moist and inhibits weeds, and eventually the mulch breaks down and begins the soil formation process. It also provides additional ground cover in your yard. Again, don't put mulch directly against your house's foundation if you are wary of snakes.

STEP 3: Replace exotic plants with species native to your region. Native plant species are adapted to the area's temperature, climate, and rainfall and often are more disease resistant. It's okay to have plants that are pretty, but if you have a small property, try to have plants that provide two or more positive attributes. For example, flowering dogwoods are native to the eastern United States, provide berries that are relished by birds, and sport a gorgeous spring bloom.

MAINTENANCE IDEAS FOR ALL LANDSCAPES

Once you've begun creating your wildscape plan, you need to consider how you will maintain the property in the future. The following guidelines provide maintenance ideas for different elements of your wildscape.

LAWNS: Convert some of your lawn into a meadow by mowing just twice in the summer to control tree and shrub invasion. You'll decrease the need for mowing if you use a native grass such as buffalo grass rather than a turf grass. As already noted, be sure to check local mowing ordinances first. Wildflowers and butterflies can thrive in a small wild meadow.

SHRUB LAYER: Encourage a variety of heights and species to increase plant diversity. Evergreen shrubs with dense or thorny branches are ideal bird cover and nesting areas. Thorny shrubs also discourage human interference. Group fruiting shrubs together for the best pollination and fruit production.

PRUNING: Remove old growth selectively to be sure plants do not overcrowd one another. Birds prefer somewhat unkempt informal hedges. Do not prune large branches during the nesting season, but wait until fall or winter when the young have left the nest.

SMALL TREES: Use native fruiting varieties that thrive without toxic sprays. Also, don't prune all dead limbs; leave some for the woodpeckers and other insectivorous birds.

LARGE TREES: Mow once a year below large trees to control unwanted seedlings. Leave dead trees and limbs standing if they are not hazardous to users of your property or adjacent areas.

PATHS: Maintain mulched or stonework paths as walkways through your yard to minimize compaction of soils and vegetation.

Sample Wildscape Plans

Although everyone's property is different, all wildscapes should contain elements of food, water, and cover. All wildlife species need a particular combination of these elements in their habitat to survive. For example, the northern cardinal needs a variety of food including insects, berries, and seeds. Dense thickets or vines, particularly evergreens, provide shelter for roosting and nesting. Cardinals also need access to shallow water for bathing and drinking. On the other hand, American toads require a permanent water source to reproduce and lay their eggs, plenty of insects to eat, and shelter during the heat of the day and for winter hibernation.

WILDSCAPE ELEMENTS

As mentioned earlier, whatever target species you decide to focus upon will determine which wildscape elements you place into your wildscape. Likewise, the amount of area dedicated for wildlife will determine which species are able to live in your wildscape and which ones will simply visit. Successful wildscapes feature at least one element in each of the categories in table 1–1.

PHASES OF WILDSCAPING

Wildscaping is a long-term investment, not something that will take place overnight. By developing your wildscape in several phases, you'll spread expenses over time, lessen your annual workload, and most important, retain your sanity! Remember that the first step in wildscaping your property is to inventory the existing landscape, including the plants, structures, and wildlife that are already present.

The following wildscape designs are simply meant to provide a starting point for your own design. These guidelines will help if you decide to certify your property as an Oklahoma Wildscape with the Oklahoma Wildlife Diversity Program (see appendix J).

In the example illustrated, Phase One (fig. 1–11a and b) is a typical backyard that already contains a Bermuda grass lawn, four red maple trees, two nandina bushes, a boxwood hedge, and four lilac shrubs. Obviously, not many creatures will call this habitat home, although some birds will probably visit, such as the American robin, European starling, house sparrow, and Western kingbird.

Phase Two (fig. 1–12a and b) contains at least one element each from the food, water, cover, and "other" categories listed in table 1–1. In this case, layers of food-producing trees and shrubs had to be planted in selected areas of the yard. A permanent water source and wren nest box were added. Food- and cover-producing plants include the existing plants plus eastern red cedar, two flowering dogwoods, five yaupon hollies, four viburnum bushes, three butterfly bushes, and a cherry laurel. Two water sources—a birdbath and a small pond 2 to 4 inches deep—were added. Certainly, more wildlife will begin visiting this wildscape, including the northern mockingbird, cedar waxwing, Carolina wren, downy woodpecker, cardinal, mourning dove, Baltimore oriole, Woodhouse's toad, and various butterflies.

Phase Three (fig. 1–13a and b) provides nectar-producing plants that are attractive to butterflies and hummingbirds; additional food-producing plants; and a bog garden. The nectar-producing plants could include Carolina allspice, bee balm, verbena, butterfly weed, purple coneflower, salvia, sunflower, trumpet vine on an arbor, groupings of glossy abelia, more butterfly bushes, cardinal flower, swamp milkweed, and perennial hibiscus. Additional food-producing plants include red oak, persimmon, more yaupon hollies and viburnums, serviceberry, and hackberry.

These additions will attract species otherwise unlikely to visit, such as American goldfinch, ruby-throated hummingbird, dark-eyed junco, white-throated and Harris's sparrows, brown thrasher, blue jay, sphinx moth, monarch butterfly, opossum, and fox squirrel.

Further enhance the wildscape in Phase Four (fig. 1–14a and b) by adding more cover sources and food-producing plants, creating a deeper pond that slopes from zero to at least 18 inches, installing a recirculating stream, and erecting a bat house and

chickadee nest box. Cover sources could include Virginia creeper and creeping cotoneaster, rock piles, brush piles, and fallen logs. Food-producing plants could include a blackberry hedge; beautyberry and hawthorn; and pickerel weed, arrowhead, and elderberry for the pond area.

These new changes will now attract box turtle, ground skink, fence lizard, gray treefrog, dragonflies, big brown bat, mosquito fish, red-bellied woodpecker, Carolina chickadee, migratory warblers, and a host of other wildlife.

NEIGHBORHOOD WILDSCAPES

Imagine you are a female cardinal in search of a mate and a place to start your nest. As you fly over the landscape, you spot a male puffing up his chest in pride, showing off the area he has staked out as his own. It's a charming little spot, with a few dogwood trees and shrubby hollies. However, some neighborhood cats are prowling the area, and it appears that they could easily get to a nest, even if it were built in the densest part of the shrubs. In addition, you only see one small water source, which might freeze in winter if it isn't filled every day.

And then you hear the call of a second male just over the ridge. Curious, you wing your way skyward again and soon spy an area that contains three or four times as much habitat. A thick knot of shrubs is surrounded by additional small and medium-sized trees. Cats do lurk in the area, but it doesn't look as if they'd be successful in finding your nest. And you spot several water sources that are easily accessible and feature running water.

You quickly make up your mind and spiral down to meet the second male.

Urban wildscapes—even small ones—can be extremely beneficial to some species of wildlife. They serve as small oases in the midst of asphalt jungles and Bermuda grass lawns. They are even

TABLE 1-1. Wildscape Elements

FOOD	WATER (YEAR-ROUND)	COVER	OTHER
Food-producing shrubs, trees, vines	Within ¼ mile of permanent water source	Vertical structure in plant layers	Plants for butterfly caterpillars
Wildflowers	Water garden	Rock pile	Snag/fallen log
Feeders	Birdbath/puddle	Brush pile	Dust bath area
Nectar-producing flowers	Artificial bog or stream	Dense hedge, thicket, evergreen plants	Nesting/roosting boxes or shelves

FIGURE 1-11. Wildscape design Phase One, a: three-dimensional view, and b: bird's-eye view. To begin wildscaping property, first inventory the existing landscape. The current plantings in this yard include Bermuda grass, four red maples, two nandinas, a boxwood hedge, and four lilac shrubs. This yard will attract wildlife species such as the American robin, European starling, house sparrow, and the western kingbird.

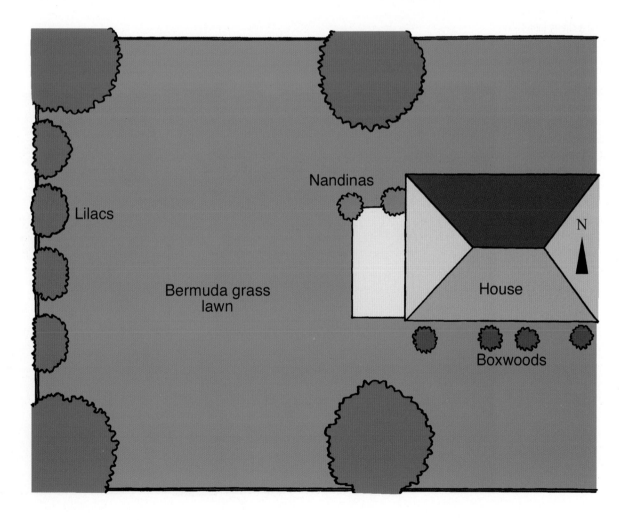

Nandinas

Lilacs

Bermuda grass lawn

N

House

Boxwoods

FIGURE 1-12. Wildscape design Phase Two, a: three-dimensional view, and b: bird's-eye view. To create a wildlife garden, plant layers of food-producing trees and shrubs in a selected area of the property. Add a permanent water source and a wren nest box. One recommendation is to remove the boxwood hedge and lilac shrubs. Instead, plant species that serve multiple functions, such as producing berries, providing nectar and shelter, and adding beauty to the property. In addition to the existing plants, some food- and cover-producing species have been added to this yard: an eastern red cedar, two flowering dogwoods, five yaupon hollies, four viburnums, three buddleia, and a cherry laurel. The water source should include a small pond two to four inches deep and a birdbath. This yard will attract species such as the American robin, northern mockingbird, cedar waxwing, Carolina wren, downy woodpecker, northern cardinal, northern oriole, mourning dove, Woodhouse's toad, various bathing songbirds, and various butterflies.

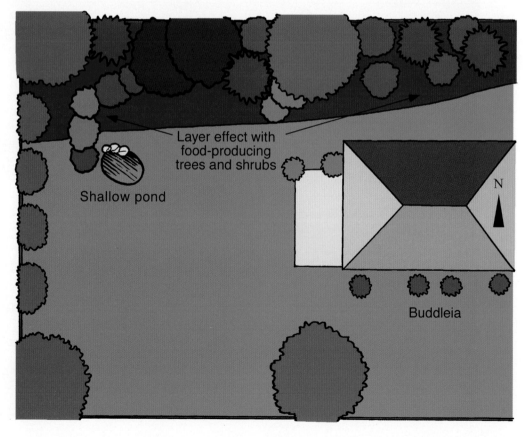

Layer effect with food-producing trees and shrubs

Shallow pond

Buddleia

N

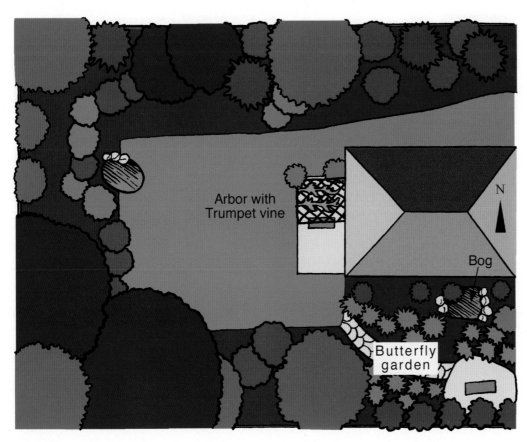

Arbor with
Trumpet vine

Bog

Butterfly
garden

N

FIGURE 1-13. Wildscape design Phase Three, a: three-dimensional view, and b: bird's-eye view. To create a wildlife habitat as shown here, provide plants that are attractive to butterflies and hummingbirds, plant additional food-producing plants, and add a bog garden. In addition to the plants mentioned in figures 1-11 and 1-12, add cardinal lobelia, swamp milkweed, monarda, and perennial hibiscus. Additional food-producing plants such as red oak, two persimmon trees, two more yaupon hollies, two more viburnums, two serviceberries, and a hackberry are recommended. To attract butterflies and hummingbirds, plant species such as Carolina allspice, bee balm, verbena, butterfly weed, purple coneflower, *Salvia coccinea,* parsley, fennel, sunflowers, a trumpet vine on an arbor, three glossy abelia, and six more buddleia. In addition to the wildlife species mentioned in figures 1-11 and 1-12, this yard will attract the American goldfinch, sphinx moth, ruby-throated hummingbird, dark-eyed junco, white-throated sparrow, Harris's sparrow, brown thrasher, monarch butterfly, opossum, fox squirrel, and blue jay.

FIGURE 1-14. Wildscape design Phase Four, a: three-dimensional view, and b: bird's-eye view. Further enhance a wildlife habitat by adding cover, more food-producing plants, a deeper pond, and a variety of nest boxes. Plants such as the Virginia creeper and creeping cotoneaster will provide cover, but should be supplemented with rock piles, a brush pile, and fallen logs. Also incorporate such additional food-producing plants as a blackberry hedge, pickerel weed, arrowroot, two elderberries, two beautyberries, and a hawthorn. To the existing small pond, add a deeper pond that slopes to eighteen inches or deeper. A recirculating stream would also be ideal. A chickadee nest box and a bat house should be added to the variety of nest boxes. This yard will attract the wildlife species mentioned in figures 1-11 through 1-13 as well as the box turtle, red-bellied woodpecker, ground skink, fence lizard, big brown bat, Carolina chickadee, gray treefrog, dragonflies, various migratory warblers, and many other species.

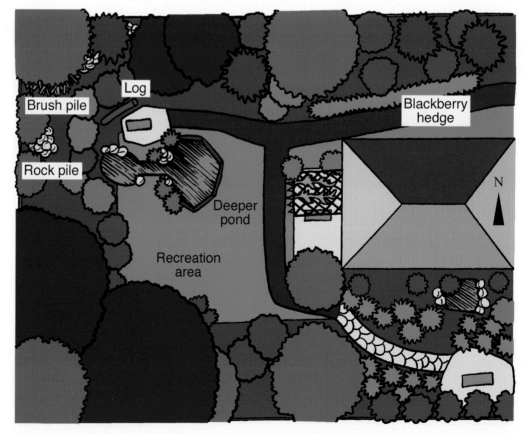

somewhat successful for wildlife to live in and raise their young, depending upon the number of predators (including cats) that also live in the area.

However, many wildlife species need larger territories and would not even consider living in a single backyard wildscape because of its limited size. To attract these size-dependent species or to broaden the diversity of species, you must increase the amount of available habitat. One way to do this within an urban area is to create a neighborhood wildscape.

A neighborhood wildscape is basically a collection of single backyard wildscapes where homeowners work together with their neighbors to create a larger habitat (fig. 1-15). Simply by creating a curving wildscape along all three sides of your back fence and connecting the area to the property of neighbors who have done the same, you will create a corridor through which wildlife can safely move. With an increase in the amount of available habitat, plant diversity is enhanced, making the whole area more attractive to wildlife. Cover sources increase, boosting nesting success. Food production will also increase because insects are able to cross-pollinate related plants more easily.

If the neighborhood wildscape includes several deep ponds and running water sources scattered throughout the area, you'll have better opportunities to see amphibians. Imagine the nighttime concerts you could hear just by stepping outside! Creating a neighborhood wildscape is a great way to forge a closer bond with your neighbors. Together, you can share in the knowledge that you are doing something to benefit wildlife, right in your own backyards.

Regional Demonstration Areas

Although it is one thing to look at a diagram of how to wildscape, it is quite another to visit a site and view wildscaping concepts in action. The following wildscape demonstration areas are found throughout Oklahoma and are publicly accessible. They should provide an idea of what can be done to adapt a yard for wildlife.

BYRON HATCHERY WATCHABLE WILDLIFE AREA (NORTHWEST)

FEATURES: Half-mile trail through cattail marsh, swamp, and midgrass prairie; Wildscape Demonstration Area around nature center featuring native regional plants and butterfly garden; bluebird trail; bat house; barn owl nest house; observation blinds and piers; various bird feeders.

PLANTS: Autumn Joy sedum, butterfly bush, Indian blanket, *Salvia greggii*, black-eyed susan, purple coneflower, Indian grass, big bluestem, little bluestem, redtop, *Verbena canadensis*, woolly paperflower, sand plum, sumac, Texas betony, sunflowers, abelia, yarrow, hackberry, rough-leaf dogwood, chittam, cottonwood, redbud, golden currant, buttonball bush, poison ivy, trumpet vine, cattail, wild grape, smilax, eastern red cedar, pokeweed, mulberry.

WILDLIFE SPECIES: Harris's sparrow, American goldfinch, purple finch, house finch, cedar waxwing, red-winged blackbird, dark-eyed junco, four woodpecker species, eastern bluebird, loggerhead shrike, great horned owl, yellow-rumped warbler, blue-gray gnatcatcher, rough green snake, kingsnake, bullsnake, glass lizard, chorus frog, leopard frog, various butterflies, deer mouse, deer, cottontail rabbit.

LOCATION: East of Cherokee, Oklahoma. Go 2 miles north from the intersection of Highways 38 and 11 (north of Great Salt Plains National Wildlife Refuge); ½ mile west to nature center.

SPECIAL NOTES: The area is open during daylight hours. To schedule a field trip, call Byron Hatchery at 580/474–2663.

SUNSHINE NURSERY (WEST-CENTRAL)

FEATURES: Native plant nursery featuring native, drought-tolerant southwestern U.S. plants; rock garden with native shrubs and flowers.

PLANTS: Desert willow, pinyon pine, dwarf sumac, flametip sumac, New Jersey tea, mountain mahogany, *Arbutus*, creosote bush, dwarf mulberry, rough-leaf dogwood, mahonia, desert hackberry, Mormon tea, red skullcap, Indian blanket, *Hymenopsis subintegra*, *Salvia greggii*, *Mirabilis*, *Psilotrophe*, evening primrose, agave, sandsage, *Delphinium*, *Zinnia grandifolia*.

WILDLIFE SPECIES: Various butterflies, various hummingbirds, lark sparrow, northern cardinal, brown thrasher, western kingbird, northern mockingbird, Woodhouse's toad, Great Plains toad, eastern collared lizard, fence lizard.

FIGURE 1-15. When neighbors work together to create a collection of backyard wildscapes, the amount of quality habitat is increased and is more attractive to wildlife. The increase of plant diversity alone makes the neighborhood at the top of the diagram more attractive to the female cardinal looking for the best habitat to raise young successfully.

LOCATION: Two miles north on Highway 183 from Highway 66 intersection in Clinton, Oklahoma. Nursery is located on west side of Clinton Auction Barn.

SPECIAL NOTES: Sunshine Nursery propagates plants that are drought-tolerant and thrive in the western Oklahoma climate. Call 580/323–6259 for nursery hours.

WICHITA MOUNTAINS NATIONAL WILDLIFE REFUGE (SOUTHWEST)

FEATURES: Restoration of highly impacted area at old visitor center; use a walk-up blind to view birds and other wildlife that visit the demonstration area's feeders and brush piles.

PLANTS: Sensitive briar, sand plum, smilax, buffalo grass, switchgrass, Indian grass, Indian blanket, prairie coneflower, prairie ragwort.

WILDLIFE SPECIES: Cardinal, chickadee, blue jay, painted bunting, most woodpeckers and flickers, turkey, eastern towhee, white-tailed deer, squirrels.

LOCATION: West from Lawton, Oklahoma, on Highway 62 and north on Highway 115; from Interstate 44, take Highway 49 west at Medicine Park exit. The Wildscape Demonstration Area is located at the Environmental Education Center on Quanah Parker Lake within the refuge.

SPECIAL NOTES: Call 580/429–3222 for more information.

OKLAHOMA CITY ZOOLOGICAL PARK (CENTRAL)

FEATURES: Butterfly garden covering 20,000 square feet with native and introduced annuals and perennials; sandstone wall for basking; water feature for puddling; tallgrass prairie plants; interpretive signs and plant lists; bird-attracting garden with feeders and fruit-producing trees, shrubs, and vines.

PLANTS: The butterfly garden features more than 200 nectar and host plants.

WILDLIFE SPECIES: Butterflies include painted lady, monarch, gulf fritillary, European cabbage white, giant swallowtail, eastern black swallowtail, viceroy, various sulphurs, various hairstreaks, various skippers. Other wildlife include fox squirrel, six-lined racerunner, Carolina wren, northern cardinal, tufted titmouse, mourning dove, house finch, northern mockingbird, white-throated sparrow, Harris's sparrow, fox sparrow.

LOCATION: 2101 Northeast 50th Street in Oklahoma City. From Interstate 44, take Martin Luther King Avenue south to 50th Street; from Interstate 35, take 50th Street west to zoo entrance.

SPECIAL NOTES: Oklahoma City Zoo is open year-round from 9:00 A.M. to 5:00 P.M. Guided group tours are available. Phone number is 405/424–3344.

OKLAHOMA GARDENING STUDIO GARDENS (NORTH-CENTRAL)

FEATURES: Butterfly gardens; shade gardens; fruit orchards; bird houses and feeding stations; amphibian hibernacula; reptile basking areas; water ponds for fish and amphibians.

PLANTS: More than 200 species of trees, shrubs, vines, perennials, and annuals are planted in the Studio Gardens.

WILDLIFE SPECIES: Cardinal, chickadee, blue jay, purple martin, bluebird, red bat, six-lined racerunner, ground skink, plains leopard frog, Woodhouse's toad, bullfrog, American toad.

LOCATION: From intersection of Highway 51 and Western Road in western Stillwater, Oklahoma, go north ½ mile on Western Road. Turn west on Farm Road for ¾ mile; follow the signs to the Studio Gardens.

SPECIAL NOTES: Call 405/744–5404 for more information.

TULSA ZOO AND LIVING MUSEUM (NORTHEAST)

FEATURES: Butterfly gardens, bog plants, shrubs, perennials, vines, shallow pond, interpretive signs.

PLANTS: More than 100 species of trees, shrubs, vines, and perennials are planted in the Habitat Demonstration Garden.

WILDLIFE SPECIES: Various butterflies, bats, toads, frogs, red-eared slider, soft-shelled turtle, dragonflies, spiders, tufted titmouse, Carolina chickadee, woodpeckers, yellow-throated warbler, Carolina wren.

LOCATION: 5701 East 36th Street North in Tulsa, Oklahoma. From Interstate 244 or Highway 11, go north on Sheridan and then east on 36th Street. Follow the signs to the zoo.

SPECIAL NOTES: The Tulsa Zoo is open year-round from

10:00 A.M. to 5:00 P.M. except on Christmas and the third Friday in June. Phone number is 918/669–6600.

CLEAR CREEK FARM AND GARDENS (EAST-CENTRAL)

FEATURES: Native plant nursery featuring trees, shrubs, and perennials adapted to eastern U.S. conditions; butterfly gardens; prairie fields; undisturbed woodlands; springs.

PLANTS: More than 125 species of trees, shrubs, vines, and perennials; butterfly nectar gardens; butterfly host plant gardens; herb and rose gardens; vegetable gardens.

WILDLIFE SPECIES: American goldfinch, purple finch, eastern bluebird, northern cardinal, summer tanager, indigo bunting, warblers, white-breasted nuthatch, ruby-throated hummingbird, tree frogs, toads, snakes, skinks, flying squirrel, chipmunk, raccoon, bats, deer, various butterflies, bees, moths.

LOCATION: Three and one-half miles east of Peggs, Oklahoma, from Highway 82; call for directions.

SPECIAL NOTES: Open to the public by appointment only; call 918/598–3782. To receive newsletter and plant list, write to Clear Creek Farm and Gardens, P.O. Box 89, Peggs, OK 74452–0089. Clear Creek also books special group tours in spring and fall.

OKLAHOMA DEPARTMENT OF WILDLIFE CONSERVATION SOUTHEAST REGIONAL OFFICE (SOUTHEAST)

FEATURES: Butterfly gardens, bog garden, recirculating stream, native plants, rock piles, dust bath.

PLANTS: More than 50 species of trees, shrubs, vines, and perennials; butterfly and hummingbird gardens; amphibian area; layered fruit-producing garden; bog garden.

WILDLIFE SPECIES: Song sparrow, field sparrow, brown thrasher, eastern towhee, fish crow, red-tailed hawk, turkey vulture, downy woodpecker, red-bellied woodpecker, pileated woodpecker, flicker, bluebird, robin, goldfinch, cardinal, white-breasted nuthatch, indigo bunting, fence lizard, chorus frog, spring peeper, leopard frog, treefrogs, moths, ladybugs, butterflies.

LOCATION: East of Hartshorne, Oklahoma, 6 miles on Highway 1/Highway 63.

SPECIAL NOTES: Office hours are 10:00 A.M.–3:00 P.M. Monday through Friday. Phone number is 918/297–0153.

Establishing Plantings for Wildlife

Most species of wildlife rely upon plants during some part of the year, either eating the fruit, seeds, or nectar provided or using the plant as a source of shelter or nesting cover. The tables in this chapter list plants that have excellent wildlife value for your wildscape, giving information on trees, shrubs, vines, native grasses, wildflowers, and butterfly nectar sources. All the species that provide wildlife benefits could not be listed, obviously, but these lists should provide a good starting point. You may want to visit local nurseries and ask them to stock the recommended plants, if they don't already.

When considering your wildscape, include some evergreen shrubs and brush piles for winter cover. Also keep in mind that some fruiting shrubs such as cherries, viburnums, elderberries, and dogwoods will produce much more fruit if you plant two or more unrelated shrubs together for cross-pollination.

Several species of trees and shrubs have separate male and female plants. To produce fruits, you will need at least one of each in close proximity. As a general rule, one male plant is sufficient to pollinate six to ten female plants. Some species that have separate sexes include red cedar, hollies, persimmon, sumacs, sassafras, wax myrtle, ash, and mulberry. The best way to learn which is female is to see which plants are fruiting—primarily in fall and winter.

Most important in selecting fruiting trees and shrubs is to choose varieties with relatively small fruits. Although birds can bite pieces out of some soft fruits, such as plums or mulberries, they cannot bite pieces out of hard fruits—they must swallow them whole. Smaller birds such as eastern bluebirds and cedar waxwings can choke on the larger fruits of nandina and Chinese hollies, so they often leave those berries uneaten. It would be better to plant small-berried producers such as Foster's holly and yaupon holly.

Native plant species that occur in your state or region are highly recommended over exotics or cultivars because they are better adapted to the local sun, water, and temperature requirements. They also are adapted to local wildlife needs. Appendix C includes contacts to determine what native plants are found in your state. For example, loblolly pines are found naturally in southeast Oklahoma. If you plant the same pine in northwest Oklahoma, it may still grow, but it won't receive enough water to grow properly. Additionally, most animals in northwest Oklahoma are not adapted to living in or feeding on pine trees. For best results, plant native trees and shrubs of your own ecoregion.

Trees, Shrubs, and Vines

Tables 2–1 and 2–2 identify where and during what season various evergreen and deciduous trees, shrubs, and vines grow in the southern Great Plains. The tables also tell you which plants are native and give their sun requirements. Wildlife and landscape comments are given in the final column of each table to help you select and grow these plants. Note the following abbreviations for tables 2–1 and 2–2:

SUITABLE NATURAL COMMUNITY: CFP = Cypress Floodplains, OHL = Ouachita Highlands, OZP = Ozark Plateau, CT = Crosstimbers, TGP = Tallgrass Prairie, MGP = Mixed Grass Prairie, SHP = Southern High Plains

LIGHT NEEDS: S = sunny, Sh = shady, PSh = partial shade

FOOD PRODUCED: berry = in general, a fleshy fruit; flower = nectar source; nut = hard-shelled fruit (e.g., acorn); seed = ripened ovule

FRUITING SEASON: F = fall, W = winter, Sp = spring, Su = summer

Native Grasses

Native grasses are commonly referred to as the "bedrock" of the prairie community. Without the presence of native grasses, the prairie wouldn't exist. Native grasses provide the food base for a host of wildlife, from large bison to tiny butterfly caterpillars and everything in between. Grown in concert with native wildflowers, grasses provide nesting cover and shelter for ground-nesting birds, and their root systems stabilize soil to prevent erosion.

FIGURE 2-1. Garden gate welcomes visitors to continue exploring this wildscape (Oklahoma Certified Wildscape #0013, Norman)

TABLE 2–1. **Evergreen Trees, Shrubs, and Vines for Wildlife**

COMMON NAME (*SCIENTIFIC NAME*)	SUITABLE NATURAL COMMUNITY (**N = NATIVE**)							LIGHT NEEDS	FOOD PRODUCED	FRUITING SEASON	VALUE TO WILDLIFE
	CFP	OHL	OZP	CT	TGP	MGP	SHP				
Large evergreen trees (30 to 60 feet)											
Magnolia, southern (*Magnolia grandiflora*)	X	X	X					S/PSh	berry	F	Birds and small mammals eat berries.
Oak, live (*Quercus virginiana*)					N			S/PSh	nut	F–W	Birds and mammals eat acorns. Good source of cover.
Pine, loblolly (*Pinus taeda*)	N	N						S	seed	F	Chickadees, jays, warblers, woodpeckers, and nuthatches eat seeds in fall and winter. Squirrels eat seeds and catkins. Live trees provide excellent nesting cover, while old pines provide nesting cavities. Butterfly host plant.
Pine, longleaf (*Pinus palustris*)	X	X	X					S	seed	F	
Pine, ponderosa (*Pinus ponderosa*)							N	S	seed	F	
Pine, shortleaf (*Pinus echinata*)	N	N	N	N				S	seed	F	
Pine, slash (*Pinus elliottii*)	X							S	seed	F	
Small evergreen trees (10 to 30 feet)											
Cherry Laurel, Carolina (*Prunus caroliniana*)	X	X	X					S/PSh	berry	F	Birds and mammals eat berries. Good cover and nesting source.
Holly, American (*Ilex opaca*)	N	N		N				S/PSh	berry	F–W	Bluebird, mockingbird, catbird, robin, and thrushes eat berries. Good cover and nesting source. Plant male and female trees. Butterfly host plant.
Holly, dahoon (*Ilex cassine*)	X							S/PSh	berry	F–W	
Holly, yaupon (*Ilex vomitoria*)	N							S/PSh	berry	F–W	
Magnolia, sweetbay (*Magnolia virginiana*)	X							S/PSh	berry	F	Birds and mammals eat fruit. Butterfly host plant.
Myrtle, wax (*Myrica cerifera*)	N							S/PSh	berry	F–W	Many birds eat berries. Butterfly host plant.
Privet, glossy (*Ligustrum lucidum*)				X	X	X		S/PSh	berry	F–W	Cedar waxwings occasionally eat berries.
Red cedar, eastern (*Juniperus virginiana*)	N	N	N	N	N	N		S	berry	F–W	Birds and mammals eat berries of female trees. Good cover and nesting source. Butterfly host plant. *Caution:* Invasive into prairies.
Evergreen shrubs											
Azalea, Piedmont (*Rhododendron canescens*)	X	X	X					S/PSh	flower	Sp	Fair nectar source for hummingbirds and butterflies. Provides cover.
Barberry, wintergreen (*Berberis juliana*)	X	X						S/PSh	berry	F–W	Limited food value. Good shelter and cover source.

TABLE 2–1. Evergreen Trees, Shrubs, and Vines for Wildlife

COMMON NAME (*SCIENTIFIC NAME*)	SUITABLE NATURAL COMMUNITY (**N = NATIVE**)							LIGHT NEEDS	FOOD PRODUCED	FRUITING SEASON	VALUE TO WILDLIFE
	CFP	OHL	OZP	CT	TGP	MGP	SHP				
Cotoneaster (*Cotoneaster* spp.)	X	X	X	X	X	X	X	S/PSh	berry	F	Many songbirds eat fruit. Flowers attract hummingbirds.
Eleagnus, thorny (*Elaeagnus pungens*)	X	X	X	X	X	X	X	all	berry	Sp	Several birds eat fruit. Provides good nesting source.
Euonymus, evergreen (*Euonymus 'Manhattan'*)	X	X	X	X	X	X	X	S/PSh	berry	F	Many songbirds eat fruit. Good cover source.
Firethorn (*Pyracantha coccinea*)	X	X	X	X	X	X	X	S/PSh	berry	F–W	Many songbirds eat fruit, which persists into winter. *Caution:* Don't plant near busy roads.
Holly, Foster (*Ilex hybrid*)	X	X	X	X	X	X	X	S	berry	F–W	Many birds eat fruit. Excellent nesting and winter cover. Butterfly host plant.
Juniper (*Juniperus communis*)	X	X	X	X	X	X	X	S	berry	F–W	Birds and mammals eat berries. Good cover and nesting source.
Mahonia, leatherleaf (*Mahonia bealei*)	X	X	X	X	X			PSh/Sh	berry	Sp–Su	Several songbirds eat fruit. Good cover and nesting.
Privet, Chinese (*Ligustrum sinense*)	X	X	X	X	X	X	X	all	berry	F–W	Birds and mammals eat berries. Good cover and nesting source.
Privet, glossy (*Ligustrum lucidum*)	X	X	X	X	X	X		S/PSh	berry	F–W	Cedar waxwings occasionally eat berries.
Viburnum, leatherleaf (*Viburnum rhytidophyllum*)	X	X	X	X	X			S/PSh	berry	Su–F	Many mammals and birds eat berries. Good cover source. Butterfly host plant for spring azure.
Vines											
Cross-vine (*Bignonia capreolata*)	N	N	N	N	N	N	N	all	seed	Su	Semi-evergreen. Good hummingbird nectar source.
Greenbrier (*Smilax rotundifolia*)	N	N	N	N	N	N	N	S/PSh	berry	F–W	Evergreen or deciduous. Fruit important in winter. Good cover and nesting source.
Honeysuckle, coral (*Lonicera sempervirens*)	N	N	N	N	N	N	N	S/PSh	berry	Su	Semi-evergreen. Hummingbird nectar source. Songbirds eat berries.
Honeysuckle, Japanese (*Lonicera japonica*)	X	X	X	X	X	X	X	all	berry	Su	Good cover for birds and rabbits. Butterfly host plant for spring azure. *Caution:* Japanese honeysuckle can be invasive.

TABLE 2–2. Deciduous Trees, Shrubs, and Vines for Wildlife

COMMON NAME (*SCIENTIFIC NAME*)	CFP	OHL	OZP	CT	TGP	MGP	SHP	LIGHT NEEDS	FOOD PRODUCED	FRUITING SEASON	VALUE TO WILDLIFE
Large deciduous trees (30 to 60 feet)											
Ash, white (*Fraxinus americana*)	N	N	N	N	N			S	seed	F–W	Some mammals and birds eat seeds, which are produced by female trees. Butterfly host plant for eastern tiger swallowtail and mourning cloak.
Ash, green (*Fraxinus pennsylvanica*)	N	N	N	N	N	N		S	seed	F–W	
Basswood, American (*Tilia americana*)		N	N		N			S/PSh	seed	F	Important bee nectar source. Squirrels and chipmunks eat seeds. Hollow trees make excellent cavities.
Beech, American (*Fagus grandifolia*)	N	N						all	nut	F	Many birds and small mammals eat nuts.
Birch, river (*Betula nigra*)	N	N	N	N	N			S/PSh	seed	Sp–Su	Pine siskins and goldfinches eat seeds. Butterfly host plant for white admiral and eastern tiger swallowtail.
Chittamwood (*Bumelia lanuginosa*)	N	N	N	N	N	N		S/PSh	berry	F–W	Fall food source for birds and summer nectar source for insects.
Elm, American (*Ulmus americana*)	N	N	N	N	N	N		all	seed	Sp	Finches attracted to trees. Orioles nest in drooping boughs. Fruits eaten by many birds. Deer browse twigs. Butterfly host plant for mourning cloak and painted lady.
Elm, slippery (*Ulmus rubra*)	N	N	N	N	N	N		S/PSh	seed	Sp–Su	
Gum, black (*Nyssa sylvatica*)	N	N	N					S/PSh	berry	Su–F	Fruit valuable to many songbirds and drops in fall. Good nectar source for bees.
Hackberry (*Celtis occidentalis*)		N	N	N	N			S/PSh	berry	Su–W	Many birds eat winter berries. Butterfly host plant for mourning cloak, hackberry emperor, and American snout.
Hickory, black (*Carya texana*)	N	N	N	N	N			S	nut	F	Nuts relished by squirrels, chipmunks, birds, and humans. Butterfly host plant.
Hickory, mockernut (*Carya tomentosa*)	N	N	N					all	nut	F	
Hickory, shagbark (*Carya ovata*)		N	N					S	nut	F	

TABLE 2-2. Deciduous Trees, Shrubs, and Vines for Wildlife

COMMON NAME (*SCIENTIFIC NAME*)	SUITABLE NATURAL COMMUNITY (N = NATIVE)							LIGHT NEEDS	FOOD PRODUCED	FRUITING SEASON	VALUE TO WILDLIFE
	CFP	OHL	OZP	CT	TGP	MGP	SHP				
Maple, red (*Acer rubrum*)	N	N	N					S/PSh	seed	Sp–Su	Flowers appear before foliage. Many birds and mammals eat buds, seeds, and flowers. Leaves and seed stalks used as nest materials. Attracts insects.
Maple, sugar (*Acer saccharum*)	N	N	N					PSh	seed	Su–F	
Mulberry, red (*Morus rubra*)	N	N	N	N	N	N		S/PSh	berry	Sp–Su	Songbirds and box turtles eat early summer food from female trees. Butterfly host plant for mourning cloak.
Oak, black (*Quercus velutina*)	N	N	N	N	N			S/PSh	nut	F–W	Oaks are of major importance to wildlife, especially in winter when other foods are scarce. Small acorns of pin, water, and willow oaks are eaten by ducks and quail. Wild turkeys swallow acorns whole regardless of size. Acorns also eaten by many songbirds and mammals. Good cover and nesting sources, especially in prairie areas. Squirrels and birds use leaves and twigs to build their nests. Butterfly host plant.
Oak, blackjack (*Quercus marilandica*)	N	N	N	N	N	N		S	nut	F–W	
Oak, bur (*Quercus macrocarpa*)		N	N	N	N	N		S	nut	F–W	
Oak, chinkapin (*Quercus muehlenbergii*)	N	N	N	N	N	N		S	nut	F–W	
Oak, northern red (*Quercus rubra*)		N	N		N			S	nut	F–W	
Oak, pin (*Quercus palustris*)		N			N			S	nut	F–W	
Oak, post (*Quercus stellata*)	N	N	N	N	N	N		S	nut	F–W	
Oak, Shumard (*Quercus shumardii*)	N	N	N	N	N			S	nut	F–W	
Oak, southern red (*Quercus falcata*)	N	N	N					S	nut	F–W	
Oak, water (*Quercus nigra*)	N	N						S/PSh	nut	F–W	
Oak, white (*Quercus alba*)	N	N	N					S/PSh	nut	F–W	
Oak, willow (*Quercus phellos*)	N							S/PSh	nut	F–W	
Pecan (*Carya illinoensis*)	N			N	N	N		S	nut	F	Squirrels, chipmunks, and birds eat nuts. Butterfly host plant for gray hairstreak.
Sugarberry (*Celtis laevigata*)	N	N	N	N	N	N		S/PSh	berry	F–W	Birds eat winter berries. Butterfly host plant for mourning cloak and hackberry emperor.
Sweetgum (*Liquidambar styraciflua*)	N	N						all	seed	F	Limited use by wildlife. Finches and small mammals eat seeds.

TABLE 2–2. Deciduous Trees, Shrubs, and Vines for Wildlife

COMMON NAME (SCIENTIFIC NAME)	SUITABLE NATURAL COMMUNITY (N = NATIVE)							LIGHT NEEDS	FOOD PRODUCED	FRUITING SEASON	VALUE TO WILDLIFE
	CFP	OHL	OZP	CT	TGP	MGP	SHP				
Tuliptree (*Liriodendron tulipifera*),	X	X	X					S	seed flower	Su–F	Birds and squirrels eat seeds. Flowers attract hummingbirds.
Walnut, black (*Juglans nigra*)	N	N	N	N	N	N		S/PSh	nut	F	Squirrels eat nuts and bury them for future use. Many songbirds eat meat from opened nuts. Butterfly host plant.

Small deciduous trees (10 to 30 feet)

COMMON NAME (SCIENTIFIC NAME)	CFP	OHL	OZP	CT	TGP	MGP	SHP	LIGHT NEEDS	FOOD PRODUCED	FRUITING SEASON	VALUE TO WILDLIFE
Box-elder (*Acer negundo*)	N	N	N	N	N			S/PSh	seed	Su–F	Fair cover source. Butterfly host plant. *Caution:* Box-elder bugs a nuisance on female trees.
Buckeye, red (*Aesculus pavia*)	N	N						all	seed, flower	Su–F	Red flowers attract hummingbirds. Squirrels eat seeds.
Buckthorn, Carolina (*Rhamnus caroliniana*)	N	N	N	N				Sh	berry	Su–F	Many birds eat fruit.
Cherry, black (*Prunus serotina*)	N	N	N		N			S	berry	Su–F	Fruit eaten by many birds and mammals. Butterfly host plant for eastern tiger swallowtail, red-spotted purple, and spring azure.
Crabapple, southern (*Malus angustifolia*)	X	X	X					S/PSh	berry	Su–W	Birds and mammals eat fruit; use small-fruited species. Good nesting source.
Dogwood, flowering (*Cornus florida*)	N	N	N					PSh/Sh	berry	F	Many birds and mammals eat fruit. Good nesting source. Butterfly host plant for spring azure.
Fringe tree (*Chionanthus virginicus*)		N						all	berry	Su–F	Many birds and mammals eat fruit. Flowers in late spring.
Hawthorn, Washington (*Crataegus phaenopyrum*)	X	X	X	X	X	X	X	S/PSh	berry	F–W	Many birds eat fruit. Thorny branches provide nesting cover. Butterfly host plant for gray hairstreak.
Holly, deciduous (*Ilex decidua*)	N	N	N	N				S/PSh	berry	F–W	Many birds eat late winter fruit off female tree. Good nesting source. Butterfly host plant.
Ironwood (*Carpinus caroliniana*)	N	N	N					Sh	nut	F	Squirrels sometimes eat nutlets.

TABLE 2–2. Deciduous Trees, Shrubs, and Vines for Wildlife

COMMON NAME (SCIENTIFIC NAME)	SUITABLE NATURAL COMMUNITY (N = NATIVE)							LIGHT NEEDS	FOOD PRODUCED	FRUITING SEASON	VALUE TO WILDLIFE
	CFP	OHL	OZP	CT	TGP	MGP	SHP				
Mimosa (*Albizia julibrissin*)	X	X	X	X	X	X	X	S/PSh	flower	F	Fragrant pink flowers attract hummingbirds and butterflies. Butterfly host plant for Reakirt's blue.
Olive, autumn (*Elaeagnus umbellata*)	X	X	X	X	X	X	X	S/PSh	berry	Su–W	Many birds, especially cedar waxwing and robin, eat winter berries.
Olive, Russian (*Elaeagnus angustifolia*)	X	X	X	X	X	X	X	S/PSh	berry	Su–W	Provides good nesting cover. *Caution:* Invasive in pastures and riparian zones.
Pawpaw (*Asimina triloba*)	N		N		N			Sh/PSh	berry	Su–W	Raccoon and opossum eat berries. Butterfly host plant.
Persimmon (*Diospyros virginiana*)	N	N	N	N	N			S/PSh	berry	F–W	Many birds and mammals eat fruit off female tree.
Plum, American (*Prunus americana*)			X	X	X			S/PSh	berry	Su–F	Many birds and mammals eat fruit. Butterfly host plant for spring azure.
Redbud, eastern (*Cercis canadensis*)	N	N	N	N	N	N		S/PSh	seed	Su–F	Flowers before the foliage. Good nectar source for bees. Dove and quail eat seeds. Butterfly host plant.
Sassafras (*Sassafras albidum*)	N	N	N					S/PSh	berry	Su–F	Birds eat fruit off female tree. Butterfly host plant for eastern tiger and spicebush swallowtails.
Serviceberry, downy (*Amelanchier arborea*)		N	N		N			S/PSh	berry	Su	Songbirds eat berries. Butterfly host plant.

Deciduous shrubs

COMMON NAME (SCIENTIFIC NAME)	CFP	OHL	OZP	CT	TGP	MGP	SHP	LIGHT NEEDS	FOOD PRODUCED	FRUITING SEASON	VALUE TO WILDLIFE
Arrow-wood, maple-leaved (*Viburnum acerifolium*)	X	X	X	X	X	X	X	PSh	berry	F	Good protective cover in summer. Several birds eat fruit. Butterfly host plant for spring azure.
Arrow-wood, southern (*Viburnum dentatum*)	X	X	X	X	X	X	X	PSh	berry	F	
Azalea, hammock-sweet (*Rhododendron serrulatum*)	X	X	X	X	X	X	X	PSh	flower	Sp	Spring to summer flowers provide nectar for butterflies.
Barberry, Japanese (*Berberis thunbergii*)	X	X	X	X	X	X	X	S	berry	F–W	Some birds eat berries. Good sparrow nesting sites.
Beauty berry, American (*Callicarpa americana*)	N	N	N					Sh/PSh	berry	Su–F	Robin, thrasher, catbird, and mockingbird eat berries.

TABLE 2–2. Deciduous Trees, Shrubs, and Vines for Wildlife

COMMON NAME (*SCIENTIFIC NAME*)	SUITABLE NATURAL COMMUNITY (**N = NATIVE**)							LIGHT NEEDS	FOOD PRODUCED	FRUITING SEASON	VALUE TO WILDLIFE
	CFP	OHL	OZP	CT	TGP	MGP	SHP				
Blackberry/Raspberry (*Rubus trivialis*)	N	N	N	N	N	N	N	S	berry	Su	Important summer food source. Excellent cover source.
Black Haw, southern (*Viburnum prunifolium*)	X	X	X	X	X			all	berry	F–W	Good nesting and cover source. Birds and mammals eat fruit.
Black Haw, rusty (*Viburnum rufidulum*)	N	N	N	N	N			all	berry	F–W	Plant unrelated shrubs for best production. Butterfly host plant for spring azure.
Blueberry (*Vaccinium* spp.)	N	N	N	N	N			Sh/PSh	berry	Su	Good late summer food. Birds and mammals eat berries. Butterfly host plant for spring azure.
Burning bush (*Euonymus atropurpureus*)		N	N	N	N			PSh	berry	F	Good food and cover source.
Butterfly Bush (*Buddleia davidii*)	X	X	X	X	X	X	X	S	flower	Su–F	Perennial. Excellent nectar source for butterflies and hummingbirds.
Buttonbush (*Cephalanthus occidentalis*)	N	N	N	N	N	N		PSh	seed, flower	Su–F	Cover and nectar source. Attractive white flower clusters.
Chokeberry, red (*Aronia arbutifolia*)	X	X	X	X	X	X	X	Sh/PSh	berry	Su–F	Good food and cover source for birds.
Choke cherry (*Prunus virginiana*)					N	N		S/PSh	berry	Su–F	Excellent food and cover source for many birds and mammals. Butterfly host plant for eastern tiger swallowtail.
Coral-berry (*Symphoricarpos orbiculatus*)	N	N	N	N	N	N	N	S/PSh	berry	F–W	Fair food source and good cover source for birds.
Dogwood, rough-leaf (*Cornus drummondii*)	N	N	N	N	N	N		all	berry	Su–F	Many mammals and birds eat berries. Good nesting site.
Elderberry (*Sambucus canadensis*)	N	N	N	N	N	N	N	S	berry	Su–F	Many birds eat berries. Good nesting site.
Hazel, American (*Corylus americana*)	N	N	N					S/PSh	seed	Su–F	Wildlife eat seeds. Good cover and nesting source.
Highbush cranberry, American (*Viburnum trilobum*)	X	X	X	X	X			S/PSh	berry	F–W	Good protective cover. Many birds and mammals eat winter berries. Plant unrelated shrubs for best fruit production. Butterfly host plant for spring azure.
Highbush cranberry, European (*Viburnum opulus*)	X	X	X	X	X	X	X	S/PSh	berry	F–W	

TABLE 2–2. **Deciduous Trees, Shrubs, and Vines for Wildlife**

COMMON NAME (SCIENTIFIC NAME)	CFP	OHL	OZP	CT	TGP	MGP	SHP	LIGHT NEEDS	FOOD PRODUCED	FRUITING SEASON	VALUE TO WILDLIFE
Honeysuckle, amur (*Lonicera maackii*)	X	X	X	X	X	X	X	S	berry	F	Many birds eat fruit. Hummingbirds feed on nectar. Good nesting site. Butterfly host plant for spring azure.
Huckleberry (*Vaccinium arboreum*)	N	N	N	N				S/PSh	berry	F–W	Several birds eat berries.
Mesquite, honey (*Prosopis glandulosa*)						N		S/PSh	seed	F–Su	Wildlife eat high-protein seeds. Butterfly host plant for Reakirt's blue.
Prairieclover, purple (*Dalea purpurea*)				N	N	N		S/PSh	seed, flower	F–Su	New growth high in protein and a valuable forage. Butterfly host plant for Reakirt's blue.
Plum, Chickasaw (*Prunus angustifolia*)				N	N	N	N	S/PSh	berry	Su	Birds, box turtles, and other wildlife eat fruit. Good cover source. Butterfly host plant.
Rose, pasture (*Rosa carolina*)	N	N	N	N	N	N	N	S	seed	F–W	Thorny shrub used as nesting site for birds.
Spicebush (*Lindera benzoin*)	N	N	N		N			S/PSh	berry, flower	F–W	Provides early flowers and scarlet fruit. Butterfly host plant for eastern tiger and spice-bush swallowtails.
Strawberry-bush (*Euonymus americanus*)	N	N	N	N	N			S/PSh	seed	F–W	Turkey and songbirds eat seeds. Favorite deer and rabbit browse.
Sumac, aromatic (*Rhus aromatica*)	N	N	N	N	N	N	N	all	berry	F–W	Quail, pheasant, and songbirds eat winter fruit. Tight-packed berry clusters hold small insects eaten by song-birds. Good cover source for ground-dwelling wildlife. Butterfly host plant.
Sumac, smooth (*Rhus glabra*)	N	N	N	N	N	N		S/PSh	berry	F–W	
Sumac, winged (*Rhus copallina*)	N	N	N	N	N			S/PSh	berry	F–W	
Viburnum, doublefile (*Viburnum plicatum*)	X	X	X	X	X	X	X	PSh	berry	F	Fruit eaten by many birds and mammals. Beware of sterile varieties. Good protective cover source in summer. Butterfly host plant for spring azure.
Viburnum, Sargent's (*Viburnum sargentii*)	X	X	X	X	X	X	X	PSh	berry	F	
Viburnum, Siebold (*Viburnum sieboldii*)	X	X	X	X	X	X	X	PSh	berry	F	
Vitex/Chastetree (*Vitex negundo*)	X	X	X	X	X	X		S	flower	Sp–F	Excellent nectar source for honey bees and butterflies. Good nesting site for birds.

TABLE 2–2. Deciduous Trees, Shrubs, and Vines for Wildlife

COMMON NAME (SCIENTIFIC NAME)	SUITABLE NATURAL COMMUNITY (N = NATIVE)							LIGHT NEEDS	FOOD PRODUCED	FRUITING SEASON	VALUE TO WILDLIFE
	CFP	OHL	OZP	CT	TGP	MGP	SHP				
Winterberry (*Ilex verticillata*)	X	X	X		X			S/PSh	berry	F–W	Songbirds eat winter berries. Both male and female plants needed to produce fruit. Butterfly host plant.
Vines											
Bean, scarlet runner (*Phaseolus coccineus*)	X	X	X	X	X	X	X	S/PSh	seed	F	Annual. Young pods and mature beans edible. Good nectar source.
Bittersweet (*Celastrus scandens*)	N	N	N	N	N	N	N	S/PSh	berry	Su–F	Deciduous. Birds eat winter berries.
Creeper, Virginia (*Parthenocissus quinquefolia*)	N	N	N	N	N	N	N	S/PSh	berry	F–W	Deciduous. Fruit important as fall and winter food.
Grape, muscadine (*Vitis rotundifolia*)	N	N	N	N	N	N	N	S/PSh	berry	Su	Deciduous. Game birds, songbirds, and mammals eat berries. Good cover source.
Greenbrier (*Smilax rotundifolia*)	N	N	N	N	N	N	N	S/PSh	berry	F–W	Evergreen or deciduous. Fruit important in winter. Good cover and nesting source.
Passionvine (*Passiflora incarnata*)	N	N	N	N	N	N	X	S/PSh	berry	Su–F	Deciduous. Birds eat fruit. Butterfly host plant for gulf fritillary.
Trumpet vine (*Campsis radicans*)	N	N	N	N	N	N	N	S/PSh	seed, flower	F–W	Deciduous. Flowers provide nectar for hummingbirds.

Table 2–3 identifies native grasses found in the southern Great Plains and lists the natural community where they grow best, their maximum height, and their value to wildlife. Note the following abbreviations for table 2–3:

Suitable Natural Community: CFP = Cypress Floodplains, OHL = Ouachita Highlands, OZP = Ozark Plateau, CT = Crosstimbers, TGP = Tallgrass Prairie, MGP = Mixed Grass Prairie, SHP = Southern High Plains

Wildflowers for Birds

Wildflowers are an important component of your wildscape, serving multiple functions. Besides serving as nectar sources for insects and hummingbirds, they also provide food sources to many seed-eating birds. Wildflowers are adapted to harsh conditions, making them easy to grow in difficult-to-maintain areas, such as corners and slopes. When wildflowers are planted near vegetable gardens, they attract butterflies and bees that help pollinate your plants. A good selection of wildflowers can beautify your wildscape with a never-ending array of colors that can provide fresh cut flowers for your home.

Wildflowers can be planted throughout the spring and summer, but for best overall results, plant wildflower seeds in early October. Wildflowers generally need at least six hours of sunlight per day to prosper, although many species tolerate light to partial shade. Watering and fertilizing the seeds will help in germination and seedling growth. Some of the seeds will germinate 10–20 days after planting if sufficient moisture is available. To reseed your wildflowers, trim the heads once the dense brown foliage offsets the floral color display.

To plant wildflowers on existing grass, except for winter grasses such as rye or fescue, mow the exist-

TABLE 2–3. Native Grasses for Wildlife

COMMON NAME (SCIENTIFIC NAME)	CFP	OHL	OZP	CT	TGP	MGP	SHP	MAXIMUM HEIGHT	VALUE TO WILDLIFE
Bluegrass, Texas (*Poa arachnifera*)		X		X	X	X		20 in.	Songbirds and rodents eat seeds; rabbits and big game graze leaves. Blades make up to 50% of coot's diet.
Bluestem, big (*Andropogon gerardi*)	X	X	X	X	X	X		6 ft.	Seeds eaten by prairie chicken, turkey, dark-eyed junco, and sparrows (chipping, field, and tree). Seeds and leaves eaten by meadow and pocket mice, while the whole plant is eaten by antelope, bison, and whitetail deer. Little bluestem provides excellent nesting cover for birds; broom-sedge bluestem considered a pasture weed. Butterfly host plant.
Bluestem, broomsedge (*Andropogon virginicus*)	X	X	X	X	X			4 ft.	
Bluestem, cane (*Andropogon barbinodis*)				X	X	X		4 ft.	
Bluestem, Elliott (*Andropogon elliottii*)	X	X	X					3 ft.	
Bluestem, little (*Andropogon scoparius*)	X	X	X	X	X	X	X	4 ft.	
Bluestem, silver (*Andropogon saccharoides*)	X			X	X	X	X	3 ft.	
Bluestem, splitbeard (*Andropogon ternarius*)	X	X	X					4 ft.	
Bristlegrass, knotroot (*Setaria geniculata*)	X	X	X	X	X	X	X	3 ft.	High-value food for rodents, mourning dove, quail, dark-eyed junco, blackbirds, buntings, cardinal, cowbird, dickcissel, blue grosbeak, horned lark, longspurs, meadowlark, pyrrhuloxia, and sparrows.
Bristlegrass, plains (*Setaria macrostachya*)						X		3 ft.	
Buffalograss (*Buchloe dactyloides*)				X	X	X	X	6 in.	Plants eaten by snow goose, antelope, bison, and whitetail deer; seeds eaten by McCown's longspur.
Bundleflower, Illinois (*Desmanthus illinoensis*)				X	X	X		4 ft.	Important legume eaten by quail, sparrows, and other wildlife.
Cane, giant (*Arundinaria gigantea*)	X	X	X					20 ft.	Butterfly host plant.
Carpetgrass, common (*Axonopus affinis*)	X	X						20 in.	Blades eaten by gadwall.
Cordgrass, prairie (*Spartina pectinata*)					X	X		6 ft.	Seeds eaten by several duck species and marsh birds. Geese and muskrats eat rootstocks. Good cover source.
Cupgrass, Texas (*Eriochloa sericea*)				X				4 ft.	Butterfly host plant.
Dropseed, meadow (*Sporobolus asper*)	X	X		X	X	X		4 ft.	Seeds important to ground-feeding birds (turkey, dark-eyed junco, and sparrows) and kangaroo rat. Plants eaten by bison and deer.
Dropseed, sand (*Sporobolus cryptandus*)		X		X	X	X	X	3 ft.	
Gamagrass, eastern (*Tripsacum dactyloides*)	X	X	X	X	X			9 ft.	Cover source. Leaves used as nesting material.
Grama, blue (*Bouteloua gracilis*)		X		X	X	X	X	3 ft.	Seeds eaten by turkey and longspurs; seeds and plants eaten by blacktail prairie dog, kangaroo rat, and prairie pocket

TABLE 2–3. Native Grasses for Wildlife

COMMON NAME (SCIENTIFIC NAME)	SUITABLE NATURAL COMMUNITY							MAXIMUM HEIGHT	VALUE TO WILDLIFE
	CFP	OHL	OZP	CT	TGP	MGP	SHP		
Grama, hairy (*Bouteloua hirsuta*)		X		X	X	X	X	12 in.	mouse. Plants eaten by antelope, mule and whitetail deer, and bison.
Grama, red (*Bouteloua trifida*)				X		X	X	10 in.	
Grama, sideoats (*Bouteloua curtipendula*)		X	X	X	X	X	X	12 in.	
Indiangrass (*Sorghastrum nutans*)	X	X	X	X	X	X	X	7 ft.	Cover source. Leaves used as nesting material.
Lovegrass, plains (*Eragrostis intermedia*)				X		X	X	3 ft.	Upland game birds eat seeds; whitetail deer eat plants. Butterfly host plant.
Lovegrass, purple (*Eragrostis spectabilis*)	X	X	X	X	X			3 ft.	
Lovegrass, sand (*Eragrostis trichodes*)				X		X	X	5 ft.	
Mesquite, curly (*Hilaria belangeri*)				X		X	X	10 in.	Eaten by antelope, bison, and deer.
Muhly, seep (*Muhlenbergia reverchoni*)				X	X	X	X	3 ft.	Eaten by turkey, dark-eyed junco, tree and song sparrows, and elk.
Needlegrass (*Stipa comata*)							X	4 ft.	Seeds eaten by buntings, longspurs, thirteen-lined ground squirrel, and grasshopper mouse. Plants eaten by elk and mule and whitetail deer.
Panicum, beaked (*Panicum anceps*)	X	X	X	X	X			4 ft.	Abundant food source for teal, geese, Wilson's snipe, mourning dove, bobwhite quail, turkey, redwing blackbird, painted bunting, cardinal, cowbird, blue grosbeak, dark-eyed junco, longspurs, sparrows, and towhees. Foliage and plants eaten by muskrat, cottontail, antelope, and white-tailed deer. Butterfly host plant.
Panicum, Scribner (*Panicum scribnerianum*)	X	X	X					18 in.	
Panicum, switchgrass (*Panicum virgatum*)	X	X	X	X	X	X	X	6 ft.	
Panicum, vine-mesquite (*Panicum obtusum*)		X		X	X	X	X	3 ft.	
Paspalum, Florida (*Paspalum floridanum*)	X	X	X		X			4 ft.	Seeds eaten by upland gamebirds, mottled duck, green-winged teal, Canada goose, purple gallinule, sora, mourning dove, bobwhite quail, turkey, redwing blackbird, cowbird, dark-eyed junco, and towhees. Plants eaten by cottontail rabbit, bison, and whitetail deer. Butterfly host plant.
Paspalum, knotgrass (*Paspalum distichum*)	X	X	X	X	X			2 ft.	
Prairieclover, purple (*Dalea purpurea*)					X	X	X	2 ft.	High-protein forage valuable to deer and other herbivores. Butterfly host plant for Reakirt's blue.
Saltgrass, inland (*Distichlis stricta*)						X	X	8 in.	Rootstocks used as nesting cover for shoveler and cinnamon teal. Seedheads, young plants and rootstocks eaten by black, redhead, and shoveler ducks; blue-winged and cinnamon teal; and Canada and snow geese. Long-billed dowitchers and sora eat seeds; whitetail deer browse plants.

TABLE 2–3. Native Grasses for Wildlife

COMMON NAME (*SCIENTIFIC NAME*)	SUITABLE NATURAL COMMUNITY							MAXIMUM HEIGHT	VALUE TO WILDLIFE
	CFP	OHL	OZP	CT	TGP	MGP	SHP		
Sandbur, mat (*Cenchrus pauciflorus*)	X	X	X	X	X	X		2 ft.	Seeds eaten by few birds, notably pyrrhuloxia; whitetail deer browse plants.
Three-awn, arrowfeather (*Aristida purpurascens*)	X	X	X	X	X			2 ft.	Hard seeds used by only a few wildlife species: dark-eyed juncos, white-footed mouse, and whitetail deer.
Three-awn, Oldfield (*Aristida oligantha*)	X	X	X	X	X	X		20 in.	
Three-awn, Wright (*Aristida wrightii*)				X		X	X	20 in.	
Tobosagrass (*Hilaria mutica*)				X		X	X	3 ft.	Eaten by antelope, bison, and deer.
Tridens, purpletop (*Tridens flavus*)	X	X	X	X	X			5 ft.	Fair seed source for birds and rodents. Butterfly host plant.
Tridens, slim (*Tridens muticus*)				X		X		1 ft.	
Wheatgrass, western (*Agropyron smithii*)				X		X		3 ft.	Plants and seeds eaten by blacktail prairie dog, antelope, whitetail and mule deer, and elk.
Wildrye, Virginia (*Elymus virginicus*)	X	X	X	X	X			4 ft.	Deer and upland gamebirds eat seeds.
Wintergrass, Texas (*Stipa leucotricha*)				X		X		3 ft.	Seeds eaten by buntings, longspurs, thirteen-lined ground squirrel, and grasshopper mouse. Plants eaten by elk and mule and whitetail deer.
Witchgrass, fall (*Leptoloma cognatum*)	X	X	X	X	X	X	X	2 ft.	Plants eaten by deer, antelope, and upland gamebirds.
Uniola, broadleaf (*Uniola latifolia*)	X	X	X					4 ft.	Butterfly host plant.
Uniola, longleaf (*Uniola sessiliflora*)	X	X	X					3 ft.	

ing vegetation as short as possible in the fall. Remove the clippings from the site and rake the area to loosen the soil surface to about a ½ inch deep. Mix the wildflower seeds to provide equal distribution and then hand broadcast them over the area to be planted. Most wildflower seeds are adapted to being carried by the wind and then germinating wherever they land. If you rake over the seeds, they may not germinate as quickly. Instead, simply stomp over the area to establish good contact with the soil.

Table 2–4 lists wildflowers that have excellent value for your wildscape. It identifies whether they are native or exotic and gives their light requirements, maximum height, flower colors, and primary blooming season in Oklahoma. Their value to birds is indicated in the final column. Note the following abbreviations for Table 2–4:

LIGHT NEEDS: S = sunny, Sh = shady, PSh = partial shade
FLOWER COLOR: W = white, P = pink, R = red, O = orange, Y = yellow, L = lavender
BLOOMING SEASON: F = fall, W = winter, Sp = spring, Su = summer

Nectar Plants for Butterflies

Butterfly gardening is a growing hobby for many backyard enthusiasts. Not only do butterfly gardens contain colorful flowers, but they also attract a variety of showy butterflies, moths, bees, and even hummingbirds. The planned butterfly garden will include both *host food plants* for the larval caterpillars and *nectar plants* for the adults. Adult butterflies will have a better chance of discovering your

TABLE 2–4. Wildflowers for Birds

COMMON NAME (SCIENTIFIC NAME)	NATIVE (N) / EXOTIC (E)	LIGHT NEEDS	MAXIMUM HEIGHT	FLOWER COLORS	BLOOMING SEASON	VALUE TO BIRDS
Annual flowers						
Cosmos (*Cosmos* spp.)	some N	S	2 ft.	W, P	Su–F	Goldfinches eat seeds.
Cypress vine (*Ipomoea* spp.)	some N	S	20 ft.	R	Su–F	Fair hummingbird nectar source.
Indian blanket (*Gaillardia pulchella*)	N	S	2 ft.	R–Y	Su–F	Oklahoma's state wildflower. Produces small seeds eaten by birds.
Partridgepea, showy (*Chamaecrista fasciculata*)	E	S	4 ft.	Y	Su–F	Seeds eaten by many game and songbird species.
Petunias (*Petunia* x *hybrida*)	E	S/PSh	18 in.	various	Sp–Su	Excellent hummingbird nectar source.
Phlox, annual (*Phlox drummondii*)	E	S	18 in.	W, P	Sp–Su	Hummingbird nectar source. Finches and sparrows eat seeds.
Sage, scarlet (*Salvia splendens*)	E	S/PSh	3 ft.	R	Sp–F	Excellent hummingbird nectar source. Seeds eaten by finches and juncos.
Sunflowers (*Helianthus* spp.)	some N	S	8 ft.	Y	Sp–Su	Seeds eaten by 46 bird species.
Touch-me-nots (*Impatiens* spp.)	E	Sh/PSh	2 ft.	R, O	Su–F	Excellent hummingbird nectar source. Some birds relish seeds.
Perennial flowers						
Bergamots (*Monarda* spp.)	some N	S/PSh	3 ft.	L, R	Su	Hummingbird nectar source.
Blazing star (*Liatris pycnostachya*)	N	S	4 ft.	P	Su–F	Excellent nectar source. Finches and juncos eat seeds.
Bluebells (*Mertensia virginica*)	E	Sh/PSh	2 ft.	L	Sp	Fair hummingbird nectar source.
Cardinal flower (*Lobelia cardinalis*)	N	S/PSh	4 ft.	R	Su–F	Excellent hummingbird nectar source.
Columbines (*Aquilegia* spp.)	some N	S/PSh	3 ft.	R	Sp	Excellent hummingbird nectar source.
Coral bells (*Heuchera sanguinea*)	E	S/PSh	18 in.	R	Sp–Su	Excellent hummingbird nectar source.
Fire pink (*Silene virginica*)	N	S	10 in.	P	Su	Hummingbird nectar source. Finches and sparrows eat seeds.
Fireweed (*Epilobium angustifolium*)	E	S/PSh	4 ft.	L	Su–F	Excellent hummingbird nectar source.
Hollyhock (*Althaea rosa*)	E	S	7 ft.	W, P	Su	Excellent hummingbird and oriole nectar source. Finches and sparrows eat seeds.
Milkweed, butterfly (*Asclepias tuberosa*)	N	S/PSh	3 ft.	O	Su–F	Good hummingbird nectar source.
Paintbrush, downy (*Castilleja sessiliflora*)	N	S	2 ft.	Y	Sp–Su	Hummingbird nectar source.
Paintbrush, Indian (*Castilleja linariaefolia*)	E	S	2 ft.	O	Sp–Su	Hummingbird nectar source.

TABLE 2–4. Wildflowers for Birds

COMMON NAME (*SCIENTIFIC NAME*)	NATIVE (N) / EXOTIC (E)	LIGHT NEEDS	MAXIMUM HEIGHT	FLOWER COLORS	BLOOMING SEASON	VALUE TO BIRDS
Penstemon (*Penstemon* spp.)	some N	S	2 ft.	W	Sp–Su	Excellent oriole and hummingbird nectar source.
Phlox (*Phlox* spp.)	some N	All	2 ft.	L, P	Su	Excellent oriole and hummingbird nectar source.
Primrose, evening showy (*Oenothera speciosa*)	N	S	4 ft.	Y	Su	Fair hummingbird nectar source.
Sunflowers (*Helianthus* spp.)	some N	S	8 ft.	Y	Sp–Su	Seeds eaten by 46 species of birds.
Thistle, prairie (*Cirsium flodmanii*)	E	S	2 ft.	P	Su–F	Seeds eaten by finches.

wildscape if you plant bright colors in clusters. For instance, plant a group of yellow flowers together, rather than mixing them with reds and purples.

Table 2–5 lists nectar sources used by butterflies; larval host plants and the butterfly species that use them are included in chapter 7 (tables 7–2 and 7–3). The table of nectar plants also identifies whether the plants are native or exotic, their light requirements, height, flower colors, and primary blooming season. Note the following abbreviations for table 2–5:

LIGHT NEEDS: S = sunny, Sh = shady,
  PSh = partial shade
FLOWER COLOR: W = white, P = pink, R = red,
  O = orange, Y = yellow, L = lavender, B = Blue
BLOOMING SEASON: F = fall, W = winter, Sp = spring,
  Su = summer

Acquiring Native Plants

Native plants should be emphasized in a wildscape over introduced or cultivated plants for several reasons. First, as has by now been noted repeatedly, native plants are adapted to your area's climate, which may include taxing heat waves and extended cold spells. Second, local animals and birds are adapted to native plants and their specific attributes. For example, some butterflies require certain host plants for their larvae. Without these plants, the butterflies would not be able to complete their life cycle.

So where do you get these native plants? Many commercial nurseries are beginning to offer native species in their stock. If your local nurseries do not, ask them to begin carrying native species. In the meantime, you may be able to find the plants you want at a site near you. Use a knowledgeable expert to learn where these species might be found and how to propagate them.

Before collecting plants from private or public land, obtain the landowner's permission or any necessary permits. Some public lands, such as nature preserves, wildlife refuges, and state parks, prohibit any plant collections because the plants are providing forage and cover for the local wildlife. In general, avoid damaging the site and its aesthetic values.

Avoid trampling vegetation or other sensitive features and stay on designated trails when possible. Do not collect from areas vulnerable to erosion, such as trailside areas. Collect only the minimum amount of plants necessary. It is highly preferable to leave whole plants when plant parts (e.g., seeds or cuttings) are sufficient. The catalog from Prairie Moon Nursery (see appendix E) has a table that includes the germination techniques needed to make prairie plant seeds sprout.

Do not overcollect plants from one site. This means not collecting the only plant at a site; in general, collect one specimen for every 20–50 plants. The more collections you and others make at one site, the greater the negative effect on local plant and wildlife populations. Whenever possible, buy commercially grown native plants that are from your region instead of digging up wild plants.

If you find a rare or protected plant species, do not collect it. Report the finding to the state office of the Nature Conservancy (see appendix I) or the state Natural Heritage Inventory.

FIGURE 2-2. Before collecting native plants from private or public land, obtain the landowner's permission or any necessary permits.

TABLE 2–5. Nectar Plants for Butterflies

COMMON NAME (SCIENTIFIC NAME)	NATIVE (N) / EXOTIC (E)	LIGHT NEEDS	MAXIMUM HEIGHT	FLOWER COLOR	BLOOMING SEASON
Annual flowers					
Alyssum, sweet (*Lobularia maritima*)	E	S/PSh	10 in.	W, P, L	Sp–F
Amaranth, globe (*Gomphrena globosa*)	E	S/PSh	18 in.	W, P, R, L	Sp–F
Beebalm, basil (*Monarda clinopodioides*)	N	S/PSh	15 in.	W, P	Sp–Su
Black-eyed susan (*Rudbeckia hirta*)	N	S/PSh	3 ft.	Y	Sp–F
Bluebonnet (*Lupinus* spp.)	some N	S/PSh	16 in.	B	W–Su
Bluets (*Hedyotis* spp.)	some N	S/PSh	5 in.	W, P, L	W–Sp
Calendula (*Calendula officinalis*)	E	S/PSh	2 ft.	O	Su–W
Catchfly (*Silene* spp.)	some N	S/PSh	2 ft.	W, P, R	Sp–F
Chrysanthemum, single-flowered (*Chrysanthemum* spp.)	some N	S/PSh	2 ft.	Y, R, L	F
Cornflower/Bachelor's button (*Centaurea cyanus*)	E	S/PSh	3 ft.	W, P, B	Sp–F
Cosmos (*Cosmos* spp.)	some N	S	4 ft.	W, P	Sp–W
Crownbeard, golden (*Verbesina encelioides*)	N	S/PSh	3 ft.	Y	All
Dandelion, common (*Taraxacum officinale*)	N	S/PSh	10 in.	Y	All
Flax, stiff-stem (*Linum berlandieri*)	N	S	20 in.	Y, R	W–F
Heliotrope (*Heliotropium arborescens*)	E	S	2 ft.	P	Su
Henbit (*Lamium amplexicaule*)	E	S/PSh	16 in.	L	W–Sp
Hollyhock, single (*Althea* spp.)	E	S	7 ft.	W, R, Y	Su–W
Impatiens (*Impatiens* spp.)	some N	Sh/PSh	2 ft.	R, O	Su–F
Indian blanket (*Gaillardia pulchella*)	N	S	2 ft.	R, Y	Sp–W
Lantana (*Lantana* spp.)	E	S	3 ft.	R, Y	Sp–F
Mallow, rose (*Lavatera trimestris*)	E	S	5 ft.	P	Su–F
Marigold (*Tagetes* spp.)	E	S	2 ft.	Y, O	Su–F
Mexican sunflower (*Tithonia rotundifolia*)	E	S	6 ft.	Y, O	Su–F
Mint, lemon (*Monarda citriodora*)	N	S	32 in.	L, W	Sp–F
Morning glory, common (*Ipomoea purpurea*)	E	S/PSh	vine	W, B, R	Sp–F

TABLE 2–5. Nectar Plants for Butterflies

COMMON NAME (*SCIENTIFIC NAME*)	NATIVE (N) / EXOTIC (E)	LIGHT NEEDS	MAXIMUM HEIGHT	FLOWER COLOR	BLOOMING SEASON
Mountain pink (*Centaurium beyrichii*)	N	S	1 ft.	W, P, R	Su
Nasturtium (*Tropaeolum majus*)	E	S/PSh	10 in.	R, O	Sp–F
Paintbrush, Texas (*Castilleja indivisa*)	N	S	16 in.	W, G, R	Su
Pansy (*Viola* spp.)	E	S/PSh	1 ft.	W, O, R, L	F–Su
Periwinkle, Madagascar (*Catharanthus roseus*)	E	S/PSh	18 in.	W, R, L	Sp–F
Petunia (*Petunia* x *hybrida*)	E	S/PSh	2 ft.	Variety	Sp–W
Phlox, annual (*Phlox drummondii*)	N	S	18 in.	W, P	Sp–Su
Sage, scarlet (*Salvia splendens*)	E	S/PSh	2 ft.	R	Su–F
Sweet william (*Dianthus barbatus*)	E	S	6 in.	W, R	Sp
Verbena, garden (*Verbena hybrida*)	E	S	1 ft.	B, L, P	Sp–F
Yellow star, Texas (*Lindheimera texana*)	N	S/PSh	20 in.	Y	Sp–Su
Zinnia (*Zinnia grandiflora*)	N	S	15 in.	Y, W	Sp–W

Perennial flowers

COMMON NAME (*SCIENTIFIC NAME*)	NATIVE (N) / EXOTIC (E)	LIGHT NEEDS	MAXIMUM HEIGHT	FLOWER COLOR	BLOOMING SEASON
Anemone, Carolina (*Anemone caroliniana*)	N	S	1 ft.	W, P, B	Sp
Antelope-horn (*Asclepias viridis*)	N	S/PSh	2 ft.	Y	Sp–F
Aster, New England (*Aster novae-angliae*)	N	S/PSh	4 ft.	B, P	Su–F
Aster, Stokes (*Stokesia laevis*)	E	S/PSh	2 ft.	L, B	Sp–F
Aster, tall (*Aster praealtus*)	N	S/PSh	4 ft.	P, Y	F
Beebalm, spotted (*Monarda punctata*)	N	S/PSh	3 ft.	Y, P, L	Su
Bergamot, showy (*Monarda didyma*)	E	All	3 ft.	W, P, R	Su
Bergamot, wild (*Monarda fistulosa*)	N	S	3 ft.	L, R	Su
Black-foot, plains (*Melampodium leucanthum*)	N	S	1 ft.	W, Y	Sp–F
Blanket flower (*Gaillardia aristata*)	E	S	2 ft.	O, Y	Sp–F
Blazing star (*Liatris* spp.)	some N	S	4 ft.	P	Su–F
Bluets, fine-leaf (*Hedyotis nigricans*)	N	S/PSh	20 in.	W, P, L	Sp–F
Bluets, summer (*Hedyotis purpurea*)	N	S/PSh	1 ft.	W, L	Su
Boltonia (*Boltonia asteroides*)	N	S	4 ft.	W, P, L	Su–F
Butterfly milkweed (*Asclepias tuberosa*)	N	S	2 ft.	O	Su–F
Cardinal flower (*Lobelia cardinalis*)	N	S/PSh	6 ft.	R	Su–W
Catnip (*Nepeta cataria*)	E	S/PSh	3 ft.	W	Sp–Su
Chicory (*Cichorium intybus*)	N	S	40 in.	B	Su–F
Clematis, autumn (*Clematis paniculata*)	E	S/PSh	vine	W	F
Clover, white (*Trifolium repens*)	E	S	10 in.	W, P	Sp–F
Columbine (*Aquilegia canadensis*)	N	Sh/PSh	2 ft.	R	Sp
Coneflower, purple (*Echinacea purpurea*)	N	S	3 ft.	L	Su–F
Coneflower, sweet (*Rudbeckia subtomentosa*)	N	S/PSh	5 ft.	Y	Su–W
Coral vine (*Antigon leptopus*)	E	S/PSh	vine	W, P	All
Coreopsis, lance-leaved (*Coreopsis lanceolata*)	N	S	5 ft.	Y	Su
Crownbeard, golden (*Verbesina encelioides*)	N	S	8 in.	Y	Su–F
Daisy, Engelmann (*Engelmannia pinnatifida*)	N	S	3 ft.	Y	Sp–F
Daisy, yellow shrub (*Euryops pectinatus*)	E	S/PSh	3 ft.	Y	All
Dogbane, spreading (*Apocynum androsaemifolium*)	N	S/PSh	20 in.	W, P	Sp–Su
Flax, prairie (*Linum lewisii*)	N	S	32 in.	W, B	Sp–F
Fleabane (*Erigeron* spp.)	some N	S/PSh	2 ft.	W	Sp–Su
Frostweed (*Verbesina virginica*)	N	S/PSh	7 ft.	W	Su–F
Gaillardia, rayless (*Gaillardia suavis*)	N	S	2 ft.	Y, R	Sp–Su
Garlic, wild (*Allium canadense*)	N	S/PSh	2 ft.	P	Sp
Gaura (*Gaura lindheimeri*)	E	S/PSh	4 ft.	P	Sp–F
Gayfeather, Kansas (*Liatris pycnostachya*)	N	S	5 ft.	L	Su–F
Gayfeather, narrow-leaf (*Liatris mucronata*)	N	S	3 ft.	L	Su–W
Gayfeather, rough (*Liatris aspera*)	N	S	4 ft.	L	Su–F
Goldenrod (*Solidago* spp.)	some N	S	6 ft.	Y	Su–F
Heliotrope, seaside (*Heliotropium curassavicum*)	N	S	16 in.	W	Sp–F
Heliopsis/Ox-eye (*Heliopsis helianthoides*)	N	S/PSh	3 ft.	Y	F
Hollyhock (*Althaea rosa*)	E	S	5 ft.	W, R, Y	Su–F

TABLE 2-5. Nectar Plants for Butterflies

COMMON NAME (SCIENTIFIC NAME)	NATIVE (N) / EXOTIC (E)	LIGHT NEEDS	MAXIMUM HEIGHT	FLOWER COLOR	BLOOMING SEASON
Hyacinth, wild (Camassia scilloides)	N	S/PSh	2 ft.	B, L	Sp–Su
Ironweed, Missouri (Vernonia missurica)	N	S	5 ft.	R, L	Su–F
Ironweed, western (Vernonia baldwinii)	N	S	5 ft.	L	Su–F
Joe-pye-weed (Eupatorium fistulosum)	N	S/PSh	7 ft.	P, L	Su–F
Lantana, Texas (Lantana horrida)	E	S	5 ft.	O, Y	Sp–F
Larkspur, prairie (Delphinium virescens)	N	S/PSh	5 ft.	W, B	Sp–Su
Lavender (Lavandula spp.)	E	S	18 in.	L	Su
Lobelia, blue (Lobelia siphilitica)	N	S/PSh	5 ft.	B	Sp–F
Lupine (Lupinus spp.)	some N	All	3 ft.	B	Sp
Mexican hat (Ratibida columnifera)	N	S	3 ft.	Y	Sp–W
Milkweed, common (Asclepias syriaca)	N	S	7 ft.	P	Su
Milkweed, Mexican (Asclepias curassavica)	E	S/PSh	3 ft.	Y, O	Sp–F
Milkweed, purple (Asclepias purpurascens)	N	S/PSh	40 in.	R, L	Sp–Su
Milkweed, swamp (Asclepias incarnata)	N	S/PSh	5 ft.	P	Su–F
Milkweed, white-flowered (Asclepias variegata)	N	S	3 ft.	W	Sp–Su
Mist-flower, blue (Eupatorium coelestinum)	N	PSh	6 ft.	B	Su–W
Mist-flower, pink (Eupatorium incarnatum)	N	Sh/PSh	6 ft.	W, P, L	F–Sp
Morning glory, bush (Ipomoea leptophylla)	N	S	5 ft.	P, L	Su
Paintbrush, downy (Castilleja sessiliflora)	N	S/PSh	1 ft.	Y, P	Su–F
Paper-flower, woolly (Psilostrophe villosa)	N	S	2 ft.	Y	Sp–F
Parsley, prairie (Polytaenia nuttallii)	N	S/PSh	3 ft.	Y	Sp–Su
Penstemon, pink plains (Penstemon ambiguus)	N	S/PSh	20 in.	W, P	Sp–Su
Pentas (Pentas lanceolata)	E	S	3 ft.	P, R	Sp–W
Peppermint (Mentha piperita)	E	S/PSh	3 ft.	L	Su–F
Phlox, moss (Phlox subulata)	E	S	6 in.	W, P, R, B	Sp–Su
Phlox, prairie (Phlox pilosa)	N	S/PSh	2 ft.	P, L	Sp
Phlox, summer (Phlox paniculata)	N	S/PSh	6 ft.	P, L	Su–F
Phlox, blue (Phlox divaricata)	N	All	2 ft.	L, W	Sp
Prairie-Coneflower (Ratibida spp.)	N	S	3 ft.	Y, R	Sp–Su
Prairie clover, purple (Dalea purpurea)	N	S	3 ft.	L	Su
Puccoon, fringed (Lithospermum incisum)	N	S	1 ft.	Y	F–Su
Queen Anne's lace (Daucus carota)	E	S	3 ft.	W	Su
Sage, blue (Salvia azurea)	N	S	5 ft.	W, B	Su–F
Sage, lyre-leaf (Salvia lyrata)	N	Sh/PSh	2 ft.	B, L	Sp–Su
Sage, mealy (Salvia farinacea)	N	S/PSh	3 ft.	B	Sp–F
Sage, pineapple (Salvia elegans)	E	S/PSh	3 ft.	R	Sp–W
Sage, cherry (Salvia greggii)	N	S	3 ft.	P, R	Su–F
Sand-verbena, sweet (Abronia fragrans)	N	S/PSh	2 ft.	W, P, L	W–Su
Sedum, autumn joy (Sedum spectabile)	E	All	2 ft.	P	Su–F
Skeleton plant (Lygodesmia aphylla texana)	N	S	2 ft.	P, L, B	Sp–F
Snakeroot, white (Eupatorium rugosum)	N	S/PSh	32 in.	W	F
Spearmint (Mentha spicata)	E	Sh/PSh	2 ft.	W	Su–F
Speedwell (Veronica spp.)	some N	S/PSh	18 in.	P, B	Su–F
Sunflower, Maximilian (Helianthus maximiliani)	N	S	10 ft.	Y	Su–F
Verbena (Verbena bonariensis)	N	S	20 in.	L	Su
Verbena, Dakota (Verbena bipinnatifida)	N	S	18 in.	P, L	All
Verbena, hoary (Verbena stricta)	N	S	6 ft.	B, L	Su–F
Verbena, rose (Verbena canadensis)	N	S/PSh	16 in.	P, L	Sp–Su
Verbena, tuberous (Verbena rigida)	E	S	2 ft.	L	Sp–F
Violet, wood (Viola spp.)	E	Sh/PSh	6 in.	L	Sp
Wild Onion, Drummond (Allium drummondii)	N	S/PSh	1 ft.	W, P	Sp
Wild Onion, fragrant (Allium perdulce)	N	S/PSh	8 in.	W, P	Sp
Wisteria, Chinese (Wisteria sinensis)	E	S/PSh	vine	W, B	Sp
Yarrow, white (Achillea millefolium)	N	S	20 in.	W	Su–F
Zexmenia (Zexmenia hispida)	E	All	3 ft.	Y	Sp–Su
Zinnia, plains (Zinnia grandiflora)	N	S	9 in.	Y	Su–F

TABLE 2–5. Nectar Plants for Butterflies

COMMON NAME (SCIENTIFIC NAME)	NATIVE (N) / EXOTIC (E)	LIGHT NEEDS	MAXIMUM HEIGHT	FLOWER COLOR	BLOOMING SEASON
Trees					
Apple (*Malus pumila*)	E	S/PSh	50 ft.	W, P	Sp
Basswood, American (*Tilia americana*)	N	S/PSh	100 ft.	W, Y	Sp
Black-haw, rusty (*Viburnum rufidulum*)	N	S/PSh	30 ft.	W	Sp
Chaste tree, lilac (*Vitex agnus-castus*)	E	S	20 ft.	L	Sp–F
Cherry, black (*Prunus serotina*)	N	S/PSh	60 ft.	W	Sp
Chittamwood (*Bumelia lanuginosa*)	N	S/PSh	45 ft.	Y, G	Su
Dogwood, flowering (*Cornus florida*)	N	S/PSh	36 ft.	W, Y	Sp
Locust, black (*Robinia pseudo acacia*)	N	S/PSh	45 ft.	W	Sp
Mesquite, honey (*Prosopis juliflora glandulosa*)	N	S/PSh	30 ft.	Y, G	Sp–F
Mimosa (*Albizia julibrissin*)	E	S/PSh	25 ft.	P	Sp–F
Mock orange (*Philadelphus inodorus*)	E	S/PSh	9 ft.	W	Sp–F
Peach (*Prunus persica*)	E	S/PSh	24 ft.	P	Sp
Plum (*Prunus americana*)	N	S	35 ft.	W	Sp
Redbud (*Cercis canadensis*)	N	S/PSh	35 ft.	P	Sp
Rose of Sharon (*Althea* spp.)	E	S/PSh	15 ft.	P	Sp–Su
Serviceberry, smooth (*Amelanchier arborea laevis*)	E	S	30 ft.	W	Sp
Tulip-tree (*Liriodendron tulipifera*)	E	S	100 ft.	Y	Sp
Shrubs					
Abelia, glossy (*Abelia* x *grandiflora*)	E	S/PSh	8 ft.	P, W	Su–F
Azalea, hoary (*Rhododendron canescens*)	N	S/PSh	6 ft.	P, W, Y	Sp–Su
Bird-of-paradise (*Caesalpinia gilliesii*)	E	S/PSh	8 ft.	Y, R	Su–F
Butterfly bush (*Buddleia davidii*)	E	S	12 ft.	W, P, L	Su–F
Buckeye, red (*Aesculus pavia*)	N	S/PSh	15 ft.	R, Y	Sp
Button-bush (*Cephalanthus occidentalis*)	N	S/PSh	15 ft.	W, P	Su–F
Choke berry, red (*Aronia arbutifolia*)	E	S/PSh	12 ft.	W, P	Sp–Su
Clematis, bush (*Clematis heracleifolia*)	E	S/PSh	3 ft.	L	Su–F
Dogwood, rough-leaf (*Cornus drummondii*)	N	S/PSh	15 ft.	W	Sp
Hawthorn, parsley (*Crataegus marshallii*)	N	S/PSh	25 ft.	W	Sp
Honeysuckle, white (*Lonicera albiflora*)	N	S/PSh	6 ft.	W	Sp
Indigo, false (*Amorpha fruticosa*)	N	S/PSh	15 ft.	L	Sp–Su
Lilac, common (*Syringa* spp.)	E	S/PSh	15 ft.	W, L	Sp–Su
Mahonia, leatherleaf (*Mahonia bealei*)	E	S/PSh	6 ft.	Y	Sp
New Jersey tea (*Ceanothus americanus*)	N	S	4 ft.	W	Sp–Su
Plum, Chickasaw (*Prunus angustifolia*)	N	S/PSh	14 ft.	W	Sp
Privet, Chinese (*Ligustrum sinense*)	E	S	20 ft.	W	Sp
Spiraea, Japanese (*Spiraea japonica*)	E	Sh/PSh	3 ft.	W, P	Sp–F
Viburnum (*Viburnum* spp.)	some N	S	15 ft.	W	Sp

FAMILY ACTIVITIES

Learn to use a plant key to identify local species

All plants have features or characteristics that set them apart from other species, but to learn all the characteristics for every species is difficult. A fun way to identify trees, shrubs, and other plants is by using a plant identification key.

A key lists side by side two statements concerning a plant's characteristics. The reader looks at different features of the plant, including leaves, size, branching, and color, and then decides which statement is the better description. The key then directs the reader to a new pair of statements. The process continues, leading the reader to the plant's species name.

Some of the best keys for family use are those with pictures or drawings. See appendix G for examples of tree and other plant identification guides.

Case Studies of Plantings

The 11 planting case studies that follow cover six kinds of settings: sunny, shady, and moist wildscapes, wildflower meadows, and butterfly and rock gardens. Each photo is accompanied by a bird's-eye or plan view and an interpretive sketch on which the plants are identified. All the case studies illustrate multilayering and provision of cover. Checking the plants named against those in tables 2–1, 2–2, 2–3, and 2–4 will show you their wildlife values. Your particular wildscape may include several kinds of settings, from sunny spaces to moist and shady corners or an area designed especially to attract butterflies.

FIGURE 2-3. A (above): An example of how a wildscape can be designed to offer food and shelter for wildlife as well as an attractive entrance to this homeowner's front door. (Oklahoma Certified Wildscape #0275, Tulsa)

B: The homeowner has created a diversity of layers by using trees, shrubs, ground covers, and perennials in combination with rocks and stone edging. Through use of a mixture of evergreens (carpet juniper, Oregon grape holly, live oak) and deciduous plantings, this wildscape has year-round curb appeal.

C: Wildlife value in this wildscape includes berry-producing shrubs (Oregon grape holly, sumac), acorns from the live oak, and nectar for butterflies and hummingbirds (butterfly bush, Autumn joy sedum, Indian blanket, *Salvia* spp.). The live oak serves as the caterpillar host plant for the white M hairstreak. Rocks provide basking areas for butterflies and reptiles, while the cooler, moister areas underneath the rocks provide shelter for amphibians and reptiles.

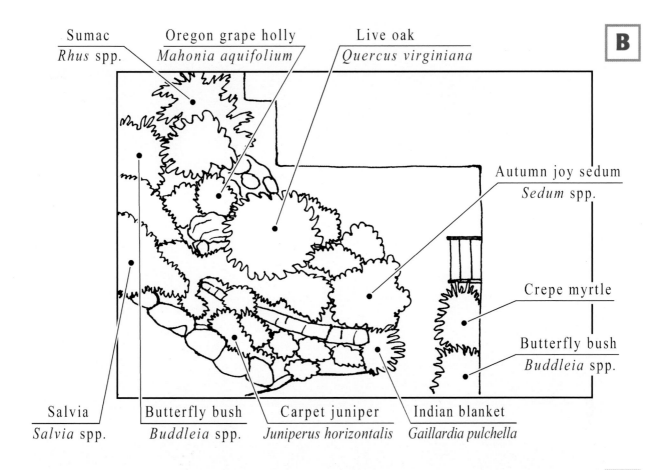

B

Sumac
Rhus spp.

Oregon grape holly
Mahonia aquifolium

Live oak
Quercus virginiana

Autumn joy sedum
Sedum spp.

Crepe myrtle

Butterfly bush
Buddleia spp.

Salvia
Salvia spp.

Butterfly bush
Buddleia spp.

Carpet juniper
Juniperus horizontalis

Indian blanket
Gaillardia pulchella

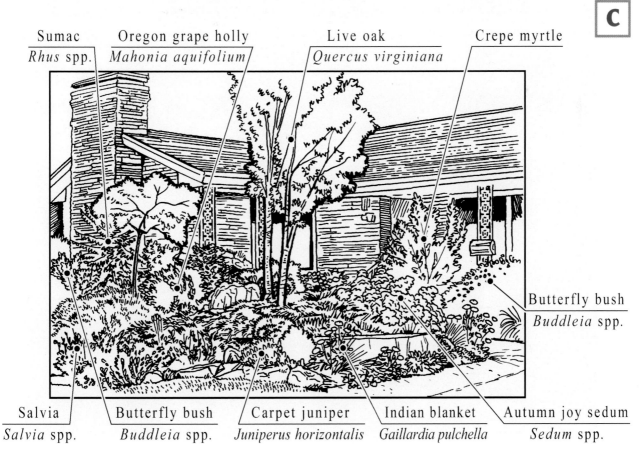

C

Sumac
Rhus spp.

Oregon grape holly
Mahonia aquifolium

Live oak
Quercus virginiana

Crepe myrtle

Butterfly bush
Buddleia spp.

Salvia
Salvia spp.

Butterfly bush
Buddleia spp.

Carpet juniper
Juniperus horizontalis

Indian blanket
Gaillardia pulchella

Autumn joy sedum
Sedum spp.

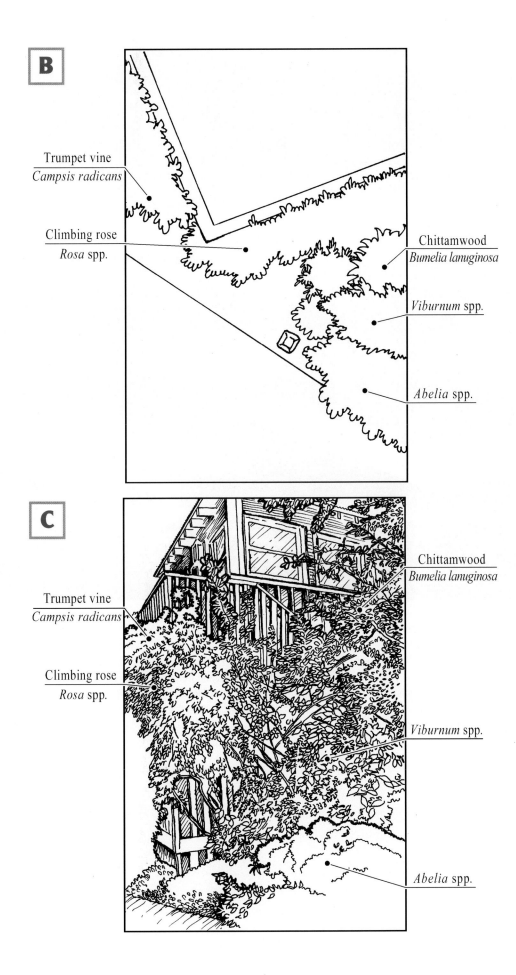

B

Trumpet vine
Campsis radicans

Climbing rose
Rosa spp.

Chittamwood
Bumelia lanuginosa

Viburnum spp.

Abelia spp.

C

Trumpet vine
Campsis radicans

Climbing rose
Rosa spp.

Chittamwood
Bumelia lanuginosa

Viburnum spp.

Abelia spp.

FIGURE 2-4. A (opposite): An example of a wildscape that provides food and shelter for wildlife through the use of deciduous trees, vines, and shrubs. This area of the wildscape receives at least six hours of sunlight.

B: Using vines to fill in the vertical space between the chittamwood tree and the low-growing *Abelia* creates a layering effect. In summer, the vines create dense, strong support and leafy concealment for nests of many songbirds, such as the cardinal, mockingbird, and brown thrasher. In winter, the density of the vine canes provides songbirds with escape cover to evade predators.

C: Wildlife value in this wildscape includes berry-producing plants (chittamwood, *Viburnum*) and nectaring plants (*Abelia*, trumpet vine) for hummingbirds. Shelter is provided by the dense vines year-round.

FIGURE 2-5. A (above): An example of a wildscape that provides food and shelter for wildlife as well as an inviting place for the homeowners to relax.

B: A layering effect is created by incorporating trees, shrubs, vines, grasses, and ground covers into the wildscape. In winter the dormant grass clumps provide important shelter for songbirds from inclement weather and predators.

C: Wildlife value in this wildscape includes berry-producing plants (sumac, holly, barberry, Virginia creeper) and nectar (*Canna* spp.) for hummingbirds. The *Vinca* creates a dense ground cover that provides shelter for toads and frogs. Some songbirds (downy woodpecker, Carolina chickadee) stash sunflower or other seeds in the deep crevices in the bark of pine trees.

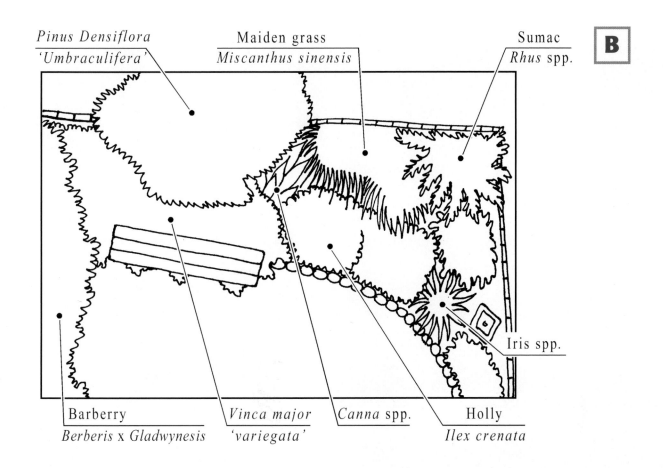

Pinus Densiflora 'Umbraculifera'

Maiden grass
Miscanthus sinensis

Sumac
Rhus spp.

B

Iris spp.

Barberry
Berberis x Gladwynesis

Vinca major 'variegata'

Canna spp.

Holly
Ilex crenata

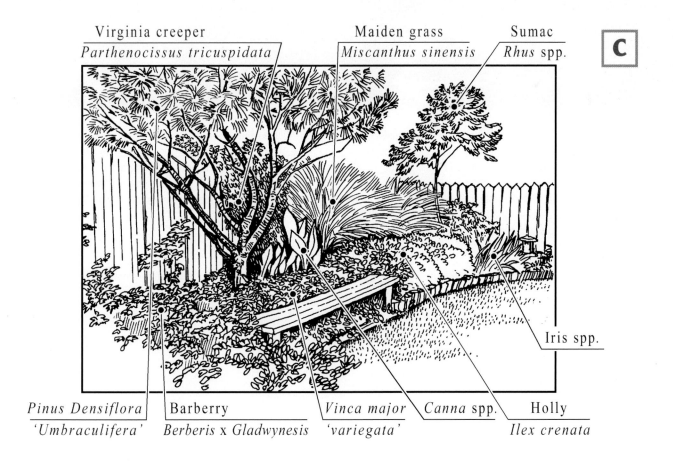

Virginia creeper
Parthenocissus tricuspidata

Maiden grass
Miscanthus sinensis

Sumac
Rhus spp.

C

Iris spp.

Pinus Densiflora 'Umbraculifera'

Barberry
Berberis x Gladwynesis

Vinca major 'variegata'

Canna spp.

Holly
Ilex crenata

FIGURE 2-6. A (above): The rock feature in this shady wildscape provides both privacy from adjoining neighbors and a natural setting for quiet repose.

B: Starting at the base, the largest rocks were carefully placed to provide nooks and crannies for plantings. The evergreen English ivy and sweet box cascade over the rocks, softening the effect.

C: Wildlife value in this wildscape includes the nectar-producing sweet box for butterflies and bees, the flowers later ripening into berries relished by songbirds. The evergreen plants provide shelter year-round for songbirds, and the nooks and crannies provide safe places for toads and lizards to hibernate in winter.

Oak tree
Quercus spp.

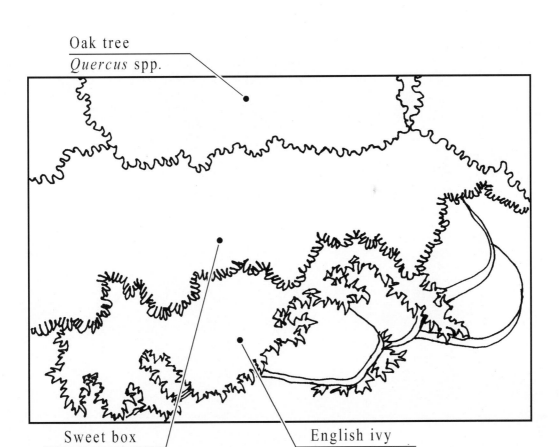

Sweet box
Sarcococca hookerana

English ivy
Hedera helix

Oak tree
Quercus spp.

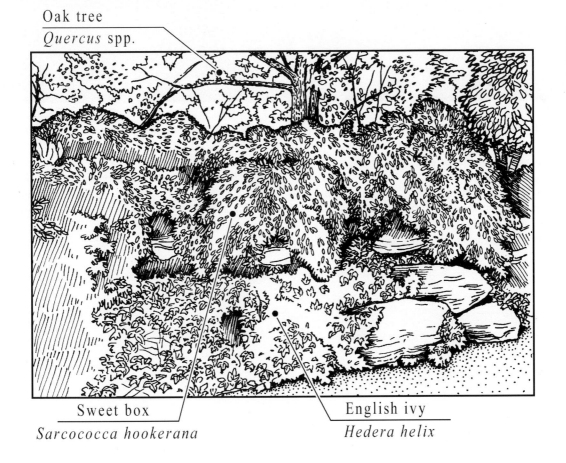

Sweet box
Sarcococca hookerana

English ivy
Hedera helix

FIGURE 2-7. A: The homeowner created a natural looking habitat by planting small trees, shrubs, and ground covers among the mature trees. (Oklahoma Certified Wildscape #0282, Ponca City)

B: The different heights of small trees, shrubs, ferns, and *Hostas* create a good multilayering effect. Vines contribute additional layering to the habitat. The curves between the wooded habitat and the lawn in this landscape mimic natural habitats; nowhere in nature will you find a straight line separating one habitat type from another.

C: Wildlife value in this wildscape includes berry and seed-producing plants (eastern red cedar, eastern redbud, burning bush, Virginia creeper) and good nesting areas in the vines and eastern red cedar.

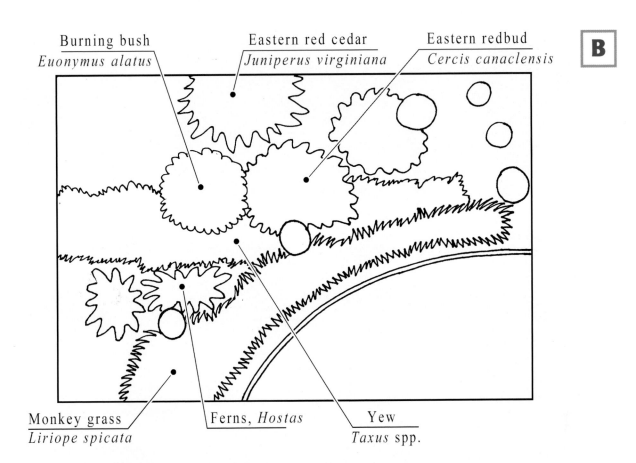

Burning bush
Euonymus alatus

Eastern red cedar
Juniperus virginiana

Eastern redbud
Cercis canaclensis

B

Monkey grass
Liriope spicata

Ferns, *Hostas*

Yew
Taxus spp.

Burning bush
Euonymus alatus

Eastern red cedar
Juniperus virginiana

Eastern redbud
Cercis canaclensis

C

Monkey grass
Liriope spicata

Ferns, *Hostas*

Yew
Taxus spp.

Virginia creeper
Parthenocissus quinquefolia

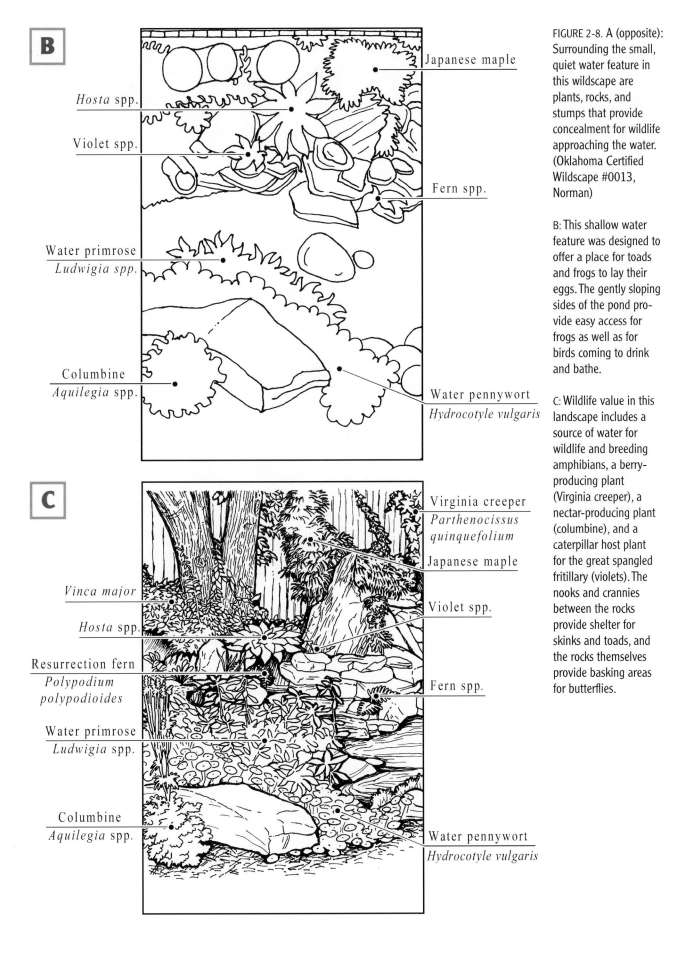

B

Hosta spp.

Violet spp.

Water primrose
Ludwigia spp.

Columbine
Aquilegia spp.

Japanese maple

Fern spp.

Water pennywort
Hydrocotyle vulgaris

C

Vinca major

Hosta spp.

Resurrection fern
*Polypodium
polypodioides*

Water primrose
Ludwigia spp.

Columbine
Aquilegia spp.

Virginia creeper
*Parthenocissus
quinquefolium*

Japanese maple

Violet spp.

Fern spp.

Water pennywort
Hydrocotyle vulgaris

FIGURE 2-8. A (opposite): Surrounding the small, quiet water feature in this wildscape are plants, rocks, and stumps that provide concealment for wildlife approaching the water. (Oklahoma Certified Wildscape #0013, Norman)

B: This shallow water feature was designed to offer a place for toads and frogs to lay their eggs. The gently sloping sides of the pond provide easy access for frogs as well as for birds coming to drink and bathe.

C: Wildlife value in this landscape includes a source of water for wildlife and breeding amphibians, a berry-producing plant (Virginia creeper), a nectar-producing plant (columbine), and a caterpillar host plant for the great spangled fritillary (violets). The nooks and crannies between the rocks provide shelter for skinks and toads, and the rocks themselves provide basking areas for butterflies.

FIGURE 2-9. A (above): A mixture of perennials, annuals, and native grasses creates a low-maintenance meadow in this opening in a pine woodland. (Oklahoma Certified Wildscape #0108, Hackett, Arkansas)

B: Prepare the area for a wildflower meadow in the spring by clearing existing vegetation, turning the soil with a plow or rotary tiller set at its deepest setting, and raking the area smooth. Select a wildflower seed mixture suitable for your region. Maintain con-stant soil moisture until the seeds germinate and seedlings reach a height of 4 to 6 inches, then water as needed. Mow in late winter with the blade at its highest setting. The wildflower meadow in this wildscape took three years to become established.

C: Wildlife value in this wildscape includes wildflowers that produce nectar for butterflies. These flowers also produce seed for winter songbirds. Native grasses serve as caterpillar host plants for many species of skippers.

Eastern red cedar
Juniperus virginiana

Shortleaf pine
Pinus echinata

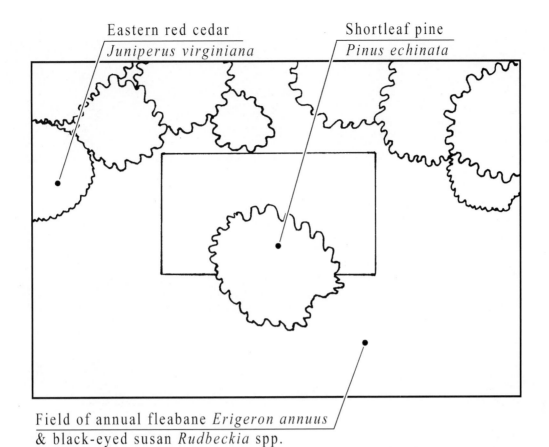

Field of annual fleabane *Erigeron annuus*
& black-eyed susan *Rudbeckia* spp.

Eastern red cedar
Juniperus virginiana

Shortleaf pine
Pinus echinata

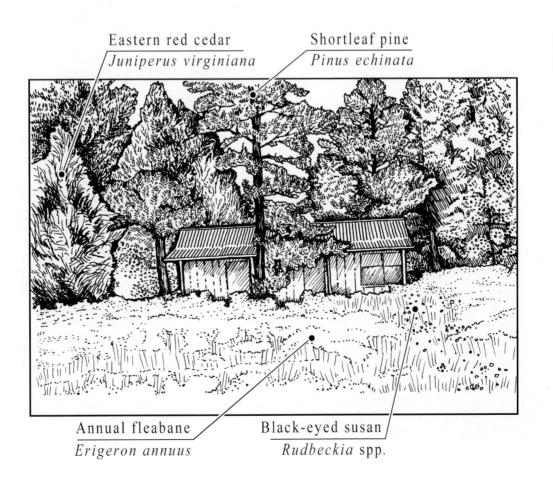

Annual fleabane
Erigeron annuus

Black-eyed susan
Rudbeckia spp.

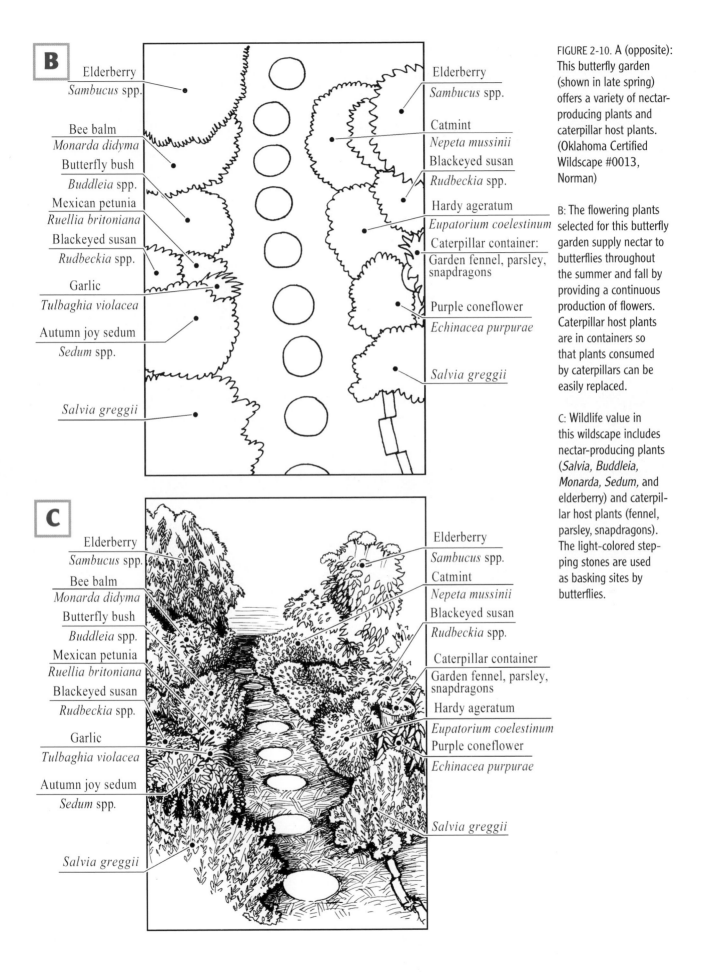

B

Elderberry
Sambucus spp.

Bee balm
Monarda didyma

Butterfly bush
Buddleia spp.

Mexican petunia
Ruellia britoniana

Blackeyed susan
Rudbeckia spp.

Garlic
Tulbaghia violacea

Autumn joy sedum
Sedum spp.

Salvia greggii

Elderberry
Sambucus spp.

Catmint
Nepeta mussinii

Blackeyed susan
Rudbeckia spp.

Hardy ageratum
Eupatorium coelestinum

Caterpillar container:
Garden fennel, parsley, snapdragons

Purple coneflower
Echinacea purpurae

Salvia greggii

FIGURE 2-10. A (opposite): This butterfly garden (shown in late spring) offers a variety of nectar-producing plants and caterpillar host plants. (Oklahoma Certified Wildscape #0013, Norman)

B: The flowering plants selected for this butterfly garden supply nectar to butterflies throughout the summer and fall by providing a continuous production of flowers. Caterpillar host plants are in containers so that plants consumed by caterpillars can be easily replaced.

C: Wildlife value in this wildscape includes nectar-producing plants (*Salvia, Buddleia, Monarda, Sedum,* and elderberry) and caterpillar host plants (fennel, parsley, snapdragons). The light-colored stepping stones are used as basking sites by butterflies.

C

Elderberry
Sambucus spp.

Bee balm
Monarda didyma

Butterfly bush
Buddleia spp.

Mexican petunia
Ruellia britoniana

Blackeyed susan
Rudbeckia spp.

Garlic
Tulbaghia violacea

Autumn joy sedum
Sedum spp.

Salvia greggii

Elderberry
Sambucus spp.

Catmint
Nepeta mussinii

Blackeyed susan
Rudbeckia spp.

Caterpillar container
Garden fennel, parsley, snapdragons

Hardy ageratum
Eupatorium coelestinum

Purple coneflower
Echinacea purpurae

Salvia greggii

FIGURE 2-11. A (above): This butterfly garden (shown in midsummer) provides masses of color that are attractive to butterflies.

B: The sunniest areas of the yard is the best location for a butterfly garden. This butterfly garden offers nectar-producing plants at different heights to accommodate a variety of butterfly species.

C: Wildlife value in this landscape includes nectar-producing plants (butterfly weed, blazing star, *Coreopsis* spp., purple coneflower). The purple coneflower is also the caterpillar host plant for the pearl crescent. All of the flowers produce seeds consumed by wintering songbirds.

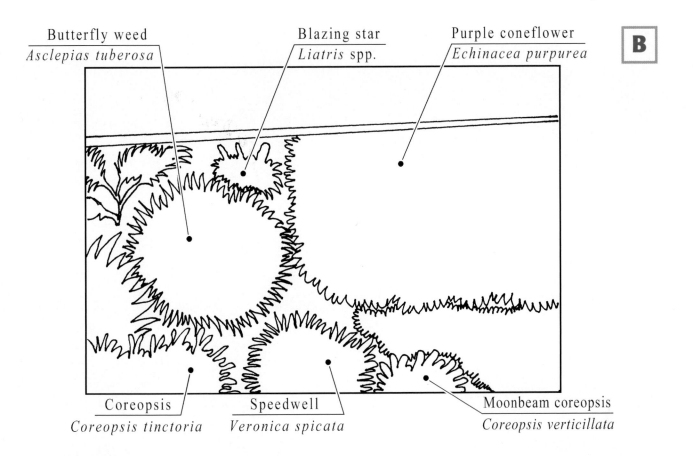

Butterfly weed
Asclepias tuberosa

Blazing star
Liatris spp.

Purple coneflower
Echinacea purpurea

B

Coreopsis
Coreopsis tinctoria

Speedwell
Veronica spicata

Moonbeam coreopsis
Coreopsis verticillata

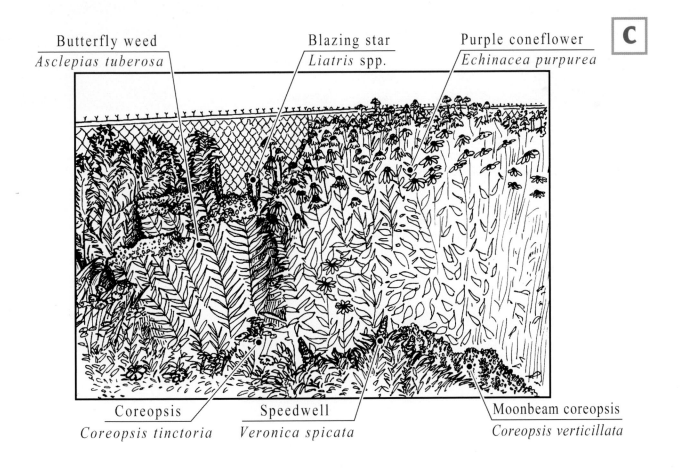

C

Butterfly weed
Asclepias tuberosa

Blazing star
Liatris spp.

Purple coneflower
Echinacea purpurea

Coreopsis
Coreopsis tinctoria

Speedwell
Veronica spicata

Moonbeam coreopsis
Coreopsis verticillata

FIGURE 2-12. A (above): The rock garden represents the lowest layer in this wildscape. Shrubs, vines, and small trees are planted out from both sides of the walkway. (Oklahoma Certified Wildscape #0013, Norman)

B: Rocks were placed in this garden to create openings for plantings. All the plantings in this rock garden require shallow, well-drained soil. Most plants selected produce tube-shaped flowers that provide nectar for hummingbirds.

C: Wildlife value in this wildscape includes nectar-producing plants for hummingbirds and butterflies. The *Viburnum* shrub and Virginia creeper produce berries, and the rocks (including the walkway) are used by butterflies and lizards for basking sites.

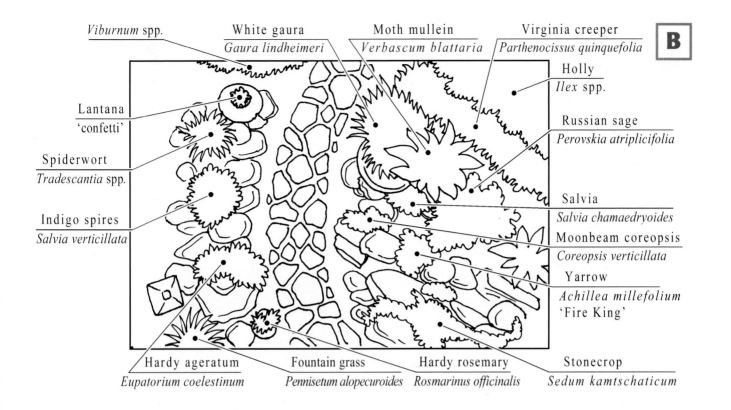

B

Viburnum spp.

White gaura
Gaura lindheimeri

Moth mullein
Verbascum blattaria

Virginia creeper
Parthenocissus quinquefolia

Holly
Ilex spp.

Lantana
'confetti'

Russian sage
Perovskia atriplicifolia

Spiderwort
Tradescantia spp.

Salvia
Salvia chamaedryoides

Indigo spires
Salvia verticillata

Moonbeam coreopsis
Coreopsis verticillata

Yarrow
Achillea millefolium
'Fire King'

Hardy ageratum
Eupatorium coelestinum

Fountain grass
Pennisetum alopecuroides

Hardy rosemary
Rosmarinus officinalis

Stonecrop
Sedum kamtschaticum

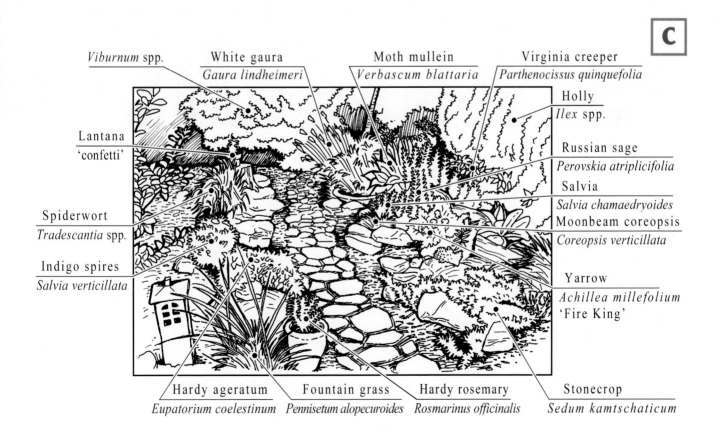

C

Viburnum spp.

White gaura
Gaura lindheimeri

Moth mullein
Verbascum blattaria

Virginia creeper
Parthenocissus quinquefolia

Holly
Ilex spp.

Lantana
'confetti'

Russian sage
Perovskia atriplicifolia

Salvia
Salvia chamaedryoides

Spiderwort
Tradescantia spp.

Moonbeam coreopsis
Coreopsis verticillata

Indigo spires
Salvia verticillata

Yarrow
Achillea millefolium
'Fire King'

Hardy ageratum
Eupatorium coelestinum

Fountain grass
Pennisetum alopecuroides

Hardy rosemary
Rosmarinus officinalis

Stonecrop
Sedum kamtschaticum

FIGURE 2-13. A (above): This rock garden was created on an existing west-facing slope. The garden receives sun from midafternoon till dusk. (Wildscape Demonstration Site, Byron Fish Hatchery, Cherokee, Oklahoma)

B: The purpose of this rock garden is to attract butterflies. The plants selected produce nectar and are drought-tolerant. Rocks were placed to create visual interest and to provide basking areas for butterflies.

C: Wildlife value in this wildscape includes nectar-producing plants and basking areas for butterflies. Staff at this site related information regarding unplanned wildlife value. A family of lizards (prairie racerunners) found that this garden provided shelter (under rocks), basking areas, and food (the butterflies!).

Texas betony
Stachys drummondii

Indian blanket
Gaillardia pulchella

Lemon mint
Monarcia citriodora

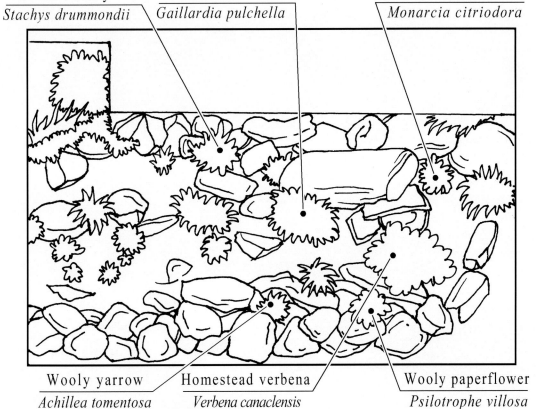

Wooly yarrow
Achillea tomentosa

Homestead verbena
Verbena canaclensis

Wooly paperflower
Psilotrophe villosa

Texas betony
Stachys drummondii

Indian blanket
Gaillardia pulchella

Lemon mint
Monarcia citriodora

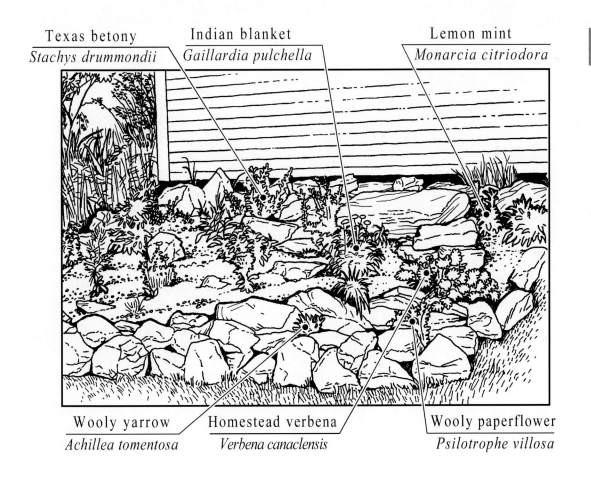

Wooly yarrow
Achillea tomentosa

Homestead verbena
Verbena canaclensis

Wooly paperflower
Psilotrophe villosa

CHAPTER 3

Water Sources

Water is a necessity for wildlife and is simple to provide. One easy way is to place a shallow birdbath in your wildscape. Keep the water level from 1 to 2 inches deep. This will allow birds to bathe in the water and to drink at their leisure. If you have a deeper bird bath, you can provide for the needs of small birds by stacking flat rocks or bricks in the water to create a shallower section. An inexpensive alternative to a concrete birdbath is to place a plastic trash can lid on the ground and fill it with water.

FIGURE 3-1. An artificial stream with protective cover close by will attract a variety of birds. (Oklahoma Certified Wildscape #0013, Norman)

Water is extremely important in winter. Birds not only drink the water; they also use it to clean their feathers, which helps them maintain better insulation from the cold. You might consider investing in a water heater to keep ice from forming in your concrete birdbath. If the water in your trash can lid freezes, simply turn it over, empty the ice, and refill the lid.

Deeper water sources will be used by a greater diversity of wildlife. Following are some examples of water sources that will provide habitat for water-dwelling plants and animals that normally wouldn't be seen in your wildscape.

MATERIALS NEEDED

Saw

¾-inch exterior plywood (4 x 8-foot sheet; have the lumber yard cut it to 3 x 6 feet)

Galvanized nails

Four 1 x 2-inch boards, each 18 inches long

Cedar or redwood for top cap (1 x 1 inches, 10 feet long)

Water-repellent paint or stain

Cardboard

6 mm to 8 mm polyethylene liner

Hair dryer

Utility knife or scissors

Concrete blocks, bricks, or rocks

Gravel

Fish

Aquatic plants

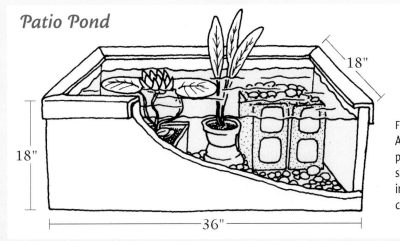

Patio Pond

FIGURE 3-2. A small patio pond can be a simple and inexpensive construction.

DIRECTIONS

1. Cut the ¾-inch plywood into four equal pieces of 18 x 36 inches. Three of these pieces will be the bottom and the two long sides. Cut the fourth piece into two equal 18 x 18-inch pieces, which will serve as the two short sides. Construct an 18 x 36-inch box from the plywood. (It can be any length, but not more than 18 inches deep.) Use the 1 x 2-inch boards to brace the four inside corners to increase the stability of the box.

2. Construct a 1-inch top cap of cedar or redwood by cutting the 10-foot board into two 38-inch lengths and two 18-inch lengths. This cap will go around the top exterior of the box to hold in the liner.

3. Use a water-repellent paint or stain on all wood surface areas, including the bottom.

4. Line the insides and bottom of the box with cardboard to protect the liner.

5. Fit the vinyl or plastic liner into the box. Use a hair dryer to soften the liner for easier folding. Allow slack for water-weight stretching. Extend the liner over the top of the box, then slide the top cap on to hold the liner in place. Trim any excess liner exposed on the outside with a utility knife or scissors.

6. Place concrete blocks, bricks, or

continued on following page

Wading-Pool Pond

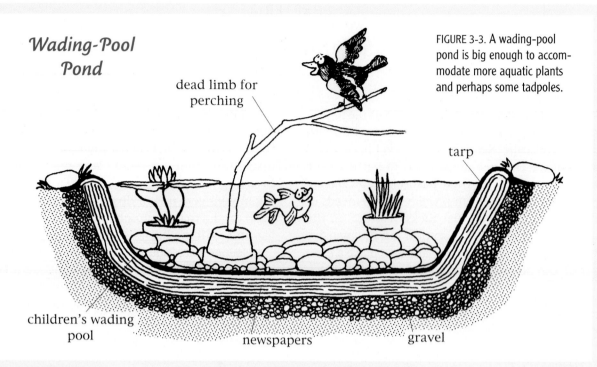

dead limb for perching

tarp

children's wading pool

newspapers

gravel

FIGURE 3-3. A wading-pool pond is big enough to accommodate more aquatic plants and perhaps some tadpoles.

MATERIALS NEEDED

Shovel

Plastic child-sized wading pool (rigid type)

Gravel

Newspapers

Plastic tarpaulin to cover pond bottom

Various sizes of rocks, including flat ones

Small tree limb

Clay pot

Aquatic plants

Fish and tadpoles (optional)

DIRECTIONS

1. Dig a hole 6 inches broader and 3 inches deeper than the size of the plastic wading pool you are using.

2. Line the cavity with 3 inches of gravel. This serves as drainage for overflow water.

3. Place a 1-inch layer of newspapers over the gravel to cushion the wading pool.

4. Put the wading pool into the hole and line it with a plastic tarpaulin. Any excess plastic will be concealed with dirt and rocks.

5. Line the inside of the pond with flat rocks. Place more rocks on one side to create a shallow area 1 to 3 inches deep, making an area for birds to drink and bathe.

6. Fill the pool with water.

7. Anchor a small limb in an upside-down clay pot for perching.

8. Add aquatic plants, fish, and tadpoles only after letting the water stand for 24 hours. This allows any chlorine gas from tap water to escape before affecting the plants and animals. During the first few weeks of your tadpoles' development, do not add water to the pond directly from the tap. Rather allow the water to sit overnight in a container so that the chlorine gas can escape. Otherwise you may accidentally kill the tadpoles.

9. Place additional rocks, plants, and logs around the pond edge to create a natural appearance.

10. To maintain the pond after your tadpoles have matured, simply add water and allow it to overflow for a few minutes each week.

Patio Pond

DIRECTIONS CONTINUED

rocks in the pond at one side to provide a shallow area for birds to drink and bathe. Use an extra layer of plastic here to protect the liner. The water should be 1–3 inches deep in the shallow end. Use gravel for a top layer and provide a small branch as a perch.

7. Provide cement blocks as cover for fish. Plant rushes or grasses in a pot and submerge this in the pond. Use extra plastic beneath pots.

8. To maintain the pond, simply add water and allow it to overflow for a few minutes each week.

FIGURE 3-4. Example of a large pond and water garden in Oklahoma City.

Large Pond

MATERIALS NEEDED

Shovel

Cardboard, newspapers, or grocery bags

Waterproof flexible liner (8 mm to 10 mm polyethylene or heavier synthetic rubber)

Hair dryer

Rocks of assorted shapes and sizes

Aquatic plants

Fish

Recirculating pump (optional)

Filter for pump (optional)

Tubing for pump (optional)

DIRECTIONS

1. Dig a hole that slopes gradually to a depth of 20 to 26 inches, removing any sharp rocks. If you want a natural bottom, you need to dig deeper to compensate for backfill above the liner. The shallowest area, 2 to 8 inches deep, should extend for at least 2 feet to allow room for bog plants and a bird bathing area. The middle level should be 9 to 14 inches deep to provide an area for pond plants. Fish and water lilies will inhabit the deepest area of the pond. Eighteen inches is the recommended depth for overwintering fish.

2. Smooth out the excavation, remove all sharp

continued on following page

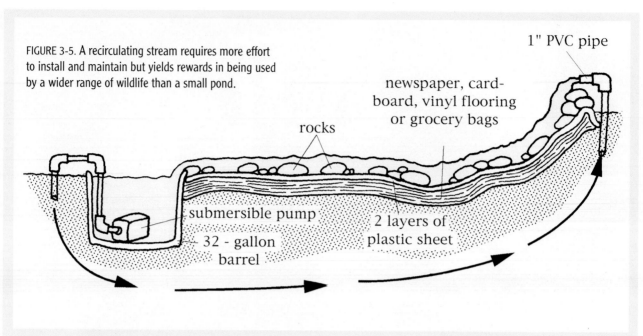

FIGURE 3-5. A recirculating stream requires more effort to install and maintain but yields rewards in being used by a wider range of wildlife than a small pond.

1" PVC pipe

newspaper, card-
board, vinyl flooring
or grocery bags

rocks

submersible pump

32 - gallon
barrel

2 layers of
plastic sheet

Recirculating Stream

MATERIALS NEEDED

Hose

Shovel

Cardboard, newspapers,
or grocery bags

Heavy waterproof liner
(at least 10 mm to 30 mm
plastic sheeting)

Duct tape

Rocks of various sizes and
shapes

Clay (such as bentonite)
for larger streams

Sand

Pea gravel

32-gallon barrel

Recirculating pump

1-inch PVC tubing

Aquatic plants

Cattle trough float

Large Pond

DIRECTIONS CONTINUED

objects, and line the cavity with at least a
1-inch layer of cardboard, newspapers, or
grocery bags to provide a cushion for the liner.

3. Place the liner into the cavity and smooth it
into place. Use a hair dryer to heat the plastic,
making it easier to shape. Any creases you create will be unnoticeable after the pond is filled
with water and will not have a negative effect
on the liner's life.

4. Cover the entire liner with natural materials,
such as earth, stones, logs, etc., to create a natural effect and a more permanent installation.

5. Leave an area of exposed mud, if possible,
for use by butterflies and nest-building birds.

6. Fill the pond with water.

7. Let the water sit for at least 24 hours before
adding aquatic plants and fish.

8. Place the pump in the lowest part of the
pond so that water flows to it by gravity. If the
pump must be installed outside the pond, run
a screen-filtered outlet from the lowest point in
the pond in a straight line to the pump. House
the pump in a box to keep it safe. Also, be sure
to filter the circulating water before pumping it
to a waterfall or the headwaters of a stream.
(See the section above for advice on building a
recirculating stream.) Always use the shortest
practical route to make the pump more efficient. To avoid siphoning solids off the pond
bottom, place the pump in a bucket.

Recirculating Stream

DIRECTIONS

1. Lay out both sides of your desired streambed with a garden hose, making it neither entirely straight nor very sharply curved. View it from all angles both outside and inside the house, making adjustments until you are completely satisfied with how it looks.

2. Excavate the streambed cavity approximately 24 inches wide and 12 inches deep at a gradual slope.

3. Line the cavity with a ½-inch layer of card-board, newspaper, or grocery bag material.

4. Line the cavity with plastic liner. Cover any seams with duct tape on both top and bottom.

5. Carefully place a layer of 4- to 6-inch-diameter rocks into the streambed.

6. Sprinkle dry clay between rocks. Bentonite is a swelling clay that allows water to flow on top of the streambed rather than beneath the rocks. Press firmly into place.

7. Add a 1- to 3-inch layer of sand across the rocks and clay.

8. Add rocks of all sizes to the sides and bottom of the streambed.

9. Sprinkle pea gravel over other material in the streambed to "lock in" the rocks.

10. Excavate a hole at the lower end of the stream deep enough to hold a 32-gallon barrel. Since the stream will run into the barrel, be sure to finish it off right up to the barrel. This is where the pump will be located.

11. Bury 1-inch PVC tubing deep enough to prevent freezing, running it from the barrel to the head of the stream by the shortest route possible. The tubing can be looped over the lip of the barrel and covered with plants, or if freezing is a problem, it can be run directly through the barrel above water level but below ground level. After putting the pump into the barrel, connect it to the PVC tubing and anchor the other end of the tubing with a rock pile at the head of the stream.

12. The barrel at the bottom of the stream can be covered by a lid and made to look natural with rocks and plants.

Note: The pump must be covered by water at all times. This can be accomplished by manually filling the barrel with water when the level is low or by installing a cattle trough float that will trigger the water valve to come on when the water level becomes too low. Such floats are available at livestock feed stores. See your feed store dealer for specifics on installation and size.

FAMILY ACTIVITIES

Take a nighttime garden pond safari

Quietly walk to your garden pond and, using a flashlight, peer down into the watery depths of a new world. You might see dragonfly nymphs moving over the bottom of the pond, tubifex worms waving their mouths in search for food, or a water boatman oaring through the water. Cast your light around the edges of the pond where you can catch the eye reflection of the toads and frogs in your wildscape.

Side Yard Marsh

MATERIALS NEEDED

Shovel

Clay

Heavy waterproof liner
(at least 10 mm to 30 mm
plastic sheeting)

Flexible plastic pipe

Sand

Compost

Peat

Rototiller

Bog-type plants

DIRECTIONS

1. Outline the perimeter of the
proposed marsh; 45 square feet
is an average size.

2. Strip sod from the area, and
then excavate the subsoil and
rock to an average depth of
14 inches.

3. If your soil is too porous,
you might line the perimeter
with clay or a plastic liner.

4. Connect a downspout from
your roof to a length of solid,
flexible plastic pipe. Angle this
pipe down and away from the
house so that water enters the
top of the marsh. After the
next rainstorm, make adjustments to the pipe angle and
ditch angle.

5. Prepare a soil mixture containing some sand,
a dozen buckets of compost, a good quantity of
the original subsoil, and as much peat as you
can afford. The marsh soil can be mixed in
place with a rototiller.

6. Create areas of differing moisture by varying
the original basin depth, then backfilling uni-
formly with your marsh soil.

7. Add a variety of plants, depending on the
wildlife species you would like to attract. Some
butterfly and hummingbird attractants found in

FIGURE 3-6. Small water garden with a variety of aquatic and bog-type plants. (Oklahoma Certified Wildscape #0275, Tulsa)

wetland habitats include spicebush, buttonbush,
prickly ash, elderberry, and willow, towering over
cardinal flower, pickerel-weed, swamp milkweed,
and arrowhead. Joe-pye-weed could be planted
over the downstream end of the marsh to provide a transition between the marsh and a
butterfly garden.

Common Aquatic and Wetland Plants

When you have finished creating your water source, you should stock it with a variety of native water plants. These will serve as an oxygen source for fish and amphibians as well as provide shade from the sun and cover from the prying eyes of predators. You can find water plants in a variety of places, but probably best and easiest is to look in a nearby pond. Not only will these plants be less expensive than nursery plants, but they also will be adapted to the soil requirements and rainfall in your area.

Transplanting water plants from a wild pond to your backyard water source should be fairly simple—most species do not have any special requirements for water quality. However, over time you will learn which species are easier to introduce to your pond. To prevent invasive plant species from overrunning your pond, place them in large pots or boxes (fig. 3–7). If soil from the roots begins to cloud the water, use a thin layer of clean sand or pea gravel to cover the bare soil and roots. One common plant species found in moist soils that should not be introduced is purple loosestrife (*Lythrum salicaria*), which has become a serious pest in waterways.

Table 3–1 lists native water plants that can be introduced into your wildscape pond, although you certainly can experiment with other species as well. Note the following abbreviations for the table: PLANTING ZONE (fig. 3–8): 1 = deep water/floating plants, 2 = shallow water plants, 3 = emergent water plants, 4 = semi-emergent water plants. HEIGHT indicates the height above water or the soil.

Wetland-Related Wildlife Species

Some species of wildlife spend all or part of their life cycles around wetland or aquatic areas, including waterfowl, shorebirds, wading birds, amphibians, and aquatic insects. Other species, including some songbirds and mammals, intermittently use wetlands as breeding areas, migratory stopovers, or food sources. Table 3–2 lists common wetland-related wildlife and how these species use wetlands. Remember, however, that most of these species will not visit a backyard water feature in an urban area. Note the following abbreviations for table 3–2: TIME OF YEAR: M = migratory stopover, S = summer/breeding, W = winter, YR = year-round resident.

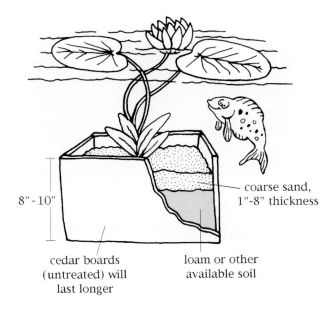

FIGURE 3-7. A method of planting aquatic plants in an outdoor pool.

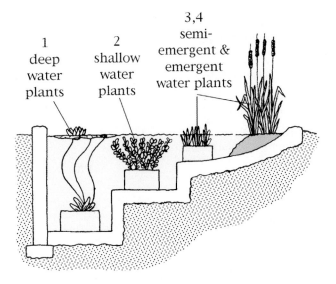

FIGURE 3-8. Cross section of a pool showing different water depths for a variety of aquatic plants.

TABLE 3–1. Aquatic Plants and Their Wildlife Value

AQUATIC PLANT	PLANTING ZONE	HEIGHT	VALUE TO WILDLIFE
Bladderwort (*Utricularia vulgaris*)	1	-	Cover for aquatic insects.
Duckmeat (*Spirodela polyrhiza*)	1	-	Waterfowl eat plants and small animal organisms attached to plants.
Duckweed (*Lemna minor*)	1	-	Waterfowl eat plants and small animal organisms attached to plants.
Watermeal (*Wolffia* spp.)	1	-	Plants eaten by 13 duck species, purple gallinule, and sora.
Coontail (*Ceratophyllum demersum*)	2	-	Plants and seeds eaten by coot and 10 duck species. Seeds eaten by stilt sandpiper.
Elodea (*Elodea densa*)	2	-	Leafy stems make up main diet of coot, mallard, ring-necked duck, wood duck, and green-winged teal.
Lotus, yellow (*Nelumbo lutea*)	2	2 ft.	Fruits eaten by wood duck and other waterfowl. Tubers eaten by muskrat. Cover source for aquatic insects and amphibians.
Pondweed (*Potamogeton nodosus*)	2	-	Seeds and plants eaten by waterfowl, shorebirds, muskrat, and deer. Cover source for aquatic insects and amphibians.
Skunkgrass (*Chara* spp.)	2	-	Plants eaten by coot; semi-palmated sandpiper; northern pintail, redhead, and ring-necked ducks; greater scaup and 20 other waterfowl species.
Waterlily, yellow (*Nuphar lutea*)	2	-	Seeds eaten by Virginia rail and four duck species.
Water milfoil (*Myriophyllum* spp.)	2	-	Seeds and foliage eaten by 11 duck species. Seeds eaten by dowitchers and pectoral and stilt sandpipers.
Water nymph (*Najas guadalupensis*)	2	-	Branches, leaves, and seeds eaten by coot, gadwall, and 16 waterfowl species. Seeds and leaves eaten by king rail.
Watershield (*Brasenia schreberi*)	2	-	Seeds eaten by ring-necked duck and five other duck species.
Arrowhead (*Sagittaria latifolia*)	3	2–3 ft.	Tubers consumed by waterfowl and muskrat.
Buckbean (*Menyanthes trifoliata*)	3	1 ft.	Hummingbird nectar source.
Cattail (*Typha latifolia*)	3	4–9 ft.	Green-winged teal and semi-palmated sandpiper eat seeds; geese eat shoots; muskrat eat all parts. Nesting cover for red-winged blackbird.
Cinquefoil, marsh (*Potentilla palustris*)	3	2 ft.	Seeds and foliage eaten by woodcock, chipmunk, and squirrel. Foliage eaten by cottontail rabbit.
Iris, yellow (*Iris pseudacorus*)	3	3–4 ft.	Hummingbird nectar source. Beaver food source.
Pickerel-weed (*Pontederia cordata*)	3	3 ft.	Seeds eaten by wood duck and muskrat. Nectar attracts butterflies and bees.
Plantain, water (*Alisma plantago-aquatica*)	3	3–4 ft.	Cardinal, grasshopper sparrow, and other songbirds eat seeds. Rabbit, squirrel, pocket mouse, and white-tailed deer eat leaves and capsules.
Rush (*Juncus* spp.)	3	4 ft.	Plants eaten by cottontail rabbit, muskrat, gopher, and quail.

TABLE 3–1. Aquatic Plants and Their Wildlife Value

AQUATIC PLANT	PLANTING ZONE	HEIGHT	VALUE TO WILDLIFE
Sweet flag (*Acorus calamus*)	3	2–4 ft.	Roots and foliage eaten by muskrat. Waterfowl eat fruit. Foliage used by muskrat for lodge construction. Nesting site for pied-billed grebe.
Ash, white (*Fraxinus americana*)	4	tree	Seeds eaten by some birds and mammals. Butterfly host plant for eastern tiger swallowtail and mourning cloak.
Beautyberry (*Callicarpa americana*)	4	shrub	Fruit eaten by quail, robin, mockingbird, brown thrasher, towhee, armadillo, and raccoon.
Buttonbush (*Cephalanthus occidentalis*)	4	shrub	Butterfly nectar source. Seeds eaten by waterfowl and songbirds.
Cardinal flower (*Lobelia cardinalis*)	4	4 ft.	Butterfly and hummingbird nectar source.
Chufa (*Cyperus esculentus*)	4	3 ft.	Seeds and tubers prized by wild turkey, ducks, mourning dove, quail, other bird species, and muskrat.
Elderberry (*Sambucus canadensis*)	4	shrub	Fruits eaten by birds and mammals. Nesting cover.
Fern, cinnamon (*Osmunda cinnamomea*)	4	3–4 ft.	Mammals eat fiddleheads (emerging fern fronds).
Fern, rattlesnake (*Botrychium virginianum*)	4	1–2 ft.	Eaten by deer. Attractive ornamental.
Gamagrass, eastern (*Tripsacum dactyloides*)	4	6–9 ft.	Seeds eaten by wild turkey and McCown's and chestnut-collared longspurs.
Holly, deciduous (*Ilex decidua*)	4	tree	Fruit eaten by birds and mammals.
Horsetail (*Equisetum hymali*)	4	3–4 ft.	Roots and stems eaten by snow goose. Plants eaten by muskrat.
Iris, blue flag (*Iris versicolor*)	4	1–2 ft.	Cover source. Nectar source.
Joe-pye-weed (*Eupatorium maculatum*)	4	5 ft.	Butterfly and hummingbird nectar source.
Milkweed, swamp (*Asclepias incarnata*)	4	3 ft.	Butterfly nectar source. Monarch caterpillar food.
Primrose, water (*Ludwigia arcuta*)	4	4 ft.	Cover source. Limited food value.
Rush, spike (*Eleocharis palustris*)	4	1–2 ft.	Seeds eaten by waterfowl. Plant eaten by cottontail rabbit and muskrat. Shelter for aquatic insects and amphibians.
Sedge (*Carex* spp.)	4	1–4 ft.	Seeds consumed by waterfowl, wild turkey, shorebirds, and songbirds. Deer browse plant. Cover source.
Smartweed (*Polygonum coccinium*)	4	2–4 in.	Seeds consumed by waterfowl, shorebirds, songbirds, and mammals.
Spicebush (*Lindera benzoin*)	4	shrub	Butterfly host plant for eastern tiger and spicebush swallowtails.
Willow (*Salix* spp.)	4	tree	Butterfly host plant for eastern tiger swallowtail, mourning cloak, and red-spotted purple. Good browse plant for white-tailed deer.

FIGURE 3-9. Ducks, herons, and egrets are among the larger birds that commonly visit even quite small wetland habitats.

TABLE 3–2. Wildlife Species and Their Wetland Use

SPECIES	TIME OF YEAR	USES OF WETLANDS
Shorebirds and wading birds		
Avocet, American	M	Eats worms and aquatic insects.
Egret, great	S	Eats amphibians, fish, reptiles, and crayfish. Nests in midstory trees.
Egret, snowy	S	Eats amphibians, fish, reptiles, and crayfish. Nests in midstory trees.
Heron, green	S	Eats amphibians, fish, and reptiles.
Heron, great blue	YR	Eats amphibians, fish, reptiles, and crayfish. Nests in tall trees next to water.
Heron, little blue	S	Eats amphibians, fish, reptiles, and crayfish. Nests in midstory trees.
Night-heron, black-crowned	S	Eats amphibians, fish, and reptiles.
Sandpiper, least	M	Eats worms and aquatic insects.
Sandpiper, semipalmated	W	Eats worms and aquatic insects.
Snipe, common	M	Eats worms and aquatic insects.
Phalarope, Wilson's	M	Eats worms and aquatic insects.
Waterfowl		
Coot, American	W	Eats aquatic plants.
Duck, wood	YR	Eats aquatic insects and plants. Nests in cavities above water.
Gadwall	W	Eats aquatic plants.
Goose, Canada	YR	Eats aquatic plants and insects. Nests on ground or islands.
Grebe, pied-billed	YR	Eats crayfish, small fish, and aquatic insects. Forms nest in floating emergents.
Mallard	YR	Eats aquatic plants and invertebrates. Nests on ground near water.
Pintail, northern	W	Eats aquatic plants, seeds and insects.
Shoveler, northern	W	Eats aquatic plants.
Teal, blue-winged	W	Eats aquatic plants.
Wigeon, American	W	Eats aquatic plants.

TABLE 3–2. Wildlife Species and Their Wetland Use

SPECIES	TIMEOFYEAR	USES OF WETLANDS
Songbirds		
Blackbird, red-winged	YR	Eats insects and seeds. Nests in cattails.
Cardinal, northern	YR	Eats seeds produced by wetland plants.
Dove, mourning	YR	Eats insects and seeds. Nests in trees.
Junco, dark-eyed	W	Eats seeds produced by wetland plants.
Lark, horned	YR	Eats seeds produced by wetland plants.
Meadowlark, eastern	YR	Eats seeds produced by wetland plants.
Quail, bobwhite	YR	Eats insects and seeds. Nests on ground in fields.
Sparrows	YR	Eat seeds produced by wetland plants.
Yellowthroat, common	S	Eats insects. Nests in emergents next to water.
Mammals		
Armadillo	YR	Eats seeds and invertebrates found in mud.
Bats	S	Eats insects. Lives in cavities and on foliage near water.
Beaver	YR	Eats aquatic plants. Builds lodges and dams from trees and shrubs.
Mink	YR	Eats frogs, fish, crayfish, and mice.
Muskrat	YR	Eats aquatic plants. Builds lodges from cattails and other aquatic vegetation.
Raccoon	YR	Eats frogs, crayfish, and aquatic plants.
Skunk, striped	YR	Eats frogs and invertebrates found in mud.
Amphibians		
Bullfrog	S	Breeds and hibernates in wetlands. Eats crayfish, insects, and other frogs.
Frog, chorus	S	Breeds in wetlands only.
Frog, cricket	S	Breeds in wetlands. Eats beetles, flies, ants, and spiders.
Frog, southern leopard	S	Breeds and hibernates in wetlands. Eats isopods, spiders, and crayfish.
Salamander, small-mouth	S	Breeds in wetlands only.
Toad, dwarf American	S	Breeds in wetlands only.
Toad, eastern narrowmouth	S	Breeds in wetlands only.
Toad, Woodhouse's	S	Breeds in wetlands. Eats insects and slugs.
Reptiles		
Slider, red-eared	YR	Eats aquatic vegetation. Basks and hibernates in wetlands.
Snake, brown	S	Eats slugs and earthworms.
Snake, garter	S	Eats frogs, small fish, and spiders.
Snake, Graham's crayfish	S	Eats crayfish, frogs, and snails. Hibernates in crayfish burrows.
Snakes, water	YR	Eat fish, frogs, salamanders, and crayfish.
Turtle, common snapping	YR	Eats aquatic invertebrates, fish, reptiles, birds, and mammals.
Turtles, mud	YR	Eat insects, mollusks, amphibians, and aquatic plants. May live in muskrat lodges.
Turtles, softshell	YR	Eat fish, amphibians, insects, mollusks, and plants. Common baskers in wetlands.
Aquatic Insects and Butterflies		
Beetle, diving	S	Eats aquatic insects, small fish, and tadpoles.
Dragonfly/Damselfly	S	Eats adult mosquitoes.
Monarch (butterfly)	S	Feeds on nectar from wetland flowers. Larvae eat milkweed species.
Mosquito	S	Larvae eat detritus; adult males feed on nectar.
Swallowtail, tiger (butterfly)	S	Feeds on nectar from wetland flowers. Larvae eat several tree species.
Viceroy (butterfly)	S	Feeds on nectar from wetland flowers.
Whirligig	S	Eats aquatic insects, small fish, and tadpoles.

CHAPTER 4

Attracting Birds

Probably the most watchable of all wildlife are birds. Most people first begin to manage their property to attract birds, primarily because birds are active during the day and readily visible. Because they can fly, birds also are the easiest to entice into urban wildscapes. Birds provide a colorful contrast to the greenery in our yards, and their songs enhance a world polluted by the noise of booming car stereos, ambulance sirens, and racing vehicles outside our homes.

This chapter describes specific management techniques needed to attract common bird species to your wildscape. If you create good habitat for these birds, you will likely attract many others. For a detailed checklist of the birds in your state, contact your state wildlife agency (see appendix I).

Birds fall into four groups: year-round residents, summer breeders, fall/winter residents and spring/fall migrants. Table 4–1 lists the times of year you may see various birds in Oklahoma and describes their preferred natural foods and nesting sites, so that you can be sure your wildscape is suitable for them. Special management and landscape considerations are given for each species. Note the following abbreviations for table 4–1:

TIME OF RESIDENCE: S = summer/breeding,
W = winter, Y = year-round resident

FIGURE 4-1 (opposite). Food availability in winter is critical to songbird survival.

FIGURE 4-2 (above). Collection of bird feeders. (Oklahoma Certified Wildscape #0059, Edmond)

Food Sources and Feeder Tips

Seeds are the favorite food of many bird species. Research has shown that the top grain choices for birds are black-oil, striped, or hulled sunflower seeds; peanuts; and white proso millet and niger thistle seed. Many people put out the commercial seed mixes that are widely available in supermarkets or discount stores. Although some of these seed mixes offer a desirable mix of the preferred seeds, many substitute less desired—and less expensive—seed types. When buying mixes, select those that contain high concentrations of sunflower and millet, while staying clear of high concentrations of fillers like buckwheat, milo, and hulled oats. Though they may be less expensive at the checkout counter, these filler grains are shunned by most songbirds. The preferred seeds will be selectively eaten and the remainder will end up on the ground, attracting European starlings, house sparrows, and mice, and sprouting weeds under your feeder.

Try putting feeders in several locations and at different heights in your habitat to satisfy the different eating styles of birds (fig. 4-2). Feeders should be located in and around areas that are easily visible from your house or other viewing locations. Birds should have quick access to brushy cover no more than 15 feet from a feeding station. This will allow them adequate time to escape predators. However, refrain from placing feeders in or right next to dense cover, because cats and other stalking predators may use this cover to ambush birds.

A varied backyard feeding program might include:

- Providing sunflower seeds, peanuts, and fruit on platform or hopper feeders about 4 feet off the ground. Also, different seed types can be offered via tube-type feeders. Cardinals, finches, and grosbeaks will readily feed from these types of feeding stations.

- Offering thistle or finch mixes, which are highly desirable to finches and pine siskins. Due to its expense compared to other seed types, thistle should be dispensed from a hanging tube feeder and not placed in a platform or hopper feeder.

- Spreading millet and cracked corn on the ground to attract doves, towhees, juncos, quail, and sparrows. Spread these foods away from brush to attract doves and near brush to attract towhees. This is especially attractive to migrant and wintering birds in fall, winter, and spring. If mice, rats, or cats are a neighborhood problem, don't feed on the ground.

- Suspending or attaching a suet feeder from a tree limb to feed insect-eating birds such as woodpeckers and bluebirds. Warm temperatures will turn suet rancid, however, so rather than feed suet or other animal fat–based foods in the summer, you might consider putting out a mixture of Miracle Meal.

TABLE 4-1. Bird Species List and Management Recommendations

BIRD SPECIES	TIME OF RESIDENCE	PREFERRED FOODS	PREFERRED NEST SITE	MANAGEMENT NEEDS
Blackbird, red-winged	YR	insects, seeds	cattails and shrubs in or near water	Open shallow wetlands with cattails; winter visitor to milo, cracked corn, and sunflower feeders.
Bluebird, eastern	YR	fruit, insects, suet	cavity in a tree or post, bird house with 1½-inch hole	Scattered trees and shrubs in open habitats; fruit-bearing trees and shrubs during winter.
Blue Jay	YR	insects, nuts, seeds	mature trees	Mature forests, especially with oak and hickory trees; visit feeders with sunflower and peanuts.
Buntings, indigo and painted	S	insects, seeds	dense shrubs or small trees	Thickets and abundant shrub cover in or near forests; rarely visit urban sunflower feeders; brown-headed cowbirds may parasitize nests.

TABLE 4-1. Bird Species List and Management Recommendations

BIRD SPECIES	TIME OF RESIDENCE	PREFERRED FOODS	PREFERRED NEST SITE	MANAGEMENT NEEDS
Cardinal, northern	YR	insects, seeds	dense shrubs or small trees	Brushy hedges, thickets, and abundant shrub cover; common visitor to urban sunflower feeders.
Catbird, gray	S	fruit, insects	dense shrubs	Brushy hedges, thickets and abundant shrub cover in forested habitat; eats fruit in late summer and fall.
Chickadee, Carolina	YR	insects, seeds, suet	cavity in a tree or post, bird house with 1⅛-inch hole	Mature trees in all forests, especially those with oak trees; common visitor to sunflower and suet feeders.
Creeper, brown	W	insects, suet	does not nest in Oklahoma	Mature trees in all forests; searches tree trunks for insects; may visit suet feeder.
Crow, American	YR	insects, nuts, seeds, suet, small animals	tree tops	Mature trees in open and forested habitats; visits suet and sunflower feeders.
Cuckoo, yellow-billed	S	insects	trees	Deciduous trees with dense canopies.
Dove, mourning	YR	seeds	small trees or shrubs; occasional ground nester	Scattered trees in open habitat; visits feeders with milo, millet, sunflower, or cracked corn.
Dove, rock (Pigeon)	YR	seeds	ledges, under eaves	Open lawns; visits feeders with milo, millet, sunflower, or cracked corn.
Duck, wood	YR	insects, plants, seeds	tree cavity, nest box with 4-inch hole	Open woodlands near ponds or rivers.
Finch, house	YR	fruit, insects, seeds	tree, hanging basket, nesting shelf	Mature trees and patches of tall forbs; common urban visitor to sunflower and hummingbird feeders; eats small fruits.
Finch, purple	W	seeds	does not nest in Oklahoma	Mature forests, especially with green ash, sweetgum and sycamore trees; visits sunflower feeders.
Flicker, northern	YR	acorns, suet, insects, seeds	cavity in mature trees, nest box with 2½-inch hole	Scattered trees, shelterbelts, and open forests; feeds on insects on ground and in trees; eats acorns in winter; visits suet feeders.
Flycatcher, great-crested	S	fruit, insects	cavity in mature tree, nest box with 1⁹⁄₁₆-inch hole	Mature forests; more common in large than in small forest tracts; rare in urban areas.
Goldfinch, American	YR	seeds	shrubs or tall forbs	Rarely nests in urban areas; common winter visitor to sunflower and thistle feeders; found in forests and open habitats with patches of tall forbs.
Grackle, common	YR	insects, seeds	trees, especially evergreens	Open habitats with scattered deciduous and evergreen trees near agricultural areas, livestock, or bird feeders.
Grackle, great-tailed	YR	insects, seeds	scattered trees, patches of cattails	Urban habitats with scattered trees and lawns; wetlands with cattails and shrubs.
Grosbeak, blue	S	insects, seeds	low thickets, scattered shrubs	Brushy pastures and open habitats with low shrub cover; cowbirds may parasitize nests; rare urban visitor.

TABLE 4–1. Bird Species List and Management Recommendations

BIRD SPECIES	TIME OF RESIDENCE	PREFERRED FOODS	PREFERRED NEST SITE	MANAGEMENT NEEDS
Hummingbird, ruby-throated	S	insects, nectar	tree or shrub	Open forests and woodland edges with abundant wildflowers; visits hummingbird feeders and flower gardens.
Junco, dark-eyed	W	insects, seeds	does not nest in Oklahoma	Patches of forbs and thickets in open forests; visits ground feeders with millet.
Kestrel, American	YR	insects, small animals	cavity in mature tree, nest box with 4-inch hole	Scattered trees in open habitats, woodland edges and highline wires.
Killdeer	YR	insects	on bare ground	Pastures and prairies, often near water; nests in short grass or on gravel.
Kingbird, eastern	S	fruit, insects	scattered trees	Open habitats with scattered trees near streams or ponds.
Kingbird, western	S	insects	scattered trees	Scattered trees in very open habitats and in urban areas.
Kinglets, golden-crowned and ruby-crowned	W	insects	do not nest in Oklahoma	Thickets, forests, and woodland edges.
Martin, purple	S	insects	martin house with 2¼-inch hole	Open habitats, including urban areas, near water.
Meadowlarks, eastern and western	YR	insects, seeds	dense clump of grass	Pastures and prairies with sparse trees and shrubs; rare in urban areas; visit seed feeders in open habitats.
Mockingbird, northern	YR	fruit, insects	shrub or small tree	Thickets and dense hedges; eats fruit in winter.
Nuthatch, red-breasted	W	insects, seeds, suet	does not nest in Oklahoma	Forests, especially with pine trees; sporadic winter visitor to sunflower and suet feeders.
Nuthatch, white-breasted	YR	insects, seeds, suet	cavity in mature tree, nest box with 1⅜-inch hole	Forests, especially with oak and hickory trees; more common in large forest tracts than in small; visits sunflower and suet feeders.
Orioles, Baltimore and Bullock's	S	fruit, insects, nectar	tall deciduous trees	Deciduous forest, especially with elm, cottonwood, and sycamore trees; often found near streams and ponds; visit hummingbird and oriole feeders.
Owl, barn	YR	insects, rodents	buildings, cavities in trees and cliffs	Open fields or marshes near suitable nesting areas.
Owl, eastern screech	YR	insects, rodents	cavity in mature tree, nest box with 3-inch hole	Woodlands of all types; forest edges; fairly common in urban areas.
Owl, great horned	YR	small mammals	abandoned hawk and crow nests	Forests and open habitats with scattered mature trees; fairly common in urban areas.
Phoebe, eastern	S	fruit, insects	stream banks, cliffs, bridges, buildings	Both forested and open habitats with scattered trees near water.
Quail, bobwhite	YR	insects, seeds	on the ground in dense, tall grass	Dense grass and low shrubs for cover; forbs such as sunflower, legumes, and ragweed.

TABLE 4–1. Bird Species List and Management Recommendations

BIRD SPECIES	TIME OF RESIDENCE	PREFERRED FOODS	PREFERRED NEST SITE	MANAGEMENT NEEDS
Robin, American	YR	fruit, insects	tree, nesting shelf	Open forests with scattered trees near water; eats fruit in winter.
Sapsucker, yellow-bellied	W	fruit, insects, sap, suet	does not nest in Oklahoma	Deciduous forests near water and forested urban areas; visits suet feeders.
Siskin, pine	W	seeds	does not nest in Oklahoma	Forests and edges with pine trees and patches of tall forbs; rare visitor to sunflower and thistle feeders.
Sparrow, field	YR	insects, seeds	shrub	Pastures, prairies, and forest edges with scattered thickets and trees; rare urban visitor to ground feeders with millet or milo.
Sparrow, fox	W	insects, seeds	does not nest in Oklahoma	Thickets and mature woodlands; rare urban visitor to feeders with millet or sunflower on or near the ground and close to dense cover.
Sparrow, Harris's	W	insects, seeds	does not nest in Oklahoma	Thickets, woodland edges, and tall-grass prairie with patches of forbs; visits ground feeders with millet, milo, and sunflower.
Sparrow, lark	S	insects, seeds	on ground or in low shrubs	Prairies and pastures with scattered shrubs and small trees; rarely visits feeders.
Sparrow, Lincoln	W	insects, seeds	does not nest in Oklahoma	Dense thickets, brush piles, and woodland edges; visits ground feeders with millet.
Sparrow, song	W	insects, seeds	does not nest in Oklahoma	Marshes, thickets, woodland edges, and patches of tall grasses and forbs; uncommon urban visitor to ground feeders.
Sparrow, white-crowned	W	insects, seeds	does not nest in Oklahoma	Thickets, patches of tall grasses and forbs, woodland edges, and pastures with scattered shrubs; visits ground feeders.
Sparrow, white-throated	W	insects, seeds	does not nest in Oklahoma	Woodlands, woodland edges, and thickets near water; fairly common in forested urban areas; visits ground feeders.
Swallow, barn	S	insects	buildings, bridges	Marshes and open habitats near water.
Swallow, rough-winged	S	insects	tree cavity near water	Woodland edges and open habitats with scattered trees near water.
Tanager, summer	S	fruit, insects	trees	Mature oak or oak/pine forest; more common in large forest tracts than in small ones; rare in urban areas.
Thrasher, brown	YR	fruit, insects	dense shrub	Thickets, dense hedges, and woodland edges; eats fruit in fall and winter; fairly common in urban areas.
Titmouse, tufted	YR	acorns, suet, insects, seeds	tree cavity, nest box with 1⅛-inch hole	Mature forests, especially with oak trees, and wooded urban areas; visits suet and sunflower feeders.

TABLE 4-1. Bird Species List and Management Recommendations

BIRD SPECIES	TIME OF RESIDENCE	PREFERRED FOODS	PREFERRED NEST SITE	MANAGEMENT NEEDS
Towhees, eastern and spotted	W	insects, seeds	do not nest in Oklahoma	Thickets, woodland edges, and brush piles; visit ground feeders close to dense cover.
Vireo, red-eyed	S	fruit, insects	small deciduous trees	More common in large forests dominated by deciduous trees; nests in understory trees in mature forest.
Warbler, pine	YR	fruit, insects, suet	pine trees	Pine-dominated forests with mature pine trees; occasional urban visitor to suet feeder.
Warbler, prothonotary	S	insects	tree cavity near water, nest box with 1⅜-inch hole	Mature forest near water; rare in urban areas.
Warbler, yellow	S	insects	shrubs near water	Willow thickets and deciduous forest along streams and rivers; rare urban visitor.
Warbler, yellow-rumped	W	fruit, insects, suet	does not nest in Oklahoma	Thickets, red cedar trees, and forested habitats; occasional urban visitor to suet feeders and red cedars.
Waxwing, cedar	W	fruit, insects	does not nest in Oklahoma	Forests with fruit-bearing trees, shrubs, and vines, especially red cedar thickets; common urban visitor to fruit-bearing plants and water sources.
Woodpecker, downy	YR	fruit, insects, seeds, suet	tree cavity, nest box with 1¼-inch hole	Forests with some mature trees and snags; fairly common urban visitor to suet and sunflower feeders.
Woodpecker, hairy	YR	insects, suet	tree cavity	More common in large mature forests with cavity-bearing trees and snags; rare urban visitor to suet feeders.
Woodpecker, pileated	YR	fruit, insects, suet	tree cavity	Found in or near large mature forests with well-developed canopy and large snags; rare urban visitor to suet feeders.
Woodpecker, red-bellied	YR	fruit, insects, seeds, suet	tree cavity	Mature forest, especially with oak and hickory trees; fairly common urban visitor to suet and sunflower feeders.
Woodpecker, red-headed	YR	acorns, fruit, insects, seeds, suet	tree cavity, nest box with 2-inch hole	Open forests and flooded forests around wetlands and beaver dams; scattered oak trees in pastures; rare urban visitor to seed and suet feeders.
Wren, Bewick's	YR	fruit, insects, suet	tree cavity, nest box with 1¼-inch hole	Common in open urban habitats with thickets, brushy pastures, woodland edges, and brush piles; visits suet feeders.
Wren, Carolina	YR	fruit, insects, suet	tree cavity, nest box with 1½-inch hole	Common in forested urban areas and woodland edges with abundant shrub cover; visits suet feeders.
Wren, house	S	insects	tree cavity, nest box with 1¼-inch hole	Fairly common in urban thickets and open habitats with scattered trees and shrubs; uses bird houses.

RAISING MEALWORMS

Mealworms are a beneficial protein source for insect eaters such as bluebirds, woodpeckers, and mockingbirds, especially during spring when bad weather prevents birds from searching for other foods. Adult birds also feed mealworms to nestlings. Offer mealworms in platform feeders or bluebird feeders.

You can raise mealworms very easily and cheaply. The U.S. Department of Agriculture recommends using a box 2 feet long, 18 inches wide, and 10 inches deep to raise mealworms. A top can be constructed by cutting a thin sheet of metal to fit inside the box and resting it on cleats attached to the sides. To raise fewer mealworms, use a plastic 5-gallon pail or a plastic shoe box with tiny air holes in the top.

Purchase ¼ pound of mealworms, which can be found at most pet stores. Also purchase mealworm food—a mixture of three parts bran to one part laying mash—again found at local feed stores. Buy equal dollar amounts of each and fill the box to within 2 inches of the top with the mixture.

Supply moisture for the mealworm colony by placing slices of apples or potatoes on a thin sheet of wood or metal on top of the mixture. Replace the slices every three to four days with new slices. Do not add water or other liquids.

Place the mealworms on top of the mixture. They will burrow beneath the surface and molt over a period of two months to nearly two years, depending upon the temperature. Temperatures above 80° Fahrenheit provide optimum growth for all mealworm stages, allowing them to mature in two months.

After the final molt, the mealworm larvae come to the surface. They are very sluggish but quickly transform into naked white pupae. Pupation lasts from six to 18 days. Pupation transforms them into the black adult beetles. The adults mate repeatedly after emerging and females lay eggs nine to 20 days after emergence, after which the adults die. Females lay from 77 to 576 eggs and the incubation period ranges from four to 19 days.

When the existing supply of food turns gray, which normally takes several months, replenish the supply with the same mixture. Before discarding the mixture, sift it through a screen to save the mealworms, pupae, and live beetles, which can then be placed directly into the fresh mixture. Do this when the number of live beetles is few. Salvage any eggs that may remain in the spent food by keeping the old mixture in a separate container for several weeks and then repeating the process.

FEEDING BLUEBIRDS

While some bluebirds migrate out of the Great Plains in winter, many people have reported wintering bluebirds on their property. These bluebirds often will stay in the area when people provide a feeder specifically for them. Because bluebirds feed primarily upon insects and various berries, they are

RECIPE FOR MIRACLE MEAL

INGREDIENTS

Carbohydrates: whole-grain flour and corn meal

Animal fats: real lard (not shortening), rendered suet (strained and crumbled) or trimmed beef fat (ground as for hamburger)

Fruits and nuts: peanut butter (plain or crunchy); chopped raisins, apples, or cranberries; finely chopped pecans, peanuts, walnuts, or sunflower hearts; *no seeds!*

PREPARATION

1. In large bowl, mix one cup wheat flour and three cups corn meal.
2. Cut in two cups of animal fats and melt on stove until mixture will press into a ball.
3. Add as many fruit and nut ingredients as available and mold into shape desired for feeding.
4. Store in refrigerator or freezer.

FEEDING

Easiest service is in a suet cage. Place it against the trunk of a tree for woodpeckers, or tie it to the end of a branch for chickadees and titmice. Put balls of Miracle Meal in a covered house for bluebirds and robins.

more difficult to attract to feeders than are seed-eating birds such as cardinals, blue jays, and chickadees. However, by offering foods that bluebirds like, you can bring them closer to your home.

Bluebirds will use suet logs, feeding platforms, and other traditional feeders, but most of them prefer to use a specialized bluebird feeder. These feeders can be built very simply. One way is to modify a roofed feeding tray (fig. 4–3) by (1) adding Plexiglas panels to the long sides of the feeder, (2) adding wood panels to the ends of the feeder, and (3) drilling a 1½-inch hole into each wood panel. Because most birds will not enter the holes to feed, you'll ensure that your food offerings will be eaten by bluebirds and not by other competitors.

Another way to construct a bluebird feeder is to build a bird house that contains a food tray inside (fig. 4–4). Use a saw to cut an opening 2 x 3 inches in the middle of the front panel and beneath the 1½-inch entrance hole. Cover the opening from the inside of the box with hardware cloth. Form two baskets from hardware cloth; place one on top of the box and the other inside the box where its contents can be seen from outside through the 2 x 3-inch opening. Place bluebird delectables in both trays until bluebirds begin using the tray inside the house. You can then discontinue placing food on the roof.

Bluebirds eat a variety of foods that are placed in specialized feeders, including the following:

Mealworms
Strawberries
Grapes
Currants
Raisins
Baked apples
Peanut hearts
Chopped peanuts
Sunflower hearts
Multiflora rose hips
Dogwood berries
Sumac berries
Miracle Meal
Suet (chopped into small pieces)

You also can plant the following trees and shrubs to attract bluebirds and other fruit-eating birds, such as cedar waxwings, mockingbirds, and robins to your wildscape year-round:

Blackberry	Honeysuckle
Black cherry	Mulberry
Blueberry	Poke
Choke cherry	Red cedar
Elderberry	Sumac
Greenbrier	Virginia creeper
Holly	Viburnum

1.5 " hole

plexiglass side panels on both sides to bottom of tray

fruit/Miracle Meal/mealworms

(this fruit is just to entice the bluebirds in)

FIGURE 4-3. Roofed feeding tray modified for bluebirds.

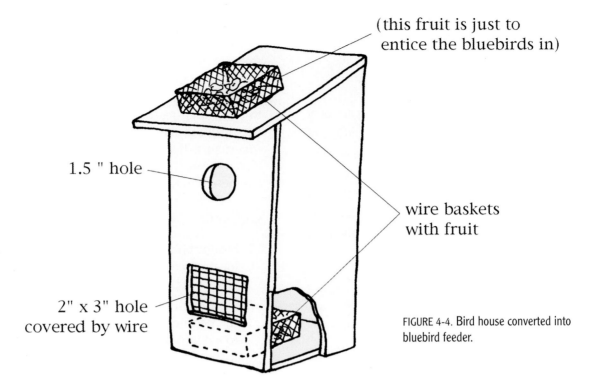

(this fruit is just to entice the bluebirds in)

1.5 " hole

wire baskets with fruit

2" x 3" hole covered by wire

FIGURE 4-4. Bird house converted into bluebird feeder.

BIRD FEEDER–RELATED DISEASES

To combat bird feeder–related diseases, all feeders should be cleaned out at least once a year. Two major diseases occur at bird feeders: aspergillosis and salmonella, both of which can be controlled by proper bird feeding sanitation. Also, periodically clean the area directly under feeders or rotate feeding sites, since disease-causing fungi can remain in the soil for several months.

ASPERGILLOSIS is caused by a fungus that occurs in moldy food. Birds inhaling the fungus spores will suffer pneumonia or bronchitis. To prevent aspergillosis, make sure your seed is clean and free of mold. After any wet weather, tip the feeder over and look for any seeds that cling to the bottom or sides. If they cling, they have become wet and should be replaced.

SALMONELLA poisoning usually occurs after flocking birds such as pine siskins, goldfinches, mourning doves, and house sparrows congregate in an area. The disease is shed in the birds' feces and can remain active on contaminated soil, vegetation, or the feeding station for several months. Birds suffering from salmonella poisoning become lethargic and may die of pneumonia.

If you observe birds dying at your feeders, stop feeding for ten days, disinfect all feeders, change the seed, and clean the areas beneath your feeders. Use a solution of nine parts water to one part bleach to clean your feeders. You may want to contact your neighbors to learn if they have seen any sick birds. Once you resume feeding, most of the infected birds will have dispersed and your clean feeders should be disease-free. Overall, fewer than one percent of birds carry diseases, so it is not a great threat to bird populations or people.

SUCCESSFUL FEEDER TIPS

1. Maintain feeders year-round. Although birds have enough other food sources in summer and don't need to visit a feeder to sustain themselves, you will enhance your chances of seeing a number of unusual species, including the colorful male goldfinch in breeding plumage, the blue grosbeak, and the elusive painted bunting.

2. Use at least eight to 12 feeders placed in two to three clusters to attract the greatest diversity of bird species. Place feeders at varying heights.

3. Keep spillage and waste to a minimum. Put out food less often if it is going to waste.

4. Provide protective cover from predators. Place the feeder 10–15 feet from a brush pile or thick shrubbery that can serve as excellent escape cover.

FAMILY ACTIVITIES

Make pine cone feeders

Collect pine cones and tie a piece of string or sturdy yarn around the base of each. Prepare a mixture of Miracle Meal (see recipe). When the mixture is liquefied, dip each cone in the liquid and set the cone on a piece of waxed paper to dry. Dip cones more than once to add more layers. Hang cones outdoors as part of your feeding station or in other parts of the yard.

5. Place the feeder where it can be easily seen and enjoyed from a patio, window, or porch.
6. Clean feeders and ground areas underneath them regularly.
7. Protect food from inclement weather. Wet, moldy grain is unhealthy for birds.

Water Sources and Birdbath Tips

Begin your wildscape plan by having water present in a shallow receptacle. As earlier noted, an inexpensive upside-down garbage can lid will work just as well as a commercial birdbath. In fact, birds will not bathe in some store-bought birdbaths because the sides are too steep. Birds prefer water depth to increase gradually from the edges. A 1- to 2-inch depth is best.

Moving water is another attraction for birds. Although a natural stream would be ideal, most people don't have such a luxury in their yards. But you can achieve the same effect in several ways. One way is to drip misting water from overhanging leaves, nozzles, or containers into a birdbath. Thin metal birdbaths magnify the sound of falling water droplets, which birds find irresistible. The best design should include a thin jet of water that shoots vertically into overhanging tree branches and then drips back into the bath.

By attaching an inexpensive mister to your garden hose, you will see a different variety of birds on your lawn (fig. 4-5). Minimize cost and wasted water by installing a timer at your hose outlet and setting it for when birds are most active—between sunrise and 10:00 A.M. and in early evening.

Although providing water in winter months can be difficult, it is more critical than at other times of the year. In many cases, your birdbath may be the only unfrozen source of fresh water in the local area. Birds will use the water both to drink and to clean their feathers. If you do not want to refill the birdbath daily during the winter, you might invest in a heater that can be inserted into the water. Heaters should only be used in ceramic or concrete bowls; plastic bowls will melt.

SUCCESSFUL BIRDBATH TIPS

1. Mount birdbaths 3 feet above ground and locate them in shade approximately 10 feet from protective cover.
2. A birdbath should have a dry edge around the perimeter and should gradually slope to a depth of 1 or 2 inches in the center. It should also have a rough bottom for safe footholds.
3. Clean the birdbath daily using a plastic scouring pad. Algae, droppings, and wind-blown debris can quickly turn the contents of a birdbath into germ-infested slush. You should occasionally clean the birdbath with a solution of nine parts water to one part bleach.
4. Provide a source of moving water to attract the greatest diversity of birds.
5. Keep birdbaths away from bird feeders so that birds don't deposit seeds or droppings in the water.
6. Refill birdbaths daily.

Managing for Birds

Holes and hollows in trees are essential for the survival of more than one-third of all forest-living birds and mammals. The scarcity of nesting and roosting cavities may drastically limit the number of kestrels, bluebirds, woodpeckers, nuthatches, owls, flying squirrels, and other desirable backyard inhabitants.

Unfortunately, people have cut down mature and dead trees for firewood and removed "unsightly" dead limbs to keep yards neat and uncluttered. Humanity is the problem as well as the solution.

If possible, leave at least one or two dead trees (snags) standing per quarter-acre lot. You also can attract more birds to your yard by "planting" a dead

FIGURE 4-5. Installing a mister may attract species otherwise unlikely to visit, such as a green heron.

tree. Do this by finding a snag in an advanced stage of decomposition and transplanting it to your yard. It will last several years and will help attract more wildlife.

Many people have begun placing artificial cavities in the form of nest boxes in their wildscape to substitute for the snags and other natural cavities that have been removed. These nest boxes help a variety of creatures, primarily birds and mammals. More specific information on nest box use is given in chapter 8.

NESTING MATERIALS

Birds use a variety of materials to line and create their nests—from string, straw, feathers, and mud to shoelaces, moss, and even snakeskin. You can provide an easy source of nesting materials by hanging out an onion bag or orange bag with loose materials. You can also provide mud by placing it on a sheet of plastic or by keeping a dust bath moist with regular water sprinkling. The following list gives the types of nesting materials several kinds of birds prefer.

Moss: Carolina chickadee, tufted titmouse

Lichen: hummingbirds

Fine straw: robin, cardinal, house finch

String (short lengths): robin, Carolina chickadee, oriole

Twigs and cedar bark: mockingbird, brown thrasher, blue jay, wrens

Feathers: barn and tree swallows

Hair: Carolina chickadee, tufted titmouse

Mud: robin; barn and cliff swallows; purple martin

Cotton, bulrush: wrens, Carolina chickadee, hummingbirds

DUST BATHS

Dust baths help birds maintain their feathers. Birds including sparrows, wrens, quail, brown thrasher, larks, and some raptors enjoy the ritual of dusting their feathers, which helps absorb excess oils and discourages parasites such as mites. When a dust bath becomes muddy, it is still valuable as a source of mud for nest builders such as the robin, purple martin, and barn swallow, besides being a place for butterflies to gather nutrients.

One way to create a dust bath area is to scrape vegetation away from a 3 x 3-foot sunny area and disturb the soil (fig. 4-6). Keep vegetation from the area. A dust bath can also be created by nailing four 3-foot pieces of 1 x 6-inch lumber together and placing them over a hole 6 inches deep. Line the hole with a heavy-duty plastic liner and poke drain holes in it. Next, add equal parts of dirt, sand, and ash into the frame and rake the mixture evenly. The fine particles in the ash help birds rid themselves of mites and other parasites.

Remember that birds using the dust bath will be vulnerable when dusting, so place the dust bath about 10 feet from bushes, a brush pile, or other low escape cover. Also, place the dust bath where you can watch birds using it. Refill the dust bath with dirt, sand, and ash as necessary and rake it after rains to loosen the dust.

Hummingbirds

Hummingbirds are a great asset to your yard. Not only do many plants depend on them for pollination, but the tiny birds help control insect pests like fruit flies. Several hummingbird species visit the Great Plains, but the ruby-throated hummingbird is the most common of these. The black-chinned hummingbird is found in the western third of the southern Great Plains, while broad-tailed and rufous hummingbirds occasionally are spotted during fall migration. Oklahoma and Texas have also been fortunate to host the green violet-eared hummingbird, which has been spotted in only six other states.

Hummingbirds have extremely high metabolic rates and energy demands, forcing them to consume up to half their weight in insects and eight times their weight in fluids every day. Their wings beat 70 times per second while hovering and up to 200 times per second during courtship dives. The small birds also expend a lot of energy when they migrate, flying 1,000 miles during two trips across the Gulf of Mexico each year.

You can help hummingbirds meet their energy requirements by planting a hummingbird garden and by setting out a sugar-water feeder. To entice hummingbirds to nest in your yard, plant evergreen or deciduous trees with dense foliage. The birds' cup-shaped nests, which are not much larger than a walnut half, are built 10–30 feet above ground, often in a fork of a downward-sloping branch. The nests are formed of spider webs, plant down, and lichens.

Most backyard naturalists like to view humming-

FIGURE 4-6. Dust bath in certified wildscape. (Oklahoma Certified Wildscape #0262, Edmond)

birds up close, so consider this before you hang your feeder or begin planting your nectar-producing plants. You may want to combine natural and artificial nectar sources by placing a hummingbird feeder in a garden designed just for hummingbirds.

CREATING A HUMMINGBIRD GARDEN

By planting native trees, shrubs, vines, and herbaceous plants that produce bright orange or red tubular blossoms, you will create a natural habitat to attract hummingbirds (fig. 4-7). Native plants are preferred because many of the popular cultivated landscape plants do not produce sufficient nectar. Single-flowered blossoms are the best choice, because they produce much more nectar than do double-flowered blossoms and sterile hybrids.

Layering the vegetation of your landscape is the best design for attracting hummingbirds. Build height into your landscape by planting flowering trees and installing trellises for vines to climb. Develop a good understory by planting shrubs under and around trees, and establish ground cover by planting annual and perennial herbaceous plants.

Table 4–2 includes some recommended hummingbird plantings for wildscapes, whether they are native or exotic, and gives their primary bloom date. Note the following abbreviations for this table: BLOOM DATE: Sp = spring, Su = summer, F = fall

ARTIFICIAL FEEDERS

Even small yards offering limited space can be attractive to hummingbirds. Backyard naturalists have found that the birds will feed from hanging potted plants or sugar-water feeders on patios and decks. The birds feed most comfortably from feeders at least 2 feet above ground.

The preferable way to attract hummingbirds is by providing nectar-producing plants in sunny areas of your yard. However, you can supplement their natural diet and draw in these little birds with sugar-water feeders. Several important guidelines should be followed when providing a sugar solution:

1. Use a solution of four parts water to one part white granulated sugar. Dissolve the sugar in warm water and then cool the mixture before using it. Refrigerate what you do not use.

2. Clean feeders every three or four days with hot water and vinegar to remove

FIGURE 4-7. Trumpet creeper will attract hummingbirds.

bacteria and fungus molds. Purchase a feeder that can be taken apart and placed in the dishwasher.

3. *Do not* use honey, which could contain fungi that may kill hummingbirds.

4. *Do not* use red dye in your solution. Use a feeder that has red ports instead.

5. To discourage bees from landing on feeder ports and the suspending wire, use vegetable oil or rub them with such low-impact insect repellents as Avon Skin-So-Soft or Off Skintastic. You also can purchase a commercial bee guard (fig. 4–8) for your feeder. The plastic guard, usually colored yellow, increases the distance from the opening to the sugar water beyond the reach of a bee's tongue.

6. *Do not* hang feeders in bright sunlight; place them in partially shaded areas.

7. Place your feeders out in April and leave them up until about November 1, unless you have observed a week without hummingbird activity. Hummingbirds will migrate whether or not your feeder is up. By providing a nectar source later in the fall, you'll provide a quick energy source for any migrating hummingbirds that may come through your area, and you are more likely to be visited by a rare hummingbird.

8. Hummingbirds are very territorial, so if you notice one hummingbird chasing another away from a feeder, set up a second feeder out of sight of the first one.

STATEWIDE HUMMINGBIRD SURVEY

Both the Oklahoma and Texas Wildlife Diversity Programs maintain databases of state hummingbirds. Biologists are interested in learning more about the habits of each state's hummingbirds, including the first and last date seen, species using hummingbird feeders, and plantings that attract hummingbirds most. If you had a hummingbird feeder up from April through November, please participate in these important surveys. Contact your state's wildlife agency (see appendix I) to learn whether it conducts similar wildlife surveys.

FIGURE 4-8. Female hummingbird at feeder. Yellow bee guard prevents bees from reaching the sugar water with their tongues.

TABLE 4–2. Hummingbird Plantings

HUMMINGBIRD PLANTINGS	NATIVE (N) OR EXOTIC (E)	BLOOM DATE
Trees and Shrubs		
Buckeye, red (*Aesculus glabra*)	N	Sp
Butterfly bush (*Buddleia davidii*)	E	Su–F
Cardinal shrub (*Weigela florida*)	E	Sp
Catalpa, southern (*Catalpa bignonioides*)	N	Su
Hibiscus, scarlet (*Hibiscus coccinea*)	E	Su
Honeysuckle, amur (*Lonicera maackii*)	E	Sp
Mimosa (*Albizia julibrissin*)	E	Su
Spirea, red (*Spirea* spp.)	E	Sp–Su
Vines		
Clematis, autumn (*Clematis virginiana*)	N	F
Cross-vine (*Bignonia capreolata*)	N	Sp
Cypress vine (*Ipomea quamoclit*)	E	Su–F
Honeysuckle, coral (*Lonicera sempervirens*)	N	Sp–F
Morning glory (*Ipomea coccinea*)	N	Su–F
Trumpet vine (*Campsis radicans*)	N	Su–F
Runner bean, scarlet (*Phaseolus coccineus*)	E	Sp–Su
Perennials		
Bergamots (*Monarda* spp.)	N	Su
Butterfly milkweed (*Asclepias tuberosa*)	N	Su–F
Canna (*Canna* spp.)	E	Su–F
Cardinal flower (*Lobelia cardinalis*)	N	F
Columbine, American (*Aquilegia canadensis*)	N	Sp
Coral bells (*Heuchera sanguinea*)	N	Sp–Su
Fire pink (*Silene virginica*)	N	Su
Fireweed (*Epilobium angustifolium*)	E	Su–F
Four O'clocks (*Mirabilis jalapa*)	E	Su–F
Hollyhock (*Althaea rosea*)	E	Su
Paintbrush, Indian (*Castilleja coccinea*)	N	Sp
Penstemon (*Penstemon gloxinoides*)	N	Sp–Su
Phlox (*Phlox* spp.)	N	Sp–Su
Primrose, evening showy (*Oenothera speciosa*)	N	Su
Red-hot-poker (*Kniphofia uvaria*)	E	Su–F
Sage, pineapple (*Salvia elegans*)	E	Su–F
Salvia, Gregg's (*Salvia greggii*)	E	Sp–F
Verbena (*Verbena bonariensis*)	N	Sp–F
Annuals		
Lantana (*Lantana* spp.)	E	Sp–F
Larkspur (*Delphinium cardinale*)	E	Sp–Su
Pentas (*Pentas lanceolata*)	E	Su–F
Petunia (*Petunia x hybrida*)	E	Sp–F
Sage, scarlet (*Salvia splendens*)	E	Sp–F
Sage, Texas (*Salvia coccinea*)	E	Su–F
Verbena (*Verbena* spp.)	E	Sp–F
Touch-me-nots (*Impatiens* spp.)	N	Su–F

Attracting Mammals

Although most mammals are not seen as often as birds, their presence can be very interesting and beneficial to your wildscape. It may be difficult to attract mammals to your property if suitable habitat is not nearby, and you certainly shouldn't expect any large mammals to visit unless a large amount of good habitat is nearby. Yet there may be more mammals visiting your yard than you realize. Many a homeowner is unaware of visiting mammals because most are nocturnal or live under heavy cover.

The following mammals are the most common species found in urban habitats and within the southern Great Plains. For photos, natural history information, and range maps on these species, use the field guides referenced in appendix G.

Common Wildscape Mammals

RACCOONS AND OPOSSUMS, which are most active at night, live in urban habitats where they have access to food, water, and daytime cover. During the day they sleep in tree cavities, underground burrows, or abandoned buildings. They forage for everything from fruits, nuts, and grains to garbage. Raccoons sometimes dunk their food in water before eating, presumably to clean it. Biologists disregard this behavior as a sign of cleanliness but are still unclear as to the purpose of this raccoon trait.

RABBITS eat mostly succulent plants and prefer to live in grassy fields with dense ground cover. They also prefer edge areas that have numerous vegetative types. Attract them to your wildscape by adding a brush pile or thicket (fig. 5-2). Their favorite foods include blackberries, tree bark, and twig ends.

DEER MICE AND WHITE-FOOTED MICE are active at night and are found in edge-type habitats, logs, brush piles, and vacant buildings. Mice provide benefits to humans by eating weed seeds, dispersing berry seeds, and consuming numerous insect pests such as grasshoppers and beetles. The exotic house mouse is the common pest found in build-

ings and should not be encouraged in your wildscape. *Caution:* Deer mice often harbor ticks that may carry Lyme disease, so use caution in handling them or their nests.

GRAY SQUIRRELS AND FOX SQUIRRELS are attracted to large trees. They nest in tree cavities or in squirrel boxes you can add to your yard (see chapter 8). As most people who maintain backyard bird feeders know, squirrels eat all kinds of seeds. They also eat acorns, pecans, fruits, and maple blossoms. Providing corn may keep them from consuming the more costly sunflower seed.

FLYING SQUIRRELS are commonly found in the eastern half of the southern Great Plains, sometimes taking up residence in bluebird houses. They aren't normally viewed, however, because of their nocturnal habits. If you have a stand of tall, mature trees, it would be worth the effort to attract these interesting creatures. By stocking a feeder with sunflower seeds, nuts, fruits, berries, and peanut butter, and by providing night lighting, you may be able to catch a glimpse of these elusive mammals gliding to the feeder from the trees.

CHIPMUNKS are pleasing to watch as they gather seeds, fruits, nuts, and insects into their cheek pouches and then scamper off into the undergrowth to eat the food alone. The eastern chipmunk lives in three-chambered burrows, especially those protected by rock piles and old logs in the eastern half of the southern Great Plains. Their most menacing urban predator is the common house cat. To attract chipmunks, provide seeds and berries in an area with lots of places to hide from predators.

DEER are found across the Great Plains and occasionally visit urban areas near green spaces. If you want to encourage them into your wildscape, plant a buffer of deciduous trees and shrubs (fig. 5-3). Some of these plants actually thrive when browsed moderately by deer, but ornamentals and evergreens may suffer. Salt blocks and garden ponds also attract deer.

SKUNKS can be the gardener's best friend; they are among the main predators of both mice and beetles and rarely consume anything else from gardens. Adult skunks must be threatened before they will

FIGURE 5-1. Fox squirrels, which are among the few mammals active during the day, are easily attracted to wildscapes that offer lots of trees, supplemental food, squirrel boxes, and water.

FIGURE 5-2. Cottontail rabbits can be attracted to your property by providing a brush pile or thicket.

FIGURE 5-3. White-tailed deer require deciduous trees and shrubs to browse for food.

discharge their highly potent spray. To survive in your wildscape, they need denning areas.

Habitat Needs for Mammals

Most urban mammals are *omnivorous,* which means they eat both plants and meat. Many mammals, such as squirrels, chipmunks and mice, are attracted to seeds that have fallen beneath your bird feeder. They also are interested in any insects that might be living in your trees.

To keep squirrels from taking over your bird feeder, offer them a separate feeder to keep them occupied. Since they can leap more than five feet, hang bird feeders at least that far away from any squirrel launching pads. You might also place your feeder on a metal post or install a metal predator guard (see chapter 8) on the post or tree.

Some mammals are strict vegetarians. In warm weather, rabbits eat dandelions, clovers, and grasses as well as some plants in your garden (fig. 5-4). You can keep them away from your garden by planting their favorite foods near brush piles, brambles, and tall grasses. You also can build a fence of 1½-inch-grid chicken wire at least 2 feet tall and buried 6 inches deep.

Deer are attracted to vegetation as well. If you don't want to welcome them, hang bundles of human hair or blood meal on fences, or spray perfumed soaps or water containing red-pepper sauce around the garden perimeter. Commercial deer repellents like Hinder and Tree Guard occasionally work to deter deer.

MANAGING FOR MAMMALS IN YOUR WILDSCAPE

The best way to manage for mammals is to protect existing cavity trees in your yard. If you have few natural cavities, you can provide nest boxes for certain species. Providing rock piles, brush piles, and artificial burrows should also enhance your wildscape for small mammals. Here are some other suggestions:

✓ Plant native trees that produce fruits and nuts.

✓ Provide ground cover as shelter from predators and the elements.

✓ Create maximum habitat diversity through edges in your backyard habitat.

Make plaster casts of animal tracks

If unsure which animals are using your wildscape, you can track your mysterious visitors in several ways. Prepare a clean area of soil, sand, or mud where an animal has walked. During one of its visits, the animal may step in the prepared area, leaving a footprint behind. Adding a little food as bait greatly increases the chance of getting tracks.

Use an animal track identification book to determine what kind of animal visited. You can create a permanent record by making a plaster of Paris cast as follows:

1. Clean the foot print of loose sand and other particles.
2. Surround the track with a 2-inch-wide strip of cardboard or tin. You could use a tuna or cat food can with top and bottom removed or a strip from a cardboard milk carton.
3. Mix plaster of Paris (available at hardware or hobby stores) and water in a can or plastic bowl until the mixture has the consistency of heavy cream.
4. Pour the liquid plaster into the mold until the plaster is near the top of the form.
5. The plaster takes at least 15 minutes to harden. Hardening takes longer on a humid day, sometimes up to an hour.
6. Gently remove the plaster and turn the cast upside down. Wipe or wash the dirt off when the cast is completely dry. To keep the plaster from chipping, shellac the cast.
7. You now have a negative of the footprint. If you prefer a positive image, don't shellac the cast. Instead, coat the track with a thin layer of Vaseline, and put the coated track in a mold as before, with the footprint side up. Pour more liquid plaster of Paris over the top, and allow it to harden for at least two hours. Once it is dry, carefully separate the two layers. Use a knife blade or very fine sandpaper to smooth any rough surfaces. Finish by washing and shellacking or painting the cast.

FIGURE 5-4. Certified wildscape and rabbit habitat. (Oklahoma Certified Wildscape #0209, Newcastle)

✓ Protect nearby streams, swamps, marshes and green spaces from destruction and water pollution.

PRECAUTIONS AGAINST RABIES

Although mammals are an important and beneficial part of wildscaping efforts, you should be aware of the potential risks associated with having them nearby. A small number of mammals are infected with the rabies virus and can transmit it to humans through close contact with saliva (i.e., bites, scratches, licks on broken skin and mucous membranes). Once symptoms appear, the disease is almost 100 percent fatal to humans, incapacitating the central nervous system.

Although the consequences of rabies can be scary, actual human deaths in the United States are few and far between. The Centers for Disease Control reported that just over 5,000 animals had tested positive for rabies in the United States between January and September 1998. However, the CDC confirmed no human cases of rabies during this time, let alone any deaths.

Dogs and cats are the most common rabies carriers in the United States, while skunks, coyotes, and raccoons top the list of wild animals that are rabies carriers. People should always be wary of handling wild animals, especially those that are exhibiting unusual behavior, such as nocturnal animals being out in the middle of the day. Animals do not always "foam at the mouth" if they are infected with the rabies virus, so be cautious. Consult an expert before moving an animal or wear heavy leather gloves and use a scoop to push the animal into a container. If you are bitten by any

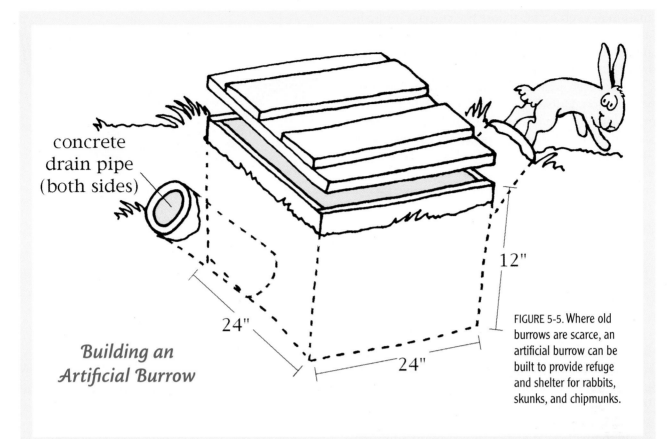

concrete
drain pipe
(both sides)

24"

12"

24"

*Building an
Artificial Burrow*

FIGURE 5-5. Where old burrows are scarce, an artificial burrow can be built to provide refuge and shelter for rabbits, skunks, and chipmunks.

Several species of small mammals, including rabbits, skunks, and mice, will use old burrows dug by woodchucks, badgers, and ground squirrels for refuge and shelter. In areas where these diggers are scarce, you can create an artificial burrow. Placing the burrow next to a bank, hedgerow, or other shrubs will increase its use by small mammals.

MATERIALS NEEDED

Shovel

Two PVC drain pipes (18 inches long, 6-inch diameter)

Four 1 x 2-foot roughened wood boards

Saw (preferably a jigsaw)

Hammer

Galvanized nails

One 2 x 2-foot compressed lumber board (used as lid for box)

DIRECTIONS

1. Dig a hole 12 inches deep and 24 inches square in an area with good drainage.

2. Dig sloping paths on opposite sides of the hole to accommodate the two PVC pipes.

3. On two pieces of 1 x 2 wood, cut an arc just over 6 inches in diameter at the bottom center of the board.

4. Nail the four pieces of 1 x 2 wood together to form the sides of a box, with the arched pieces on opposite sides.

5. Place the box—fitted with a 2 x 2-foot lid but no bottom—in the hole and install the pipes in the arches.

6. Cover the pipes and around the box with dirt so that it is partially or totally buried. To enhance the natural appearance of the lid, cover it with dirt, soil, rocks, or brush.

mammal, even a pet, report the contact immediately to a personal physician or local health department worker. Let medical professionals decide the best course of action.

The best precaution against rabies is pre-vaccination. Outside pets have the greatest chance of coming into contact with a rabid animal, so it is critical to ensure that your pets have current rabies shots. If they do not, and they are scratched or bitten by a rabid animal, they may have to be quarantined for six months or even euthanized. People who commonly work with wild animals should receive a pre-exposure immunization treatment.

Bats

Through the efforts of organizations like Bat Conservation International and state wildlife agencies, many people have learned of the benefits of having bats near their homes. These gentle mammals are the only major predator of night-flying insects such as moths, mosquitoes, cucumber beetles, June beetles, and leafhoppers. Some bats consume more than 2,000 mosquitoes each night, while the pallid bat even eats scorpions from the ground!

Although bats have relatively good eyesight, they depend primarily on a well-developed echolocation system similar to sonar. Bats emit pulses of very high frequency sound, which are inaudible to humans, at a rate of a few to more than 500 per second. By listening to the echoes that reflect back to them, bats are able to maneuver around objects in their path and capture tiny flying insects.

Bats generally mate in fall and delay fertilization until spring, when the female usually gives birth to one offspring. Red bats, a tree-dwelling species commonly seen in urban areas, may produce twins or even quadruplets.

The southern Great Plains has about 25 bat species, several of which are migratory and leave the region for the winter. Seven bat species are more likely to occupy bat houses in both urban and rural areas. In general, any species that naturally roosts in buildings, under bridges, or in tree cavities is a bat house candidate.

BAT HOUSE CANDIDATES

LITTLE BROWN BATS (*Myotis lucifugus*) are found throughout eastern Kansas and Oklahoma; males

FIGURE 5-6. Bats, like this pallid bat, are the only nighttime predators of flying insects. Pallid bats are remarkable in that they will actually grab scorpions and millipedes from the ground.

might use houses for summer roosts.

CAVE MYOTIS (*Myotis velifer*) are found in New Mexico, southern Colorado, southwest Kansas, and western Oklahoma and Texas. They probably would use houses for late summer and early fall roosts.

PALLID BATS (*Antrozous pallidus*) also are found in New Mexico, southern Colorado, southwest Kansas, and western Oklahoma and Texas. They probably would use houses for summer roosts.

MEXICAN FREE-TAILED BATS (*Tadarida brasiliensis*) migrate each fall to Central and South America but return in spring to set up nursery colonies in gypsum and limestone caves in New Mexico, Colorado, southwest Kansas, Oklahoma, and Texas. Large houses could be used to rear young, although houses are more likely to be used by bachelor colonies or as roosts by transients.

EASTERN PIPISTRELS (*Pipistrellus subflavus*) and EVENING BATS (*Nycticeius humeralis*) are found in Missouri, Arkansas, Louisiana, and eastern Kansas, Oklahoma, and Texas. Both bat species probably would use houses for rearing young and for summer roosts.

BIG BROWN BATS (*Eptesicus fuscus*) are widespread throughout the United States and use houses for nursery colonies or summer roosts.

FOOD AND WATER SOURCES

Because most bats eat only insects, it is important not to use pesticides if you suspect bats are in the area. The use of pesticides is cited as one of the three main reasons for the decline in bat populations, along with loss of habitat and cave vandalism. Because bats depend on insects, areas with high pesticide concentrations will not attract them.

Water is also an important consideration for attracting bats. Studies by Bat Conservation International have shown that areas located a quarter mile or less from at least three acres of water have the best chance of having bats present. Insects such as mosquitoes breed in and around ponds, streams, and rivers, so these areas have a higher concentration of bats. Bats obtain most of their moisture requirements from the insects they eat, but they also can drink by swooping down on a body of water to gather liquid.

MANAGING FOR BATS

Although most bats live in caves or in trees, some can be attracted into bat houses (see chapter 8 for designs). A successful bat house depends upon many factors, but biologists have found that variety is the key. The more variety you can provide for the bats, the better the chance of attracting them. In general, a successful bat house should:

1. Be located a quarter mile or less from a stream, river, lake, or standing pond.

2. Receive six to eight hours of daily sun. For best results, face the house toward the south, southwest, or west.

3. Be painted light brown to absorb additional heat. Caulk all seams, especially around the roof, before painting. Apply two coats of exterior latex paint to all outer surfaces and entry areas. Do not paint or stain inside the house.

4. Contain a ½-inch horizontal vent across the front of the bat house and about 5 inches from the bottom. This vent prevents the bats from overheating and may also assist bats in locating the house.

5. Be mounted at least 15 feet above ground. Houses mounted on the sides of buildings or on poles are twice as attractive to bats as houses placed on trees. Bat houses placed under the eaves of wood or stone buildings are especially successful when exposed to the sun.

6. Be erected in groups of three or more,

offering more variety of temperatures. Houses on the sides of buildings should be placed close together but at different heights. Pole-mounted houses should be placed back to back, ¾ of an inch apart, and covered by a tin roof. They should have a north-south orientation for maximum temperature gradients.

If bats don't occupy houses after two summers, experiment! Bat roosting preferences are still not completely understood. Try moving the house a few feet to receive more or less sun, try raising it higher off the ground, or paint the house a darker or lighter color. Double check your assessment of the house's location. Have all criteria for bat house placement been met?

Bats may not live in your bat house due to heavy pesticide use nearby or inadequate food supply or perhaps because they already have sufficient local roosts. Generally, do not expect bats to use your house during winter. Other management recommendations include:

- If wasps become a problem in your bat house, blast them with a high-pressure hose. Scrape mud dauber nests early in the season for better control. *Do not* use pesticides!

- Check bat houses for bats once or twice a month in summer and then once each fall and winter. After bats are established, check only a few times per season. To check bat houses, briefly shine a flashlight into the house, being careful not to touch the house and being as quiet as possible. Another way to check the house is by watching it at dusk or dawn and seeing if any bats fly into or out of the house. Also, look for bat droppings under the house.

- If the wood of your bat houses begins to warp, especially near the top, seal any gaps with silicon caulking. If the warping is significant, build a new house. Drafts keep bats from trapping body heat efficiently and from maintaining optimum conditions for rearing young.

- Besides mounting bat houses, you might consider loosely wrapping corrugated metal around tree trunks to provide

CHAPTER 6

Attracting Amphibians and Reptiles

Many people often overlook amphibians and reptiles in their wildscapes, even though they occasionally see snakes, lizards, frogs, salamanders, and turtles. These "creepy-crawlies" provide many beneficial actions: almost all reptiles and amphibians eat pest species such as insects and rodents; frogs and toads help to loosen up soil in our gardens; and all of these species serve as prey for other wildlife.

In recent years, biologists have noticed a decline in several species of frogs and lizards, including the beloved Texas horned lizard. These species could be declining for several reasons: habitat destruction or manipulation, insecticide use killing their food source, and increased predation by cats, raccoons, and other urban predators. If you find reptiles and amphibians in your urban wildscape, encourage them to stay, but do not keep them as pets.

Another recent development has been the discovery of deformed frogs and toads in northern states such as Minnesota and Michigan. At one Minnesota pond, 70 percent of the frogs found there had deformities like missing legs or extra ones, missing eyes, or missing jaws. Although the southern Great Plains states have not experienced this phenomenon to such a degree, it is still a possibility in the near future, making all our efforts to provide habitat for amphibians and reptiles extremely important.

Table 6–1 lists the most common amphibians and reptiles found in urban wildscapes. If you are lucky enough to live near woods, a stream, or a pond, you may see some species not listed. For photographs, natural history information, and range maps on these species, use the field guides mentioned in appendix G.

Use the following abbreviations for table 6–1:
SUITABLE NATURAL COMMUNITY: CFP = Cypress Floodplains, OHL = Ouachita Highlands, OZP = Ozark Plateau, CT = Crosstimbers, TGP = Tallgrass Prairie, MGP = Mixed Grass Prairie, SHP = Southern High Plains

FIGURE 6-1. The gray treefrog enjoys shaded trees along the water's edge.

Food and Water Sources

Most amphibians and reptiles have different food and water requirements at varying stages of their life cycles. For example, all amphibians (salamanders, toads, and frogs) hatch in water, but most live on land after metamorphosing from tadpoles. Red-eared sliders are carnivorous during earlier stages of life but gradually switch to a vegetarian diet.

Certainly, having a source of fresh water will improve the chances of attracting amphibians to your wildscape. Even a small 3 x 3-foot pond would provide enough water for tadpoles to develop. Such a breeding pond would serve as a reliable source for frogs or toads to return to each spring. A larger pond would attract water turtles, including red-eared sliders and softshell turtles. Some water snakes may also make a larger pond their home. However, if you want to help frogs, you should not put minnows or goldfish in the pond—they eat frog eggs. Mosquito fish would be acceptable and would help control the mosquitoes that would otherwise develop in standing water.

Insects are the mainstay of many reptiles' diet, as are small rodents. If you notice more snakes in your yard, it could be because they are preying on these pests. By leaving these harmless animals in your yard, you will provide natural pest control.

A way to entice insect-eating lizards into your yard is by setting out rotten fruit, such as a banana or peach, in a shady location. This may attract fruit flies, in turn attracting lizards such as green anoles in Louisiana, southeast Oklahoma, east Texas, and southern Arkansas.

Amphibians and Reptiles in Urban Wildscapes

Reptiles and amphibians are small and secretive, usually hiding and finding their food in heavy cover. Although you may not even see these species, you can improve habitat in your yard for them when you:

- Provide toad holes (fig. 6–3) and toad lights. Dig a hole several inches deep and

TABLE 6–1. Common Wildscape Amphibians and Reptiles

SPECIES COMMON NAME (*SCIENTIFIC NAME*)	SUITABLE NATURAL COMMUNITY							FOOD	HABITAT
	CFP	OHL	OZP	CT	TGP	MGP	SHP		
Amphibians									
Barred tiger salamander (*Ambystoma tigrinum*)				X	X	X	X	insects, aquatic animals	shallow wetlands
Woodhouse's toad (*Bufo woodhousii*)	X	X		X	X	X	X	insects, spiders	backyards and gardens
Great Plains toad (*Bufo cognatus*)				X	X	X	X	insects	backyards, gardens, shallow pools
Gray treefrog (*Hyla versicolor*)	X	X	X	X	X			insects	shaded trees along water's edge
Blanchard's cricket frog (*Acris crepitans*)	X	X	X	X	X	X	X	insects, spiders	muddy banks along permanent waters
Bullfrog (*Rana catesbeiana*)	X	X	X	X	X	X	X	insects, birds, frogs, fish	streams and ponds
Leopard frogs (*Rana* spp.)	X	X	X	X	X	X	X	insects, worms, snails	near water sources, gardens
Reptiles									
Red-eared turtle (*Trachemys scripta*)	X	X	X	X	X	X	X	Young-fish and insects; adults-insects and plants	streams and ponds
Box turtles (*Terrapene* spp.)	X	X	X	X	X	X	X	insects, fleshy fruits	moist open areas and prairies
Fence lizard (*Sceloporus undulatus*)	X	X	X	X	X	X	X	insects, spiders	woodlands and sandy regions
Texas horned lizard (*Phrynosoma cornutum*)	X	X	X	X	X	X	X	harvester ants	sandy areas with little vegetation
Racerunners (*Cnemidophorus sexlineatus*)	X	X	X	X	X	X	X	insects, spiders, scorpions, snails	open sunny areas
Ground skink (*Scincella lateralis*)	X	X	X	X	X	X		insects, spiders, worms	forest floor of woodlands
Five-lined skink (*Eumeces fasciatus*)	X	X	X	X	X			insects, spiders, worms, snails, mice, lizards	woodlands, rock piles, logs, debris
Ringneck snake (*Diadophis punctatus*)	X	X	X	X	X	X	X	insects, worms	rocks or debris in moist areas
Western earth snake (*Virginia valeriae*)	X	X	X	X				insects, worms	moist woodlands, wooded urban areas
Racers (*Coluber constrictor*)		X	X	X	X	X	X	insects, lizards, frogs, rodents, birds, snakes	open habitats
Water snakes (*Nerodia* spp.)	X	X	X	X	X	X	X	fish, tadpoles, salamanders, crayfish	permanent water sources
Western cottonmouth (*Agkistrodon piscivorus*)	X	X	X	X				amphibians, fish, snakes, birds	permanent water sources
Hognose snakes (*Heterodon* spp.)	X	X	X	X	X	X	X	toads, frogs, insects, birds, rodents	sandy areas, meadows, fields
Great Plains rat snake (*Elaphe guttata*)		X	X	X	X	X	X	rodents, birds, frogs, bats	waterways, canyons, barnyards, houses

FIGURE 6-2. Natural pond in a certified wildscape. (Oklahoma Certified Wildscape #0113, Moyers)

TABLE 6–1. Common Wildscape Amphibians and Reptiles

SPECIES COMMON NAME (*SCIENTIFIC NAME*)	SUITABLE NATURAL COMMUNITY							FOOD	HABITAT
	CFP	OHL	OZP	CT	TGP	MGP	SHP		
Black rat snake (*Elaphe obsoleta*)	X	X	X	X	X	X		mice, birds, eggs, lizards	forests, fields, canyons, barnyards
Bullsnake (*Pituophis melanoleucus*)			X	X	X	X	X	rodents, birds, lizards	woodlands, fields, prairies
Prairie kingsnake (*Lampropeltis calligaster*)	X	X	X	X	X	X		snakes, lizards, rodents	woodlands, fields, prairies
Milksnakes (*Lampropeltis triangulum*)	X	X	X	X	X	X	X	rodents, snakes, lizards	woodlands, fields, prairies
Graham's crayfishsnake (*Regina grahamii*)	X			X	X	X	X	crayfish	slow-moving water, crayfish burrows
Brown snake (*Storeria dekayi*)	X	X	X	X	X	X		earthworms, slugs	urban areas, wetlands, woodlands
Common garter snake (*Thamnophis sirtalis*)	X	X	X	X	X	X	X	rodents, earthworms, fish, birds, amphibians	variety of habitats
Lined snake (*Tropidoclonion lineatum*)				X	X	X		earthworms	debris in vacant city lots and parks

line it with peat or compost. Cover it with a flat rock or board and scoop out an entrance into the cavity. By placing a low voltage light a few feet above the ground near the toad hole, you will attract insects closer to where the toads are hiding.

- Encourage native ground cover, grasses, and wildflowers. A finely trimmed lawn is not very attractive to reptiles, amphibians, or other wildlife.

- Leave stumps, rotting logs, and stones where possible. Leaf litter left under trees and shrubs and in gardens can also serve to produce reptile and amphibian homes by decomposing and providing loose, moist soil.

- Provide breeding ponds for amphibians or turtles. Do not try to introduce adult amphibians and reptiles into your wildscape. Instead, gather tadpoles from area streams and ponds, or wait for adults to make your wildscape their home.

- Provide brush, wood, and rock piles as valuable shelter and basking sites for amphibians and reptiles. Build rock walls with plenty of cracks and crevices.

- Discourage cats from using your yard. These efficient hunters frequently wipe out populations of amphibians, reptiles, and small mammals.

- Provide perches, such as wooden rail or slat fences, for lizards to bask, catch insects, and set up territories.

Managing Ponds for Amphibians and Reptiles

Owners of rural wildscapes know that ponds are vital to many reptiles and amphibians as well as to other wildlife species. Although shallow ponds may not support fish because they dry up in the heat of summer, they do provide valuable water holes for amphibians and reptiles in spring. Ponds with a wide variety of wildlife and plants also provide aesthetic values to the owner.

Many people mistakenly assume that turtles and snakes eat large numbers of fish, depleting the stock in a pond or river. However, these species actually enhance fishing opportunities by eating dead or diseased fish. This allows the remaining fish to prosper.

Ponds are fairly simple to manage for reptiles and amphibians—just let nature take its course after the plants and wildlife are introduced and established. However, you can still do several things to enhance your pond for amphibian and reptile species:

- Fence the pond and a portion of its watershed to keep livestock out of the water.

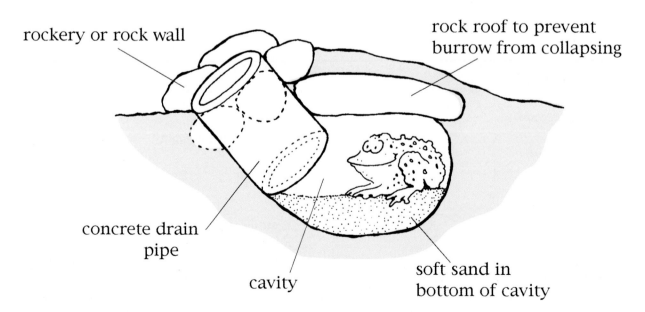

rockery or rock wall

rock roof to prevent burrow from collapsing

concrete drain pipe

cavity

soft sand in bottom of cavity

FIGURE 6-3. Construction details of a toad hole.

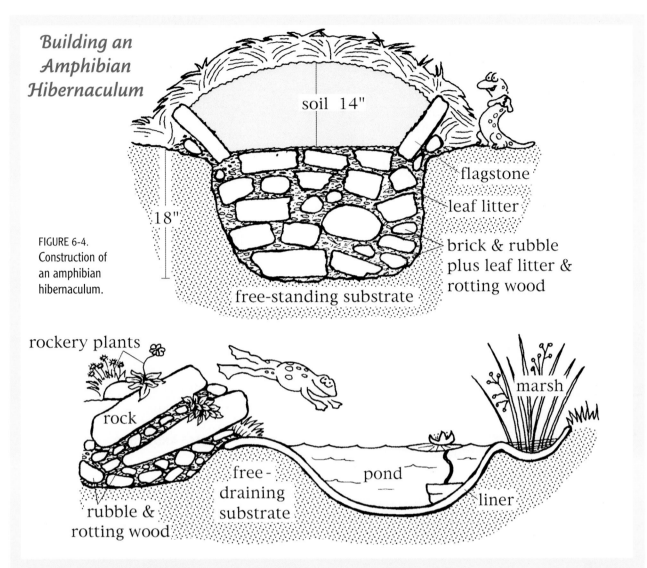

Building an Amphibian Hibernaculum

soil 14"

18"

FIGURE 6-4. Construction of an amphibian hibernaculum.

flagstone

leaf litter

brick & rubble plus leaf litter & rotting wood

free-standing substrate

rockery plants

rock

rubble & rotting wood

free-draining substrate

pond

liner

marsh

Although ponds and streams provide summer breeding habitats for frogs, toads, and salamanders, you can provide for their needs year-round by creating a place where amphibians can hibernate in the winter. Hibernacula are especially important in urbanized areas where natural habitats have been destroyed or severely degraded. You can build an amphibian hibernaculum on a well-drained site, a poorly drained site, or even merged into the plan for your garden pond.

MATERIALS NEEDED

Shovel

Bricks (broken and unbroken)

Wood and lumber scraps

Leaf litter

Flagstone or concrete slabs

Straw

Rocks (optional)

Plants (optional)

DIRECTIONS

1. Dig a hole 18 inches deep, so that the total area is a minimum of two square yards.

2. Fill the opening with whole and half brick rubble, creating plenty of spaces among the bricks. Mix in bits of wood and leaf litter to provide sources of humidity.

3. Place flagstone, concrete slabs, or other flat, heavy material so that it covers the edge of the bricks. Make sure entry gaps lead under the flagstone.

4. Cover the entire area with soil, making sure the entry gaps remain clear.

5. Top the mound with straw.

6. For a garden pond hibernaculum, place rocks around the edge. You can include rock garden plants as long as the entry gaps remain open. Trees and garden plantings near the pond provide important habitat for reptiles and amphibians during the terrestrial part of their life cycle.

You can place a stock tank below the dam and outside the fence to provide water for livestock. This ensures a cleaner water source free from the bacteria and ammonia in livestock droppings (fig. 6-5).

- Do not plow or allow grazing in the immediate vicinity of the pond. This will improve water quality in the pond and will leave ground cover that can be used as "wildlife corridors" to other habitats.
- Provide food and cover sources for amphibians and aquatic turtles by introducing plants into new ponds or ponds formerly used by livestock. In general, ponds managed for amphibians and reptiles can be covered by aquatic plants. See chapter 3 for a listing of recommended aquatic plants.
- For aquatic turtles, anchor several logs in open water away from the bank to serve as basking sites. Red cedar logs are ideal for this purpose. See figure 8–15 for instructions on building a loafing platform.
- Log piles, rock piles, and brush piles around the pond's edge provide valuable basking sites and cover.

Many amphibians and reptiles benefit from ponds and water sources, including:

SALAMANDERS
Barred tiger salamander
Central newt
Ringed salamander
Marbled salamander
Spotted salamander

SNAKES
Broad-banded water snake
Brown snake
Common garter snake
Diamondback water snake
Graham's crayfish snake
Northern water snake
Plainbelly water snake
Speckled kingsnake
Western cottonmouth
Western plains garter snake
Western pygmy rattlesnake
Western ribbon snake

TOADS AND FROGS
Blanchard's cricket frog
Bullfrog
Crawfish frog
Dwarf American toad

FIGURE 6-5. To ensure better quality water in your pond for amphibians and fish, fence off the pond from livestock and provide stock ponds below the pond dam.

Gray treefrog

Green frog

Northern spring peeper

Pickerel frog

Plains leopard frog

Southern leopard frog

TURTLES

Common musk turtle (stinkpot)

Common snapping turtle

Midland smooth softshell

Ouachita map turtle

Painted turtle

Red-eared slider

Western chicken turtle

Yellow mud turtle

FIGURE 6-6. An oak stump provides basking areas and insects for the fence lizard. By holding still when threatened, the fence lizard becomes camouflaged against the stump.

Woodland and Prairie Habitats

Many of the actions that constitute a normal part of managing a forested or prairie area can have spin-off benefits for wildlife.

MANAGING WOODLANDS FOR AMPHIBIANS AND REPTILES

Selective thinning creates open spaces that allow shrubs and nonwoody plants to develop. The thinned trees can either be sold, if they are of high quality, or used as firewood. The branches can be used to form brushpiles on the forest floor or around ponds. Other things that can be done in woodlands to benefit reptiles and amphibians include:

- Excluding livestock grazing to allow the growth of nonwoody plants that provide additional cover sources for ground-dwelling amphibians and reptiles.

- Leaving several snags standing per acre for lizards and black rat snakes to use for shelter; skinks also lay their eggs in snags. Produce snags by girdling old or deformed trees.

- Leaving natural shelters such as stumps, fallen logs, and brush piles on the forest floor to provide cover and shelter sources. Red-backed and slimy salamanders burrow under logs on forested slopes. Ground skinks, fence lizards, and small forest snakes such as brown snakes, redbelly snakes, earth snakes, and red milk snakes also benefit from additional cover sources.

- Planting fruiting shrubs and trees, such as pokeweed, sand plum, mulberry, and raspberry, in the understory to attract box turtles.

- Leaving thick undergrowth as cover sources for frogs like spring peepers and gray treefrogs. This undergrowth attracts the insects that reptiles and amphibians eat.

- Building ponds in and near the edge of woodlands for species such as spotted and tiger salamanders to lay their eggs. Other species, such as the central newt, live in woodland ponds as adults.

- Many amphibians and reptiles may be found in woodlands, including:

TURTLES

Three-toed box turtle

SNAKES

Black rat snake

Brown snake

Bullsnake

Coachwhip

Search for chorus frogs at local ponds

Across the southern Great Plains in late spring, chorus frogs emerge from hibernation and gather in small ponds to breed. Chorus frogs are ¾ to 1½ inches long and brownish green, and they have three dark stripes on their backs. They have a dark stripe on each side from the nose across the eyes and down the length of the body. A chorus frog's call sounds like someone rubbing a finger over the teeth of a hard plastic comb.

Dress warmly and wear waterproof boots. Take one flashlight for each person. Visit a wetland with shallow, quiet water. Listen to the chorus frogs and try to walk slowly into the marsh toward them. Make sure you keep your kids in sight! When the frogs feel threatened, they will quit singing. Simply remain perfectly still until they begin again, and then continue your stalk. The object is to find a chorus frog in the beam of your flashlight. This activity is tricky and takes great patience, but it is fun!

Copperhead
Flathead snake
Ground snake
Milk snake
Northern redbelly snake
Northern scarlet snake
Prairie kingsnake
Ringneck snake
Rough earth snake
Speckled kingsnake
Western earth snake
Western ribbon snake
Western worm snake

TOADS AND FROGS
Crawfish frog
Dwarf American toad
Eastern narrow-mouth toad
Gray treefrog
Green frog
Northern spring peeper
Strecker's chorus frog
Woodhouse's toad

SALAMANDERS
Barred tiger salamander
Central newt
Many-ribbed salamander
Smallmouth salamander
Southern redback salamander
Spotted salamander
Western slimy salamander

LIZARDS
Broadhead skink
Fence lizard
Five-lined skink
Ground skink
Southern coal skink
Western slender glass lizard

MANAGING PRAIRIES FOR AMPHIBIANS AND REPTILES

Many reptiles and amphibians are found in prairie habitats throughout the southern Great Plains. By managing fields and prairies for a variety of native grasses and other plants, you'll encourage additional insects and rodents, which in turn will attract amphibians and reptiles that prey on these pest species.

To manage your prairie, consider the following:

- For old fields that have been extensively grazed or plowed, reseed with native grasses and wildflowers. The *seed bank*— native seeds found naturally in the area but that have had their growth suppressed by human actions—may still exist and may help bring back these plant species.

FIGURE 6-7. The spadefoot toad, with its catlike eyes, comes out after the infrequent rains in the arid west to lay eggs in temporary puddles.

- Separate the prairie into several plots of equal size. If the prairie has a growing number of invasive species such as red cedar, Siberian elm, tamarisk (also called tamarack or salt cedar), and herbaceous weeds like ragweed, either mow or burn one of these blocks every three to five years on a rotational basis; that is, burn or mow block A the first year, block B the second, block C the third, block A the fourth, etc. This rotational mowing or burning will ensure that thatch and other ground cover are left for hiding places. If the prairie doesn't have a high number of invader species, don't do anything to it—leave it alone. Otherwise, your actions may inadvertently open up the prairie to these invasive species.

- Provide rock piles for shelter along fence rows, near the edges of woodlots, and on south-facing slopes of hillsides.

- Leave or construct shallow ponds and marshes (3–5 inches deep) in your prairie. You may wish to protect these water sources from livestock by fencing around them.

Some of the more common amphibians and reptiles found in Great Plains prairies include:

SALAMANDERS

Barred tiger salamander

SNAKES

Black rat snake

Blind snake

Bullsnake

Checkered garter snake

Coachwhip

Common garter snake

Eastern hognose snake

Flathead snake

Great Plains rat snake

Ground snake

Kansas glossy snake

Lined snake

Milk snake

Plains blackhead snake

Prairie kingsnake

Prairie rattlesnake

Racer

Speckled kingsnake

Texas longnose snake

Western hognose snake

Western massasauga

FROGS AND TOADS

Couch's spadefoot

Crawfish frog

Great Plains narrowmouth toad

Great Plains toad

Green toad

Hurter's spadefoot

New Mexico spadefoot

Plains spadefoot

Red-spotted toad

Spotted chorus frog

Strecker's chorus frog

Texas toad

Western chorus frog

LIZARDS

Fence lizard

Great Plains skink

Racerunner

Southern prairie skink

Texas horned lizard

Texas spotted whiptail

Western slender glass lizard

TURTLE

Ornate box turtle

Texas Horned Lizards

Probably one of the best known reptiles in the southern Great Plains is the Texas horned lizard, also called the "horny toad" (fig. 6-8). These are indeed lizards, not toads, and they have suffered a decline in recent years for a variety of reasons. Probably the greatest threat to these unique lizards has been increased use of pesticides; although pesticide use doesn't kill the horned lizard, it does reduce the populations of harvester ants (commonly called "red ants") that are the lizard's main food supply. Another threat has been the collection of horned lizards as pets or for the commercial pet trade. Finally, simple human development has decreased the amount of habitat available for horned lizard use.

The Texas horned lizard is classified as a "species of special concern," and regulations in Oklahoma, Texas, and New Mexico have established a year-round closed season on these lizards and other species of reptiles and amphibians. It is unlawful to kill, capture, keep as pets or sell Texas horned lizards in these three states without specific written permission from the state wildlife agency. While the horned lizard is not listed federally as an endangered or threatened species, its widespread decline has caused concern for its future status. The closed season is designed to protect it from unnecessary collection.

You can help Texas horned lizards in several ways:

- Refrain from extensive use of insecticides if you suspect horned lizards in the area. In particular, leave harvester ant mounds if they do not threaten humans or livestock.

- Do not keep horned lizards as pets; it's okay to examine them, but return them to where they were found.

- Keep pets inside or on leashes. The increase in feral cats is a possible reason for the horned lizard's decline.

- Report any horned lizard sightings to your state wildlife agency (see appendix I); in Oklahoma, contact the Oklahoma Wildlife Diversity Program at

FIGURE 6-8. The Texas horned lizard, also called the "horny toad," is dependent on ants, sandy soils, and scattered cover in its habitat.

405/521–4616; e-mail:
nr@odwc.state.ok.us.

- Financially support efforts to assist the horned lizard by donating to state wildlife agencies or to nonprofit organizations such as the Horned Lizard Conservation Society (see appendix I).

Venomous Snakes

Many people unnecessarily fear snakes, thinking that all snakes are venomous and will strike at them. In truth, most snakes are small and harmless and usually attempt to escape from humans to avoid conflict. If you think of it from a snake's perspective, humans are about 100 times larger, much too large for a snake to swallow. The urban landowner should encourage snakes because of the benefits they provide in eating insects, rodents, slugs, and other undesirable pest species.

One popular misconception people have is that if a snake "rattles" its tail, it must be a rattlesnake. Not so. Any given rattlesnake cannot be relied upon to rattle its tail, and some nonvenomous snakes make rattling noises to mimic their venomous cousins, thus avoiding conflict with humans or other larger predators. This "rattling" is accomplished by vibrating the tail rapidly in dry grass or leaves.

Oklahoma has seven species of native venomous snakes, which are distinguishable from the other 50 nonvenomous snakes by the vertical slits in the pupils of the venomous species and the facial pits between their eyes and nostrils. The head is also shaped differently in venomous species; because of the poison glands in their cheeks, venomous species have a more triangular head. Nonvenomous Oklahoma snakes have rounded heads with no apparent "neck."

To avoid any unpleasant encounters with venomous snakes, know what type of habitats they may occupy. Watch where you step when hiking in wooded areas, especially around cliffs and over logs and rock piles. Avoid going under bushes or shrubs when near water sources. If you use caution in the outdoors and respect snakes and other wildlife, you shouldn't have any problems.

In general, most of the snakes found in urban areas are nonvenomous. The copperhead is occasionally found in wooded suburban or rural properties in Missouri, Arkansas, Louisiana, eastern

FIGURE 6-9. This hognose snake needs downed wood or a brush pile for shelter.

Kansas, and central Oklahoma and Texas. The western cottonmouth (or water moccasin) is found near permanent water sources in Louisiana, Arkansas, south-central Oklahoma, eastern Texas, and southern Missouri.

The rattlesnake species of the Great Plains are found in a variety of habitats. The western massasauga inhabits hillsides, prairies, and grasslands in Kansas, western Oklahoma, southeast Nebraska, and central Texas. Western pygmy rattlesnakes stay near a permanent water source in Arkansas, Louisiana, southeast Oklahoma, and eastern Texas. Timber rattlesnakes are found on rocky hillsides and in swamp wetlands in Missouri, Arkansas, Louisiana, and eastern Kansas, Oklahoma, and Texas. The western diamondback rattlesnake is found in arid areas, rocky outcrops, and bluffs in scattered locations in Oklahoma, New Mexico, and Texas. Prairie rattlesnakes inhabit rocky outcrops or canyons, open grasslands, and prairie dog towns in New Mexico, eastern Colorado, and western Nebraska, Kansas, Oklahoma, and Texas.

Beneficial Insects and Spiders

Insects and spiders are an often forgotten but immensely valuable component of any wildscape. The sheer number of these *arthropods* (the category includes insects, spiders, and ticks) makes them the dominant animal species everywhere. Biologists estimate that Oklahoma contains at least 10,000 species of insects, far outnumbering the 634 native vertebrate species. In fact, 3,600 species of beetles have been identified in Oklahoma's Latimer County alone, with additional species found only a few miles away in LeFlore County.

Insects and spiders are the "glue" keeping ecosystems together through their roles of pollination, decomposition, and as food sources for fish and other wildlife. Many bees, butterflies, moths, and flies are essential pollinators of cultivated and native plants. Termites and beetles aid in decomposition of organic matter and nutrient recycling. Insects make up the primary diet for many kinds of birds during summer as well as for amphibians and reptiles year-round. In addition, growing numbers of people are now spending time and money to observe butterflies and other colorful insects, much as bird-watchers have done for decades.

When you develop your wildscape, remember to include habitat requirements for insects and spiders as well as for birds, mammals, reptiles, and amphibians. Several arthropod species such as ants, grasshoppers, mosquitoes, hornets, spiders, and ticks are considered pests and will enter your wildscape unasked. For this reason, it is also important to provide for the habitat requirements of predators of these pest species.

Depending upon what type of wildscape you have created, you will see a variety of insect and spider species. Most insects require sunny areas, nectar-producing plants, or small ponds to fulfill part or all of their life requirements. Table 7–1 gives needs and characteristics of some of the more common backyard insects and spiders.

FIGURE 7-1. Garden spider in web.

Managing for Butterflies

Butterflies probably are most people's favorite insects. Besides serving as important pollinators of native and cultivated plants, butterflies are a joy to watch and are relatively easy to attract to nectar-producing flowers.

Butterflies are also excellent indicators of the health of the local environment. Healthy ecosystems generally have large numbers of butterflies and other insects; ecosystems that have been degraded due to insecticide and herbicide use or because of local development do not have many insects. By designing a garden for butterflies, you can conserve the health of your area through your use of native plants and reduced applications of insecticide. Many native plants serve not only as nectar sources for adult butterflies but also as host species for their earlier life stages. A single native plant bed with larval host plants and nectar-producing flowers can be a central attraction for both butterflies and butterfly watchers.

Butterflies undergo four distinct life-cycle stages: egg, larva (caterpillar), pupa (chrysalis) and adult. Soon after the adult butterfly lays her eggs, the larval caterpillars will hatch and begin voraciously eating various plants. Once the caterpillars have grown large enough, they will enter the pupa stage, when the caterpillar's wormlike appearance gives way to a seemingly magical transformation. A wrinkle-winged adult emerges from the chrysalis shell. After stretching and drying its wings, it will probably begin feeding on nectar, sap, or detritus.

FOOD AND WATER SOURCES

Because butterflies are attracted to larval host plants and nectar-producing flowers, the easiest way to bring them to you is by planting a butterfly garden. Your own garden can be as simple as a few nectar plants in pots or as complex as a home landscape designed with sequentially flowering nectar plants. Before you begin a butterfly garden, decide from the start how much time, expense, and effort you want to invest in your butterfly habitat project. Creating a successful habitat requires more than

TABLE 7–1. Characteristics of Common Insects and Spiders

INSECT OR SPIDER	MANAGEMENT NEEDS	INTERESTING CHARACTERISTICS
Cricket	Sunny area with loose cover	Chorus on warm summer evenings
Grasshopper	Sunny, grassy location	May damage garden plants
Ladybird/ladybug beetle	Sunny garden	Feeds on aphids and scale insects
Hover fly	Sunny area with flowers	Harmless mimic of bees and wasps; larvae feed on aphids
Bumblebee	Nectar-rich flowers	Colorful buzzers, seldom sting
Hornet or Yellowjacket	Dry overhang	Makes paper; sting may be allergic
Ant	Cracks in wall or stones	Colonial workers with flying adults
Butterfly	Larval and host plants, sunny areas	Bright, colorful fliers
Moth	Night-blooming flowers	Large species most attractive; hummingbird, sphinx, and bumblebee moths mistaken as hummingbirds
Dragonfly	Open areas near pools with emergent vegetation	Noisy, colorful fliers control black flies and mosquitoes
Damselfly	Pool with emergent plants	Dainty and colorful; eat mosquitoes
Orb spider	Shrubbery	Large webs trap insects
Wolf spider	Sunny vegetation near walls	Female carries egg case on back
Jumping spider	Sunshine, crevices	Colorful leapers, change eye color
Garden spider	Shrubbery	Retreats to rolled-up leaf near web
Crab spider	Leaves, bark, flowers	Waits in ambush for insects
Daddy-long-legs	Dark corners, flat stones	Long thin legs with flexible ends

one season of planting, so you should keep that in mind from the beginning.

Next, discover what butterfly species you already have. You can only expect to attract butterflies that already occur in your area, so concentrate on these. Identify and list the butterflies that visit your yard during the season. Also, survey the plants in your yard, including the "weeds." Field guides should assist you in making the correct identifications. Although plant species appropriate for butterfly gardens vary across the country, the plant species listed in chapter 2 will give the best chance of attracting a wide variety of butterflies to your property.

Nectar-feeding butterflies are attracted to red, orange, pink, and purple flowers arranged in clusters in sunny areas of your yard. Butterflies prefer blossoms with large petals that provide a platform where they can feed securely on nectar. The best butterfly gardens combine annual and perennial cultivated flowers with wildflowers at staggered blooming intervals to provide a continuous nectar supply.

Butterflies prefer open, sunny spaces—a full-sun wildflower garden is ideal. Butterflies often perch on flat, light-colored stones to raise their body temperature by basking in the sun. A wind-sheltered garden with a fence or a windbreak of trees and large shrubs also attracts winged visitors. However, some caterpillars may require food plants in shaded areas.

Water is essential. Most butterflies obtain the water they need from flowers they visit, but many species enjoy a damp area from which to drink. Although butterflies are unable to drink from open water, you can easily provide a small puddle or seep for their use. Wet sand in a shallow dish filled with rocks or gravel can serve as a butterfly oasis.

To make your wildscape more attractive to additional butterflies, provide rotting apples, peaches, bananas, and other fleshy fruits. Some butterfly and moth species can be attracted by setting out a bait mixture.

FIGURE 7-2. Pearl crescent on butterfly weed.

BUTTERFLY AND MOTH BAIT

INGREDIENTS

1 quart beer

1 lb. brown sugar

1 tablespoon rum

1 tablespoon honey

1 slice brown bread

1 apple (cut and dried)

DIRECTIONS

Mix ingredients together and let stand 12–24 hours. To set out bait, take 3 x 3-inch pieces of sponge and soak them in the solution. Remove them and tie with string to trees or posts.

BUTTERFLY LARVAL HOST PLANTS

Providing larval food plants as well as nectar blossoms will increase your chances of attracting more butterflies. Another advantage of providing larval food plants is that you can observe the caterpillars on their food plants. If you care to rear them in captivity, you have the added bonus of learning about the life-cycles of the various species. Tables 7–2 and 7–3 list common flowers, trees, shrubs, and vines that are used as larval food sources, also showing the butterflies that will visit these plants.

SUCCESSFUL BUTTERFLY HABITAT TIPS

1. Use large splashes of color in your landscape design. Butterflies are first attracted to flowers by their color. Groupings of colors are easier for butterflies flying overhead to locate than are isolated plants.

2. Refrain from mowing the selected area so that grasses and wildflowers native to your area can grow into a meadow. Over time, add seeds from other nectar-producing plants to these natural food patches. Be sure to check your local mowing ordinances.

3. Mow your meadow in February and set the cut height to the highest setting. Some butterfly species overwinter as caterpillars or in chrysalis form in the lower part of the vegetation.

4. Probably most important of all, *do not* use insecticides or herbicides in your meadow.

5. Provide shelter for hibernating butterflies and moths. You can do this by creating a brush pile or by erecting a roost box (see figure 8–16) with bark perches inside the box. Mount the box 3½ to 4 feet above ground on a pole or post. The box should be placed in an area around trees, flowers, or a garden, preferably in the shade. Recent surveys have shown that such roost boxes are used about 10 percent of the time by hibernating butterflies.

FIGURE 7-3. Magnified butterfly wing scales.

TABLE 7–2. Common Wildscape Butterflies and Their Host Plants: Annual and Perennial Flowers

HOST PLANT	BLACK SWALLOWTAIL	PIPEVINE SWALLOWTAIL	CABBAGE WHITE	CLOUDED SULPHUR	CLOUDLESS SULPHUR	ORANGE SULPHUR	GRAY HAIRSTREAK	EASTERN TAILED-BLUE	MARINE BLUE	SPRING AZURE	AMERICAN LADY	COMMON BUCKEYE	PAINTED LADY	PEARL CRESCENT	GOATWEED LEAFWING	MONARCH	COMMON CHECKERSPOT	COMMON SOOTYWING	HAYHURST'S SCALLOPWING	HOARY SKIPPER	SILVER-SPOTTED SKIPPER	FIERY SKIPPER	NYSA ROADSIDE-SKIPPER
Alyssum, sweet			X																				
Amaranth, globe																		X	X				
Asters													X	X									
Bluebonnet, Texas							X																
Bluegrass, Kentucky																						X	X
Broccoli/Cabbage/Cauliflower			X																				
Bush-clover/Tick-clover							X	X												X	X		
Carrot/Dill/Fennel	X																						
Clover				X	X	X		X															
Corn/Okra							X																
Croton, woolly							X								X								
Daisy, ox-eye										X													
Hollyhock							X				X		X				X						
Lettuce													X										
Mallows							X						X				X						
Milkweeds							X									X							
Nasturtium			X																				
Paintbrush, Indian										X													
Parsley/Queen Anne's lace	X																						
Partridge pea, showy				X	X	X																	
Peas				X		X	X	X	X				X										
Plantain												X											
Ragwort, golden											X		X										
Snakeroot, white		X								X													
Snapdragon												X											
Sunflower											X		X										
Thistles											X		X										
Vetch						X	X	X															
Yarrow													X										

HOST PLANT	EASTERN TIGER SWALLOWTAIL	PIPEVINE SWALLOWTAIL	SPICEBUSH SWALLOWTAIL	GRAY HAIRSTREAK	REAKIRT'S BLUE	SPRING AZURE	GULF FRITILLARY	AMERICAN LADY	MOURNING CLOAK	PAINTED LADY	RED ADMIRAL	RED-SPOTTED PURPLE	HACKBERRY EMPEROR	SILVER-SPOTTED SKIPPER
Apple				X		X						X		
Ash	X								X					
Birch	X													
Blueberry						X								
Cherry	X					X						X		
Chokecherry	X													
Cottonwood	X								X					
Dogwood						X								
Elm									X	X				
Hackberry/Sugarberry									X				X	
Hawthorn				X								X		
Honeysuckle						X								
Lantana								X		X				
Lilac	X													
Locust														X
Mimosa					X									
Mock-orange	X													
Mulberry									X					
New Jersey tea						X								
Nettle, stinging										X	X			
Passionvine							X							
Peach	X													
Pear									X					
Pecan				X										
Pipevine, Dutchman's		X												
Plum						X								
Poplar									X			X		
Rose of Sharon				X										
Sassafras	X		X											
Spicebush	X		X											
Spirea						X								
Viburnum						X								
Willow	X								X			X		
Wisteria														X

FIGURE 7-4. Painted lady in meadow.

Talk to fireflies and sniff for spiders in your wildscape

During early to midsummer evenings, the edges of woods and moist areas are alive with small, dancing lights. The flying male fireflies, also called lightningbugs, are advertising their presence to the grounded female fireflies. When a female firefly recognizes the flash of the male, she flashes back. You can mimic the answering female by using a small flashlight such as the small squeeze-light key chains.

Place the bulb end of the flashlight down in the grass. When you see a male firefly flash, count three seconds and then flash (squeeze) your flashlight three times. If the male is interested, he will turn and fly toward you. Repeat the procedure after every flash. If the male lands on the ground nearby, he will start a series of flashes. Without pausing, mimic the exact number of flashes. For example, if he flashes four times, you flash four times. The male firefly will move over the ground closer and closer until he is on the flashlight. At this point he will probably figure out his mistake and fly away.

On a dry evening in mid- to late summer, try "sniffing" for spiders. For this activity everyone needs a flashlight. A good place to sniff for spiders is at the edge of weedy areas and mown lawn. Place your flashlight along the bridge of your nose, directing the light toward the ground. By looking down the beam of the flashlight you can easily see the greenish-white sparkle of the light from the compound eyes of spiders. Zero in on the sparkle and you should have a spider.

Learn your neighborhood moths

Choose a summer night to hang an old, white bed sheet in the door of your garage. Put a black light in front of the sheet. You can purchase a black light from an army surplus store or make your own with black cellophane wrapped around a flashlight or electric lantern. Moths flying toward the light flutter against or hang on the sheet. Use a butterfly and moth identification book (see appendix G) to learn the names of the moths attracted to the light.

CHAPTER 8
Woodworking for Wildlife

Woodworking for wildlife involves two major kinds of installations: building nest boxes or other artificial structures for birds and mammals, and building wildlife feeders. The construction of nest boxes and nesting structures is important to fill the void caused by human destruction of habitat and the loss of natural cavities such as snags and hollows. Feeders are not quite as necessary to wildlife. They are mainly convenient for our own enjoyment, serving to bring wildlife closer to us, although they can be beneficial during extended periods of icy weather.

A scarcity of nesting and roosting cavities may limit populations of kestrels, bluebirds, nuthatches, owls, flying squirrels, bats, and other desirable backyard inhabitants. Unfortunately, people have cut down mature and dead trees for firewood and have removed "unsightly" dead limbs to keep yards neat and uncluttered. In doing so, we have removed microhabitats valuable for many species. However, with a little ingenuity, we can fill the gap by providing safe nesting and roosting areas.

If they do not present a potential hazard from falling limbs, leave at least one or two snags standing per quarter-acre lot. These dead trees not only provide homes to wildlife but also serve as a place to store and find food. As insects attack the dying trees, woodpeckers and other insectivores move in to feed. The woodpeckers eventually carve out holes that are also used by other cavity-nesting birds. If you don't have any snags in your wildscape, you can transplant a snag in an advanced stage of decomposition to your property. It will last several years and will help attract more wildlife.

But if you are the kind of property owner who can't face having a dead tree in the yard, there are other things you can do to provide homes for wildlife. By mimicking what nature provides, you can develop a number of nesting and roosting structures that wildlife readily adopt in the absence of natural sites.

FIGURE 8-1. Eastern bluebird populations, once in decline due to lack of nesting cavities and competition with house sparrows and starlings, are rebounding thanks to the many people who install and maintain bluebird nest boxes.

Nest Box Designs

Lack of suitable nest sites often prevents wildlife—primarily birds—from utilizing otherwise good habitat. This is especially the case in many urban areas where natural tree cavities have been removed. In some instances, artificial cavities are especially useful in reducing competition by European starlings. Natural cavities may have entrance sizes large enough to allow access by these pests, but nest boxes can be tailored for specific songbirds by using smaller holes. Also, an artificial nesting structure may provide a more secure site than a natural cavity. These structures can be built to resist predators, parasites, and destruction by winds, storms, and floods.

Providing nest boxes in your yard affords a myriad of benefits. Besides aiding local bird populations, you can see all of the bird's life stages. About 30 species of cavity-nesting birds are found in the southern Great Plains and can be enticed to some type of bird house. It may even be possible to "trick" woodpeckers into using an artificial nest box rather than having to create their own nest.

A good nest box should be made of rough wood and should have a roof over all sections to protect adults and young. Small holes are especially important for drainage and ventilation. Houses should be built for a particular species, using the proper cavity size, depth, and entrance hole diameter.

To build nest boxes, begin with the correct materials. Nest boxes should be made from ¾-inch rough cedar, exterior grade plywood, pine, or redwood. Rough-textured wood blends into the natural habitat and aids young birds in climbing out of the nest. As a rule, stay away from plastic and metal boxes, except for commercially made purple martin houses, because these may get too hot in the summer.

Nest boxes should be constructed to keep adults, young, and eggs as dry as possible. To prevent water dripping into the box, extend the roof at least one to three inches beyond the front of the nest box. Providing for interior drainage is very important. Either cut the corners off the floor of the box or drill ⅜-inch drainage holes in the floor near each corner.

Extremely hot summer conditions can be a big problem for nesting birds. Natural cavities usually have large enough openings for ventilation to not be a problem. However, artificial structures need to be modified to keep birds cool. This can be accomplished by drilling several vent holes near the top of the sides or by dropping the front or sides of the box down from the roof a quarter of an inch. Do not use milk carton or cardboard nest boxes—they are not adequately insulated against hot weather and provide no protection from predators.

Nest boxes should be monitored weekly, particularly in urban areas, to note any problems with nest parasites or losses from predators and to remove intruding house sparrow and starling nests. Keeping records will help in managing birds and recognizing problems.

Birds will not use a nest box that houses wasps. To discourage wasps from using the nest box, coat the inside of the roof completely with Vaseline. The Vaseline will prohibit the wasps from constructing their hanging nests. Although a small nest of wasps will keep birds out, small numbers of mites, lice, and flies that naturally occur in bird nests are not dangerous. However, larger numbers may cause bird deaths. If you find such a problem, sprinkle half a teaspoon of diatomaceous earth or powdered sulfur in the bird house, no more than twice a season; both can be found at local feed stores. Do not apply these directly to eggs or young. Only in extreme cases should you remove infested nesting material and replace it with clean, dry straw or cedar shavings.

Boxes should be checked in February and March to prepare for the upcoming nesting season. Mice and other small animals sometimes take refuge in these ready-made shelters during the cold winter months. After each nesting cycle, old nesting material should be removed to keep parasites from reproducing.

Most nest boxes are based on the simple bluebird house style, although differing in floor size, cavity depth, and entry hole height and diameter. Use table 8–1 to create your own nest box for the species you wish to attract. Diagrams of the actual sizes of entrance holes are also included (figs. 8–2 and 8–3).

BUILDING STRUCTURES FOR WILDLIFE

Several kinds of wildlife will use the common bluebird-style house (fig. 8-4). To attract bluebirds, erect the house 5–6 feet high in an open spot with mixed hardwoods and perching areas (fig. 8-5). Carolina chickadees are common users of nest boxes placed 5–15 feet high in mature hardwoods or woodlots in agricultural areas that receive around 40–60 percent sunlight. Bewick's and house wrens aren't quite so picky; they will use hanging houses located 5–10 feet up under house eaves or in trees. To encourage wrens, a horizontal slot 1⅛ inches high and 4 inches wide is recommended so that males are able to bring twigs in for the nest. Tufted titmice also are common users of nest boxes located 5–15 feet high in old orchards and woodlands.

The bluebird house may attract some uncommon visitors, including nuthatches, which will nest in houses placed 12–20 feet high in mature hardwood forests. Prothonotary warblers nest 3–5 feet above shallow woodland pools or oxbow ponds of river bottom habitat, with the hole facing open water. To attract tree swallows, place boxes 4 feet above ground around marshes or ponds and face the hole east. Downy woodpeckers nest 5–15 feet above ground on poles or tall trees overlooking open areas; to attract these birds, fill the interior of the bird house to the top with packed sawdust. Birds are not the only kind of wildlife that may favor a bluebird house—white-footed mice and woodland deer mice use east-facing houses 3–4 feet high on fence posts. And in heavily wooded sites in Missouri, Arkansas, Louisiana, and eastern Oklahoma and Texas, you might find flying squirrels using bluebird houses.

The barred owl will use a nest box (fig. 8-6) that is placed 20–30 feet high in a mature hardwood tree within 200 feet of water but not within 150 feet of a human home. Ensure that the bird house is not obscured by branches but offers nearby perches for the young. Erect it in January with a 2- to 3-inch layer of small wood chips inside. The pileated woodpecker will use this nest box if it is placed facing south or east in the interior of a mature hardwood stand. To encourage woodpeckers, erect the nest box 20–30 feet up on a live or dead hardwood and pack the interior to the top with sawdust, which the woodpeckers then hollow out. Raccoons will use emptied houses placed 10–20 feet above ground on live or dead trees at least 12 inches in trunk diameter.

TABLE 8–1. Specifications for Nest Boxes

INSECT OR SPIDER	MANAGEMENT NEEDS			INTERESTING CHARACTERISTICS		
SPECIES THAT USES HOUSE	HOUSE DESIGN FIGURE	FLOOR DIMENSION (IN.)	CAVITY DEPTH) (IN.)	ENTRANCE ABOVE FLOOR (IN.)	ENTRANCE DIAMETER (IN.)	HEIGHT ABOVE GROUND (FT.)
Bluebird, eastern	8-4	4 x 4	9	6	1½	5
Chickadee, Carolina	8-4	4 x 4	9	7	1⅛	5
Duck, wood	8-9	12 x 12	22	17	4	3–20 on water
Flicker, northern	8-9	7 x 7	16–18	14–16	2½	6–30
Flycatcher, great-crested	8-8	6 x 6	8–10	6–8	1 9/16	10–20
Kestrel, American	8-8	8 x 8	16	11	3	10–30
Martin, purple	—	6 x 6	6	1	2¼	10–20
Mouse, white-footed	8-4	4 x 4	9	6	1⅛	3–4
Mouse, woodland deer	8-4	4 x 4	9	6	1⅛	3–4
Nuthatch	8-4	4 x 4	9	7	1⅜	12–20
Owl, barn	8-7	12 x 40	16	7	6	20–25
Owl, barred	8-6	12 x 12	23	12	7	20–30
Owl, screech	8-8	8 x 8	16	11	3	10–30
Phoebe, eastern	8-10	6 x 6	6	1–3 sides open		8–12
Raccoon	8-6	10 x 10	24	19	6	20–30
Robin, American	8-10	6 x 8	8	1–3 sides open		6–15
Squirrel, flying	8-4	4 x 4	9	6	1½	5
Squirrel (gray or fox)	8-8	8 x 8	16	11	3	10–30
Swallow, barn	8-10	6 x 6	6	1–3 sides open		8–12
Swallow, tree	8-4	4 x 4	9	6	1½	4
Titmouse, tufted	8-4	4 x 4	9	7	1⅜	5–15
Warbler, prothonotary	8-4	4 x 4	6	4	1⅜	3–5
Woodpecker, downy	8-4	4 x 4	9	7	1¼	5–15
Woodpecker, red-headed	8-8	6 x 6	12	9	2	10–20
Woodpecker, pileated	8-6	10 x 10	24	19	4	20–30
Wren, Bewick's	8-4	4 x 4	6–8	4–6	1¼	5–10
Wren, Carolina	8-4	4 x 4	6–8	4–6	1⅜	5–10
Wren, house	8-4	4 x 4	6–8	4–6	1⅛	5–10

TRACE ONTO WOOD WITH CARBON PAPER

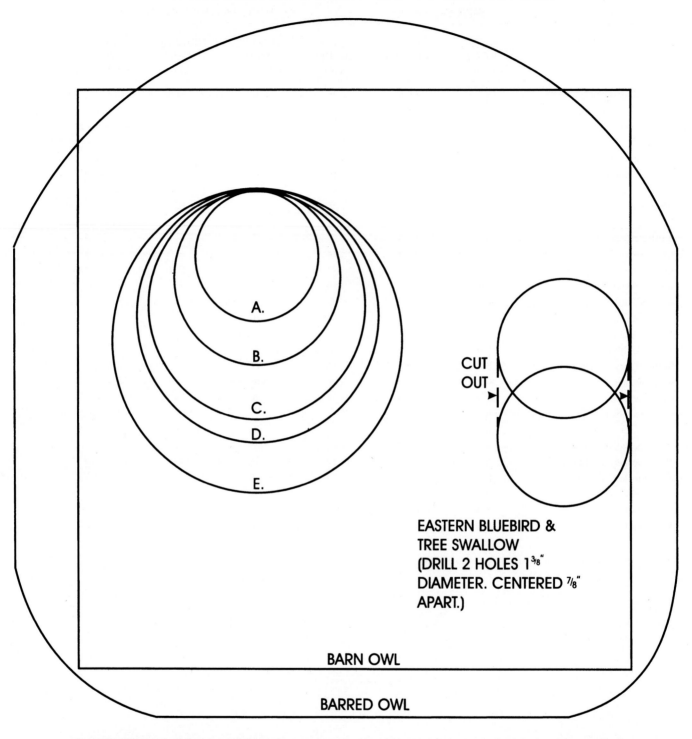

CUT
OUT

EASTERN BLUEBIRD &
TREE SWALLOW
(DRILL 2 HOLES 1³⁄₈″
DIAMETER. CENTERED ⁷⁄₈″
APART.)

BARN OWL

BARRED OWL

A. HOUSE WREN, BLACK-CAPPED CHICKADEE, WHITE-BREASTED NUTHATCH, TUFTED TITMOUSE
   AND PROTHONOTARY WARBLER.
B. GREAT CRESTED FLYCATCHER.
C. PURPLE MARTIN
D. COMMON FLICKER.
E. GRAY AND FOX SQUIRREL, SCREECH OWL, AND AMERICAN KESTREL

FIGURE 8-2. Entrance hole sizes for songbird, woodpecker, and squirrel boxes.

TRACE ONTO WOOD WITH CARBON PAPER

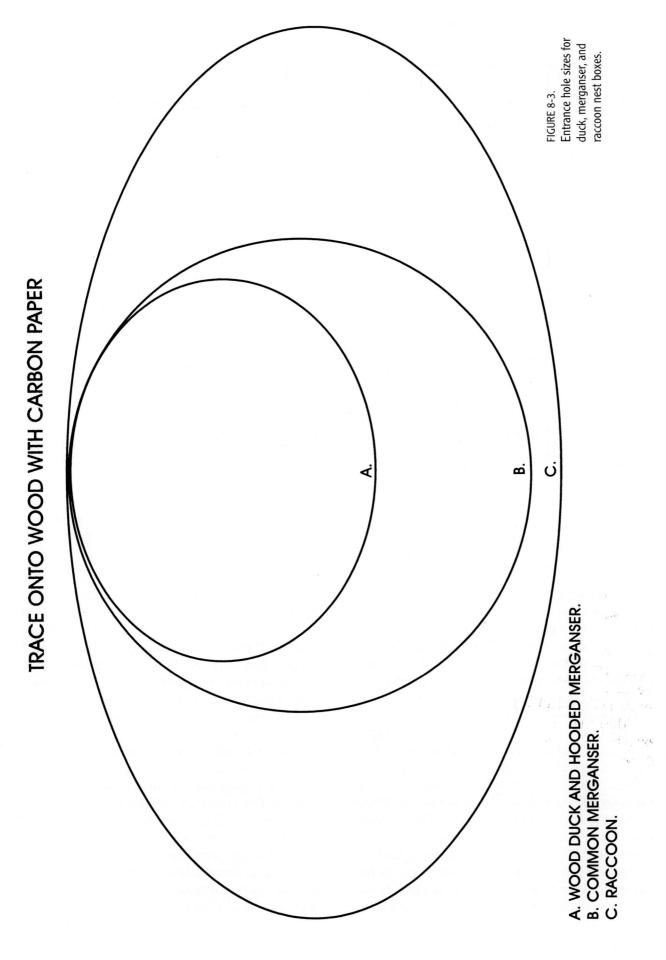

A. WOOD DUCK AND HOODED MERGANSER.
B. COMMON MERGANSER.
C. RACCOON.

A.

B.

C.

FIGURE 8-3.
Entrance hole sizes for duck, merganser, and raccoon nest boxes.

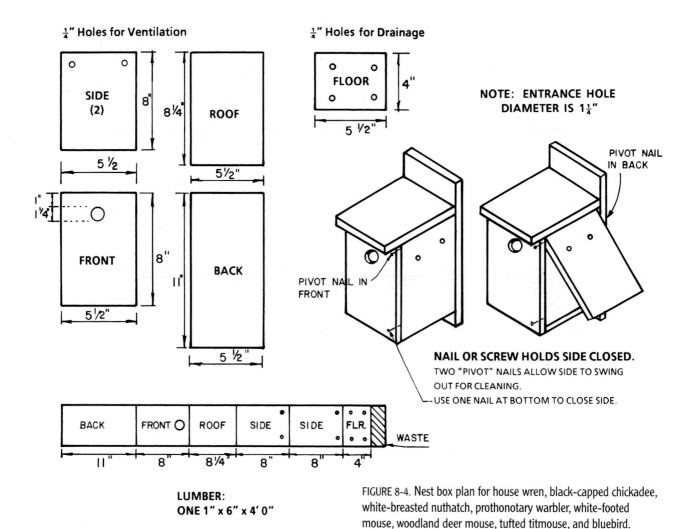

¼" Holes for Ventilation   ¼" Holes for Drainage

SIDE (2) 8" 8¼" ROOF 5½" 5½"

FLOOR 4" 5 ½"

NOTE: ENTRANCE HOLE DIAMETER IS 1¼"

1" 1¼" FRONT 8" BACK 11" 5½" 5 ½" 5 ½"

PIVOT NAIL IN BACK

PIVOT NAIL IN FRONT

NAIL OR SCREW HOLDS SIDE CLOSED.
TWO "PIVOT" NAILS ALLOW SIDE TO SWING OUT FOR CLEANING.
USE ONE NAIL AT BOTTOM TO CLOSE SIDE.

BACK	FRONT O	ROOF	SIDE	SIDE	FLR.	WASTE
11"	8"	8¼"	8"	8"	4"	

LUMBER:
ONE 1" x 6" x 4' 0"

FIGURE 8-4. Nest box plan for house wren, black-capped chickadee, white-breasted nuthatch, prothonotary warbler, white-footed mouse, woodland deer mouse, tufted titmouse, and bluebird.

The barn owl requires a specific house (fig. 8–7) to accommodate its nesting needs. These aggressive mousers can help landowners and farmers by ridding them of mice and other rodents that get into feed. The box should be placed 20–25 feet up in a covered silo or seldom-used barn with nearby hayfields. Don't disturb the house during April or May or the adults might abandon the site.

The kestrel house (fig. 8–8) should be installed by February 1 at least 10–30 feet above ground on a pole or tree. Place the nest box in an orchard or in open country with the hole facing south or west. Great-crested flycatchers will use houses 10–20 feet up in pine trees, mixed conifers, and hardwoods, while screech-owls need houses in hardwood forests on the edge of woods adjacent to fields or wetlands. Place 2–3 inches of wood chips in the bottom for screech-owls. Gray and fox squirrels will use this perfectly sized box to raise their young or

as a winter food storage site. For squirrels, place the box 15–30 feet above ground in trees at least 10 inches in diameter; fill the box halfway with dry leaves and face the hole south or east. Red-headed woodpeckers may use houses 10–20 feet above ground on poles or trees on the edge of woodlands next to open habitat; as when aiming to attract other woodpeckers, pack the bird house interior to the top with sawdust.

Due to the efforts of sportsmen and conservationists across the country, wood ducks are again common throughout the Great Plains. Many people helped by erecting wood duck nest boxes (fig. 8–9) in ponds and marshes. Isolate houses so they are not visible from each other; place each house three feet above standing water or 20 feet high in trees on land. Before filling the interior of the house with four inches of cedar shavings, provide roughened toeholds just below the hole. Flickers will also

FIGURE 8-5. Bluebird house in certified wildscape. (Oklahoma Certified Wildscape #0209, Newcastle)

use the wood duck box. To appeal to them, place the house 6–30 feet high in a farm orchard, woodlot, or urban area and pack the interior to the top with sawdust.

People interested in attracting purple martins should probably purchase a commercially available plastic or aluminum house rather than constructing a wood house. These purple martin houses are light, which makes them easy to raise and lower to pull out unwanted sparrow and starling nests, and they provide good ventilation for the growing chicks.

The American robin is a favorite of backyard bird-watchers. Robins will use a nesting ledge (fig. 8–10) placed 6–15 feet above ground sheltered under house eaves and light fixtures or on a tree trunk. Eastern phoebes use ledges 8–12 feet high under eaves near water sources, while barn swallows will use ledges on house or garage walls.

Landowners with prairie dog towns nearby in western Kansas, Oklahoma, and Texas and in eastern Colorado and New Mexico might consider constructing a burrowing owl nest tunnel (fig. 8–11). Since the number of prairie dog towns has decreased, this has resulted in decreased habitat for burrowing owls. These unique owls make their homes in old prairie dog tunnels and are fairly receptive to using the new nest tunnels if these are placed in the proper habitat. Bury the nest tunnel 6 inches deep and use 2-inch-thick lumber and 8-inch septic tank tubing.

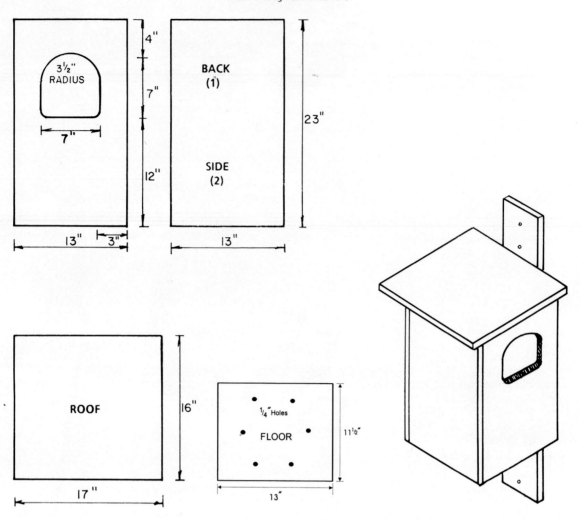

NOTE: No hinged door needed
Clean through entrance hole

3½" RADIUS

7"

BACK (1)

SIDE (2)

4"

7"

12"

23"

13" 3"

13"

ROOF

16"

17"

¼" Holes

FLOOR

11½"

13"

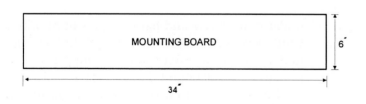

MOUNTING BOARD

6"

34"

LUMBER: One 4' x 4' x ¾"
sheet exterior plywood

FIGURE 8-6. Barred owl nest box.

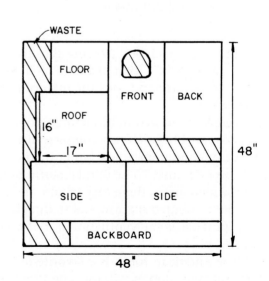

WASTE

FLOOR

FRONT

BACK

ROOF

16"

17"

SIDE

SIDE

BACKBOARD

48"

48"

Chimney swifts also face a decline in nesting structures. They used to nest in deep, hollow cavities in trees, but when people created chimneys, they found an even better place to nest. However, this close contact with man has led to some misunderstandings, eventually resulting in the use of chimney caps to keep birds out. Contrary to popular belief, people cannot get histoplasmosis or other diseases from these birds, and chimney swift nests are very small. They will not clog a chimney or create a significant fire hazard. The chimney swift tower (fig. 8–12) mimics a chimney by creating a hollow shaft 8–12 feet deep. Attach the tower to the north or east side of the existing structure, extending the top 4–6 feet above that structure. Free-standing towers should be located in a small (30 feet square) treeless area and elevated 3 feet above ground.

Bats are becoming more popular, now that more people understand this unique mammal and want to attract it to their property. Both small and large bat houses (figs. 8–13 and 8–14) should be placed at least 15–30 feet above ground on a building or pole—not in trees with close-hanging shrubbery. Face the house south or southwest, where it will receive at least six hours of sun daily, and place it within a quarter mile of a permanent water source such as a river, lake, or pond. Bat houses in particular must be sealed tightly, painted, and caulked to create a constant temperature for the bats. See chapter 5 for more specific information on attracting bats.

Another way property owners can help wildlife is by anchoring a nesting/loafing platform (fig. 8–15) in a pond where the water is 2–4 feet deep. Turtles and ducks use such a platform as a predator-free sunning and loafing site, while Canada geese will nest on the platform if a 22-inch metal washtub is placed on it.

Although most butterflies simply die off when the first frost hits, individuals of a small number of butterfly species hibernate in brush piles and woodpiles, feeding off running tree sap, rotted fruit, dung, and animal carcasses. If you don't have any brush piles, you might consider providing a butterfly hibernation box (fig. 8–16). The box should be placed 4 feet high in a shaded area near butterfly plants. Only about 10 percent of these boxes are known to harbor hibernating moths and butterflies.

FAMILY ACTIVITIES

Create a poster of wildlife visiting your wildscape

Use a large sheet of plain newsprint or paper to create a family wildlife poster, which can be a visual record of the wildlife you see in your wildscape or neighborhood. For pictures, use a field guide or back issues of children's wildlife and nature magazines. As you and your family see animals, cut out and glue a picture of that animal onto the poster. If you wish, add labels with the animal's common name and the date it was seen.

IMPORTANCE OF PREDATOR GUARDS

Although erecting a nest box provides a good home for birds, it can also make them an easy meal for predators such as cats, raccoons, and snakes. To protect birds from these predators, various predator guards are available or can be built. New information indicates that the most effective predator guards are either pole wrappings or circular baffles placed around the pole holding the bird house.

To install wrapping after placing a nest box on a pole, clear the vegetation from the pole base. Wrap a 2-foot (or longer) section of either 4-inch PVC pipe or sheet metal around the mounting pole and just beneath the nest box to deter leaping predators such as cats and raccoons. Another way to prevent access by snakes or other climbing predators is to use a cone of smooth metal or plastic that umbrellas downward away from the pole. These baffles (fig. 8–18), which should be at least 40 inches wide, will foil most predators.

Contrary to past practice, the 1- to 2-inch-thick wooden predator guard surrounding the entrance hole to a bluebird house may actually have done more harm than good. It was thought that this

4-inch x 4-inch x ⅝-inch CDX exterior plywood

1-inch x 12-inch x 6-foot pine board (SPF)

2-inch x 4-inch x 10-foot (SPF) for silo ladder, plan #3

Electric screwdriver

Two 2-inch eye-bolts for plan #1

1½-inch long galvanized drywall screws (1 lb.)

Two hinges

One hasp

3-inch long deck screws for plans #1 and 3

6 feet of #12 wire for plans #1 and 3

Two 1⅜-inch x 12-inch slotted flat steel strips to bend into hangers for box, plan #3

DIRECTIONS

1. Cut out top, side, end, and bottom pieces of nest box. Cut entrance hole at appropriate location for plan being used.

2. Assemble nest box with 1½ inch screws, hinges, and hasp. If building plan #3, it may be easier to attach 2-inch x 4-inch supports before top is installed. Ladder width must be known beforehand.

3. Provide support for box in plan #1 by attaching the #12 wire from the lower outside corners to the wall with eye-bolts.

4. For plan #3: After cutting out 2-inch x 4-inch boards, bend flat metal strips to form mounting hooks and then attach them to the 2-inch x 4-inch boards.

5. For plan #3: Cut out and attach 2-inch x 4-inch supports.

6. Cut out appropriately sized platform and associated railings. Attach railings to platform. It may be easier to attach the assembled platform to the box after box is mounted at location.

7. For plan #2: Platform length can be extended along beam as far as is possible—the longer, the better.

8. Plans 1 and 2 require cutting an entrance hole in barn wall for owl access. Locate hole 12 inches above platform.

If interior site location is likely to be disturbed by cats and raccoons, align box hole with barn wall hole and place the platform on exterior of barn below the entrance hole.

Although any barn can be used, the best building in which to install a barn owl nest box is an abandoned or seldom-used barn on a farmstead. Select the "clean face," or end of the barn having few or no openings. Choose a crossbeam on which to mount the box. Mount the box by screwing it to the beam.

Provide additional support as necessary by bracing the box with 2-inch x 4-inch lumber or by attaching wire cable or ½-inch nylon or marine rope from the lower outside corners of the box to the wall.

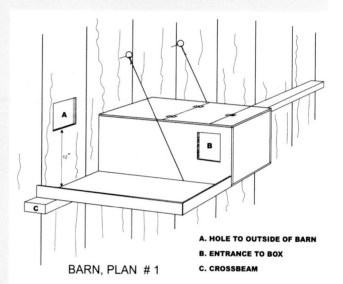

A. HOLE TO OUTSIDE OF BARN

B. ENTRANCE TO BOX

C. CROSSBEAM

BARN, PLAN # 1

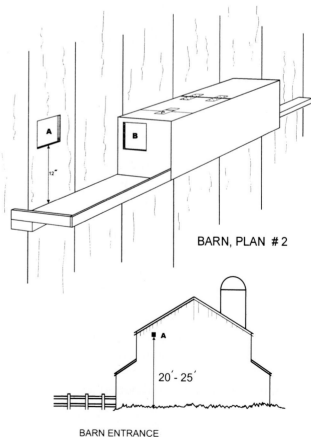

BARN, PLAN # 2

BARN ENTRANCE

FIGURE 8-7. Barn owl nest boxes.

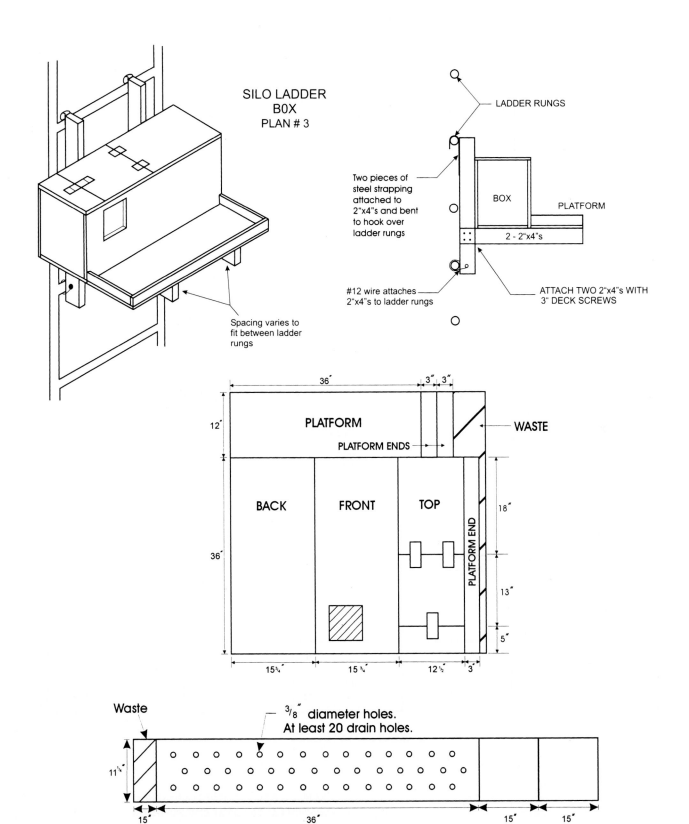

SILO LADDER
BOX
PLAN # 3

LADDER RUNGS

Two pieces of
steel strapping
attached to
2"x4"s and bent
to hook over
ladder rungs

BOX

PLATFORM

2 - 2"x4"s

#12 wire attaches
2"x4"s to ladder rungs

ATTACH TWO 2"x4"s WITH
3" DECK SCREWS

Spacing varies to
fit between ladder
rungs

36" 3" 3"

12"

PLATFORM

WASTE

PLATFORM ENDS

BACK   FRONT   TOP

PLATFORM END

18"

36"

13"

5"

15 ¾"   15 ¾"   12 ½"   3"

Waste

³⁄₈" diameter holes.
At least 20 drain holes.

11 ¼"

15"   36"   15"   15"

2" x 4" x 10' FOR MOUNTING SUPPORTS FOR SILO LADDER, PLAN # 3

VERTICAL SUPPORT	VERTICAL SUPPORT	HORIZONTAL SUPPORT	HORIZONTAL SUPPORT	

3 ¼"

31"   31"   28 ¼"   28 ¼"

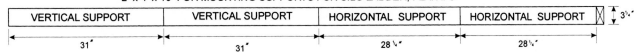

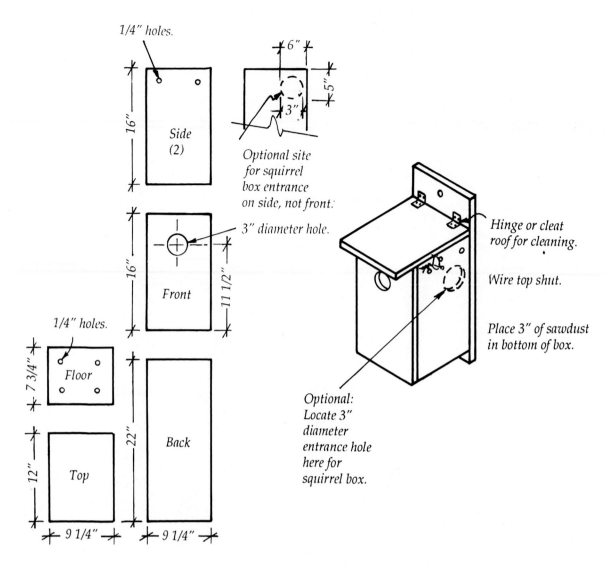

1/4" holes.

Side
(2)

16"

6"

5"

3"

Optional site
for squirrel
box entrance
on side, not front.

3" diameter hole.

Front

16"

11 1/2"

1/4" holes.

7 3/4"

Floor

12"

Top

22"

Back

9 1/4"

9 1/4"

Hinge or cleat
roof for cleaning.

Wire top shut.

Place 3" of sawdust
in bottom of box.

Optional:
Locate 3"
diameter
entrance hole
here for
squirrel box.

Lumber: One 1" x 10" x 8' 0"

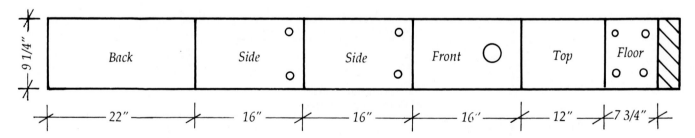

9 1/4"

Back	Side	Side	Front	Top	Floor

22"   16"   16"   16"   12"   7 3/4"

FIGURE 8-8. American kestrel, eastern screech-owl, northern
saw-whet owl, boreal owl, gray squirrel, red squirrel, and
fox squirrel nest box.

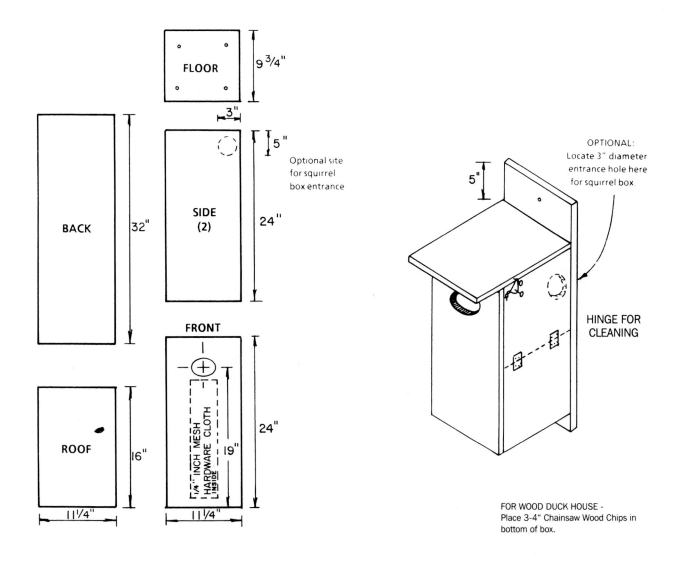

FLOOR

9¾"

3"

SIDE
(2)

5"

Optional site
for squirrel
box entrance

24"

BACK

32"

FRONT

24"

¼" INCH MESH
HARDWARE CLOTH
INSIDE

19"

ROOF

16"

11¼"

11¼"

5"

OPTIONAL:
Locate 3" diameter
entrance hole here
for squirrel box.

HINGE FOR
CLEANING

FOR WOOD DUCK HOUSE -
Place 3-4" Chainsaw Wood Chips in
bottom of box.

LUMBER:
ONE 1" X 12" X 12'0"

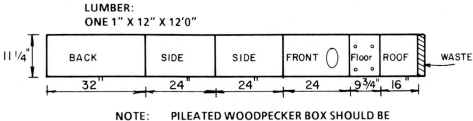

	BACK	SIDE	SIDE	FRONT ◯	Floor	ROOF	WASTE

11¼"

32"   24"   24"   24   9¾"   16"

NOTE: PILEATED WOODPECKER BOX SHOULD BE
CONSTRUCTED FROM ONE 2" X 12" X 12'0" CEDAR, AND
FLOOR MUST BE 8¼" LONG INSTEAD OF 9¾"
FOR USE OF 1½" THICK LUMBER.

FIGURE 8-9. This nest box can be adapted for use by various wild
animals. For a common merganser, the entrance hole should be
round with a minimum diameter of 5 inches. For a wood duck or
hooded merganser, the oval entrance hole should be 3 inches high
and 4 inches wide. For a raccoon, the oval entrance hole should
be 5 inches high and 9 inches wide. For a gray or fox squirrel, the
entrance hole should be round with a diameter of 3 inches.

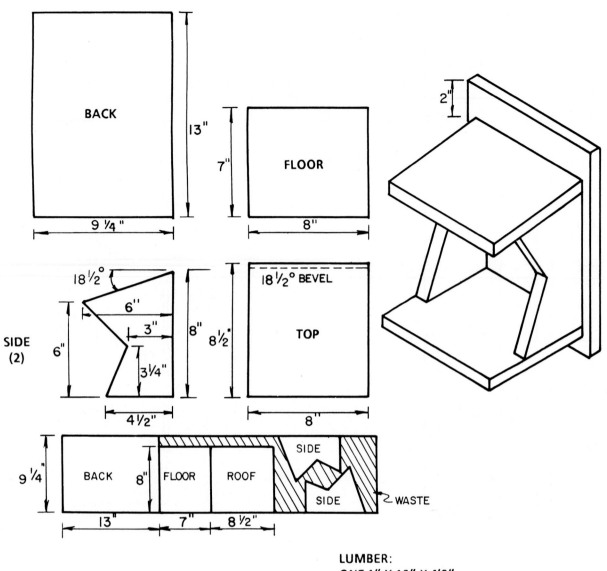

BACK

13"

9 ¼ "

FLOOR

7"

8"

SIDE
(2)

18 ½°

6"

3"

6"

3¼"

8"

8½"

4½"

18 ½° BEVEL

TOP

8"

2"

9 ¼"

BACK

8"

FLOOR

ROOF

SIDE

SIDE

WASTE

13"

7"

8 ½"

LUMBER:
ONE 1" X 10" X 4'0"

FIGURE 8-10. Nest box for American robin.

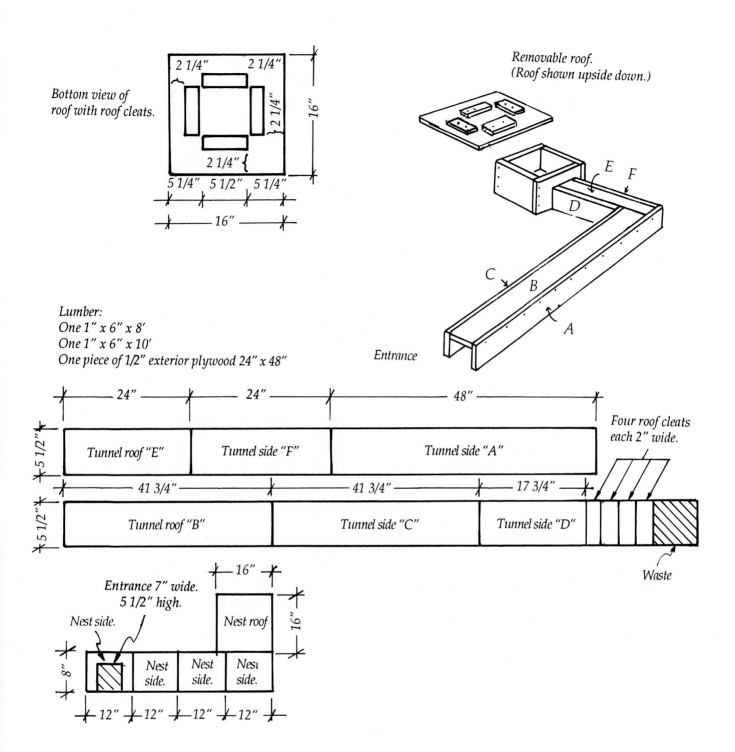

Bottom view of roof with roof cleats.

2 1/4" 2 1/4"
2 1/4"
16"
2 1/4"
5 1/4" 5 1/2" 5 1/4"
16"

Removable roof.
(Roof shown upside down.)

E F
D
C
B
A

Entrance

Lumber:
One 1" x 6" x 8'
One 1" x 6" x 10'
One piece of 1/2" exterior plywood 24" x 48"

24" 24" 48"

5 1/2"

Tunnel roof "E" Tunnel side "F" Tunnel side "A"

Four roof cleats each 2" wide.

41 3/4" 41 3/4" 17 3/4"

5 1/2"

Tunnel roof "B" Tunnel side "C" Tunnel side "D"

Waste

Entrance 7" wide.
5 1/2" high.

16"

Nest side.

Nest roof

16"

8"

Nest side. Nest side. Nest side.

12" 12" 12" 12"

FIGURE 8-11. Burrowing owl nest tunnel. Select a site on high ground that is well drained. Bury nest box and tunnel 6 inches below ground surface. The entrance should simulate a badger den entrance.

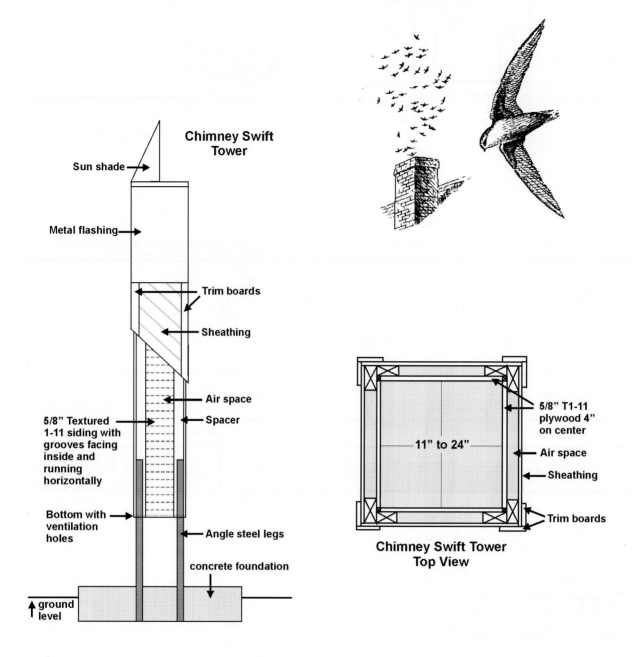

Chimney Swift Tower

Sun shade →

Metal flashing →

Trim boards

Sheathing

Air space

Spacer

5/8" Textured 1-11 siding with grooves facing inside and running horizontally

Bottom with ventilation holes

Angle steel legs

concrete foundation

↑ ground level

Chimney Swift Tower Top View

5/8" T1-11 plywood 4" on center

11" to 24"

Air space

Sheathing

Trim boards

FIGURE 8-12. Chimney swift tower, a: side view; b: top view; c: swifts at chimney.

MATERIALS

4-foot x 4-foot x ½-inch CDX exterior plywood

1-inch x 4-inch x 6-foot board

DIRECTIONS

Note: Bat roosting requirements are strict, necessitating adherence to construction details.

1. Cut out parts as illustrated.

2. Apply a bead of caulk to front edges of box sides and attach box fronts, being sure to leave ½ inch between top and bottom front panels, with 6–8 screws per side. Clean excess caulk that squeezes out the edges.

3. The landing plate and interior surfaces of the bat house must be roughened. Score inside of front and sides with utility knife to roughen. Also score bottom 5½ inches on outside of box front below vent. Make horizontal scratches ¼ inches apart. In addition, score both sides of roosting baffles and the inside of the box back. These are landing/roosting footholds and are very important. Do not use a saw to roughen the wood, as it will cause plywood to delaminate.

4. Check placement for 2 baffle spacers for the inside corners of the box front and sides. Place spacers 2 inches from top of box front and ¾ inches from edges. Attach the baffle spacers with 2 screws each, all of which are screwed in from the outside front of box. Lay assembled parts front down on table or floor.

5. Attach roost baffle 1 inch from top of baffle spacers using 2 screws on each side.

6. Attach 2 more baffle spacers, as before, to the back of the first roost baffle.

7. Attach the second roost baffle, as before, to these baffle spacers using 4 screws on each side.

continued on following page

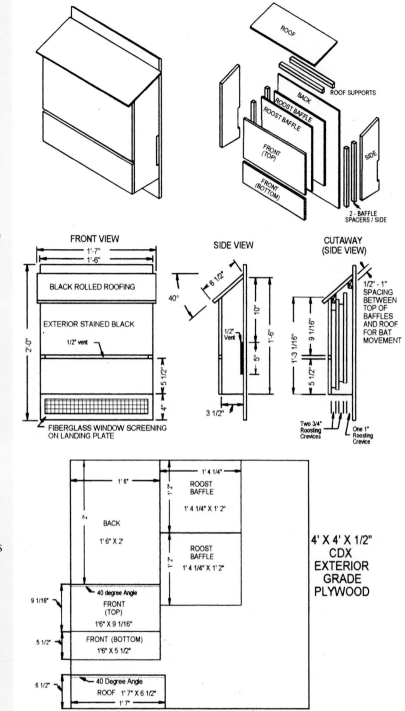

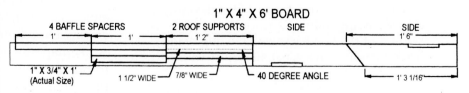

FIGURE 8-13. This small bat house can provide daytime roost space for up to 80 bats.

continued from previous page

8. Caulk back edges of box sides—excluding the indented vent areas—and attach box back with scored side in. The back should extend 2 inches above top of sides. Use 6–8 screws on each side. Clean excess caulk that squeezes out the edges.

9. Center the first roof support on the inside top of box front. Align the lower slant of the angled piece with top edge of the front and sides. Attach with 3 screws that are inserted from the outside front of box.

10. Center the second roof support 2 inches below the top inside of box back. Align the upper slant of the angled piece with the top edges of sides. Attach with 3 screws that are inserted from the outside back of box.

11. Caulk top edges of sides, front, the two roof supports, and the angled back edge of the roof.

12. Lay roof in position and attach with at least 3 screws on each of sides, front, and back. Clean excess caulk that squeezes out the edges.

13. The top of the box must be airtight so that it can hold heat. Caulk the top edge of the roof where it buts against the back of box. Smooth with a damp towel. Inspect all other caulked seams and caulk exterior seams as needed.

14. Apply 2–3 coats of black stain to exterior, including the landing plate.

15. Cut section of black rolled roofing to fit on roof top. Apply a thin bead of caulk around top edges of roof. Set roofing into position and staple down. Caulk back edge of roofing where it butts against the back of box. Also caulk all staples on roofing surface to insure the roof is airtight.

16. Score the lower exposed portion of the box back using same technique as above in case the window screening for this landing area falls off. Cut out piece of fiberglass window screening to fit on the lower exposed portion of the box back, which will provide a good landing area. Coat all staples with black stain.

piece of wood would give nestlings increased protection from marauding raccoons and cats by making it difficult for hunters to bend a foreleg to reach inside the box. Unfortunately, this fixture provided a perfect ledge for aggressive house sparrows to attack and drive off adult bluebirds, chickadees, and tufted titmice. If you have noticed this occurrence, you may want to remove this wood piece.

SUCCESSFUL NEST BOX TIPS

1. Monitor your nest boxes weekly to ensure that undesirable bird species—European starlings and house sparrows—and nest parasites are not present. If they are, take steps to rid the house of their presence. See chapter 9 for information on controlling starlings and house sparrows.

2. Clean the nest box about seven to 10 days after each nesting season to provide a fresh, clean home for birds.

3. Repair damage to the nest box. If the box leaks, or if it allows predators to gain access, fix the damage, or replace the house with a new one.

4. Remove vegetation from beneath nest boxes to discourage predators.

5. *Do not* erect nest boxes without installing some form of predator guard.

Wildlife Feeder Designs

Feeders are an important component of many wildscapes. Although they are necessary only during extended periods of bad weather, their use provides instant gratification the first time a timid titmouse darts in for a bite to eat or cardinals stop in for a few minutes. For the most part, wild animals and birds use feeders only to supplement the seeds or insects they get from other places; they don't want to compete for food resources with other wildlife. However, on cold winter days, it is much easier for animals to tolerate their competitors if they receive an easy food source in return.

Perhaps the main reason to construct feeders is to bring wildlife closer to you for easier viewing from your home. Following are several designs for small feeders that will be visited primarily by birds but also by other wildlife. By placing different feeder types at different heights and putting out a

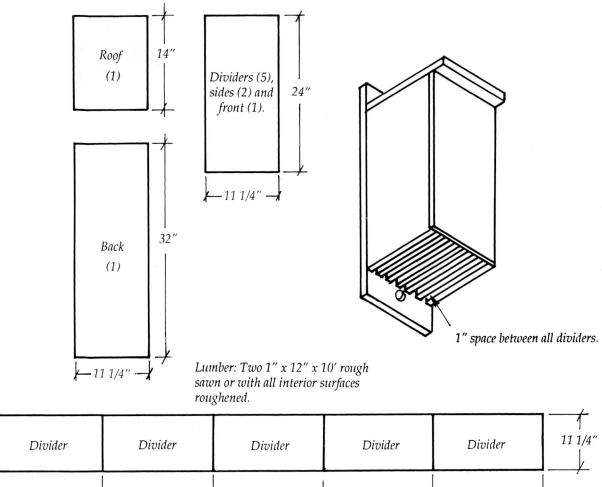

Roof
(1)

14"

Dividers (5),
sides (2) and
front (1).

24"

11 1/4"

Back
(1)

32"

11 1/4"

*Lumber: Two 1" x 12" x 10' rough
sawn or with all interior surfaces
roughened.*

1" space between all dividers.

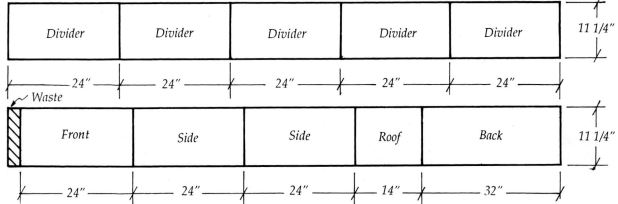

Divider	Divider	Divider	Divider	Divider	11 1/4"

24" — 24" — 24" — 24" — 24"

~ Waste

Front	Side	Side	Roof	Back	11 1/4"

24" — 24" — 24" — 14" — 32"

Note: All external seams and joints should be caulked if not
tight fitting. Divider boards are spaced 1 inch apart.

FIGURE 8-14. Johnson bat house.

MATERIALS

One 8-inch-diameter utility pole, 12 feet long

Four 2-inch x 6-inch x 8-foot pine boards

About 20 feet of welded-link chain (more or less depending on water depth)

Four bolts, nuts, and washers

Two 8-inch x 8-inch x 16-inch cement foundation blocks

Four dozen galvanized nails

DIRECTIONS

1. Cut the utility pole into three sections 4 feet long. Lay the post lengths parallel to form a base for a 4-foot x 4-foot platform.

2. Nail 4-foot lengths of the pine boards perpendicular across the posts, spacing the boards about 1 inch apart. The exact width and length dimensions of the platform are less important than the platform's height above the water.

3. Choose a location for the platform in water that is 2–3 feet deep. Measure the exact depth at platform location. Cut two lengths of welded-link chain that are both 3 feet longer than the depth of water.

4. Bolt the lengths of chain to posts at opposite corners of the platform. The other end of each chain should be bolted to a concrete foundation block.

5. The blocks should be dropped at least 6 feet apart to prevent the platform from pivoting in the wind.

Note: The platform should float low enough in the water for easy access by a turtle. Waterlogged platforms can be "raised" by inserting pieces of Styrofoam between the poles.

Anchor chain

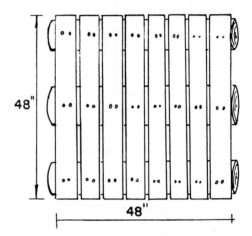

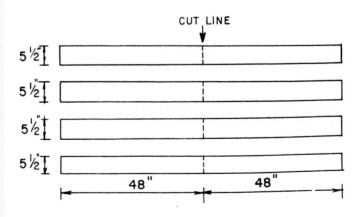

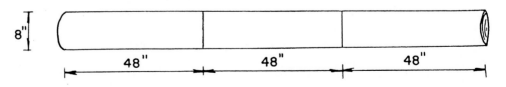

FIGURE 8-15. Turtle and duck loafing platform.

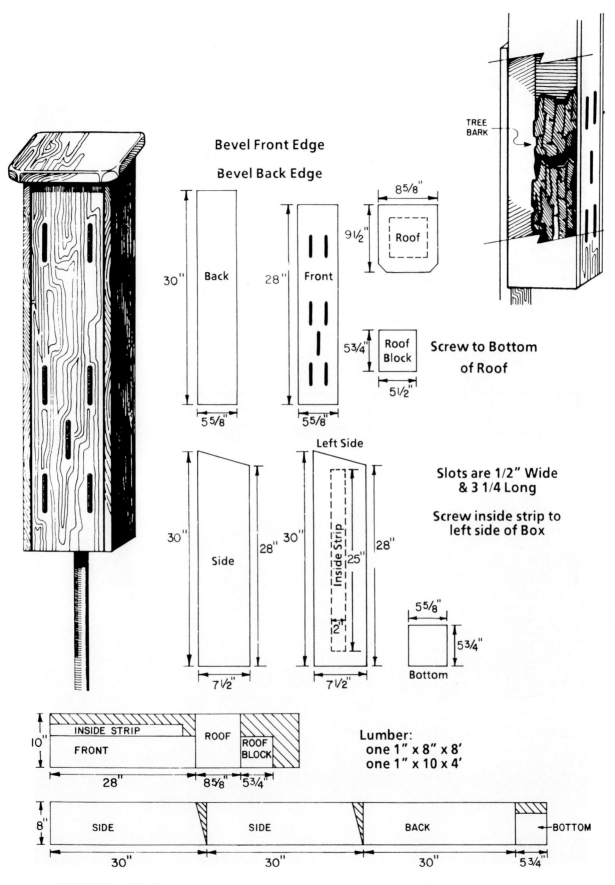

Bevel Front Edge

Bevel Back Edge

Back 30" 5 5/8"

Front 28" 5 5/8"

TREE BARK

Roof 8 5/8" 9 1/2"

Roof Block 5 3/4" 5 1/2"

Screw to Bottom of Roof

Side 30" 28" 7 1/2"

Left Side

Inside Strip 30" 28" 25" 2"

Slots are 1/2" Wide & 3 1/4 Long

Screw inside strip to left side of Box

Bottom 5 5/8" 5 3/4"

INSIDE STRIP
FRONT
ROOF
ROOF BLOCK
10"
28" 8 5/8" 5 3/4"

Lumber:
one 1" x 8" x 8'
one 1" x 10 x 4'

SIDE SIDE BACK BOTTOM
8"
30" 30" 30" 5 3/4"

FIGURE 8-16. Butterfly hibernation box.

FIGURE 8-17. Kitty at feeder in certified Wildscape.

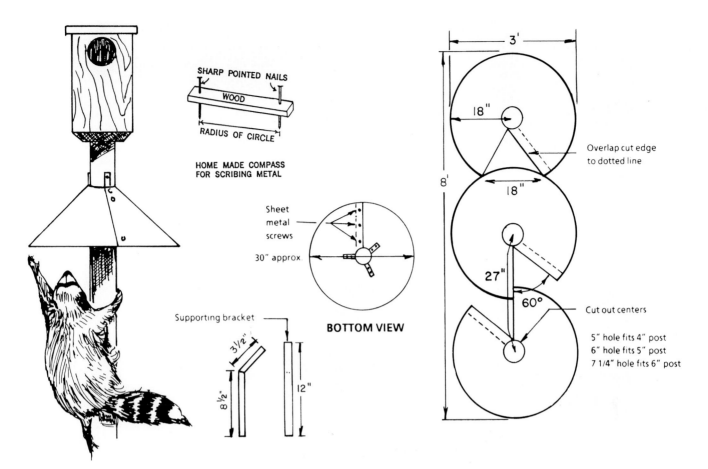

SHARP POINTED NAILS

WOOD

RADIUS OF CIRCLE

HOME MADE COMPASS
FOR SCRIBING METAL

Sheet
metal
screws

30" approx.

BOTTOM VIEW

Supporting bracket

3½"

8½"

12"

3'

18"

18"

8'

27"

60°

Overlap cut edge
to dotted line

Cut out centers

5" hole fits 4" post
6" hole fits 5" post
7 1/4" hole fits 6" post

FIGURE 8-18. This predator guard will help prevent nest boxes from becoming liabilities, which can happen if no effort is made to protect the boxes from predators. Raccoons are the most serious predators of nesting birds; they will eat the eggs and even kill the incubating adults. A predator guard is easy to make and will prevent raccoons, squirrels, and other predators from climbing up to the entrance hole of a nest box. Three guards can be cut from one 3-foot x 8-foot sheet of galvanized steel, as shown. Use three pieces of 12-inch x ³⁄₁₆-inch strap iron per guard to make support brackets for attaching guard to post. Secure the straight edges with three sheet-metal screws per guard.

diverse selection of seeds and fruits, you'll attract the greatest variety of birds (see chapter 4 for tips on how best to stock feeders).

The small tray feeder (fig. 8–20) is very versatile, attracting a variety of common wildlife such as cardinals, chickadees, blue jays, purple and house finches, grackles, squirrels, and chipmunks. Although its flat design gives birds a wider scope of vision to spot any lurking predators, it also means this kind of feeder is easily dominated by an aggressive blue jay or squirrel. These feeders can be placed 1–5 feet above ground on a stump or pole in a small yard, deck, or garden area. Place sunflower seed, corn, millet or safflower in the feeder.

The small fly-through feeder (fig. 8–21) is built upon the small tray feeder. Basically it has a roof supported by four corner posts, keeping both birds and food dry in inclement weather. Like the small

tray feeder, this type enables birds to see any approaching predators. Besides the familiar cardinals and chickadees, you'll also see dark-eyed juncos and house finches visiting these feeders.

The small self-feeder (fig. 8–22), or hopper feeder, has a bin, which means this kind of feeder need not be refilled as frequently as the others. The seed flows out and is eaten by many songbirds that perch on the small ledge, including evening grosbeaks, tufted titmice, nuthatches, American goldfinches, and brown thrashers. Construct the feeder sides of Plexiglas so that you'll be able to see what birds visit the feeder and when it needs to be refilled. The feeder should be checked every three to four days to clean out any seed that has accumulated and stopped the flow. If squirrels chew through the Plexiglas to get at the seeds, replace it with glass.

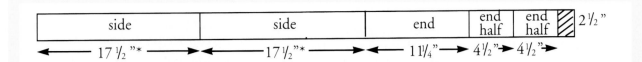

* This dimension assumes a ¾" thick board.
Sides should be 17¾" if board is ⅞" thick.

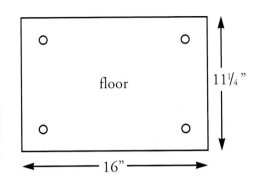

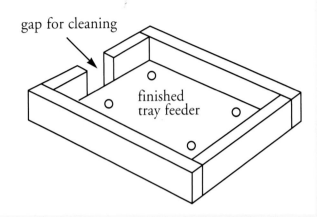

gap for cleaning

finished
tray feeder

FIGURE 8-20. Small tray feeder.

MATERIALS

One 1-inch x 12-inch x 16-inch sheet
of plywood

One 1-inch x 4-inch x 6-foot board

DIRECTIONS

1. Cut board and plywood sheet as shown.

2. Drill four small drain holes near corners
of plywood sheet.

3. Assemble as shown using nails or screws. Be
sure to leave the cleaning gap on one side to
make it easier to scrape out old or moldy seeds.

4. Feeder may be placed on the ground or fas-
tened to a post or stump. Be sure to attach
feeder securely so it will not tip.

PAINTING SUGGESTIONS FOR
WILDLIFE HOUSES AND FEEDERS

1. Boxes and feeders can be left unfinished
and allowed to weather.

2. The entire structure can be finished with
weatherproof stain. Most stains become
nontoxic after the nest box or feeder
weathers for about 30 days.

3. Painting exterior surfaces with exterior
latex paint is okay, but *do not* paint a

feeder floor, the interior of a nest box, or
the area around the entrance hole.
Weatherproof stain on feeder floors and
nest box interiors is okay, but you should
allow about 30 days before putting a
stained structure out for birds.

4. *Caution: Do not* use paint that is toxic or
contains lead.

5. A good rule of thumb is that if paint is
safe for children's toys and furniture, it is
safe for birds.

FIGURE 8-19. Bird feeders come in a variety of designs, and selecting one is a matter of personal taste rather than one being better
than another. However, be sure that the feeder style chosen can
be easily cleaned.

MATERIALS

One 1-inch x 12-inch x 16-inch sheet of plywood

One 1-inch x 8-inch x 36-inch board

One 1-inch x 6-inch x 58-inch board

DIRECTIONS

1. Cut boards and plywood sheet as shown, making sure to cut the joined sides of the roof halves at a 19° angle.

2. Assemble floor and sides for floor as shown in figure 8-20.

3. Assemble the roof and gables, making sure the gables are set 16 inches apart.

4. Fasten the angled ends of the corner posts to the inside of the gables, using two screws or nails per post.

5. Set the roof section with attached legs into the floor tray. Fasten the posts to the end boards of the tray with two screws or nails per post.

FIGURE 8-21. Small fly-through feeder.

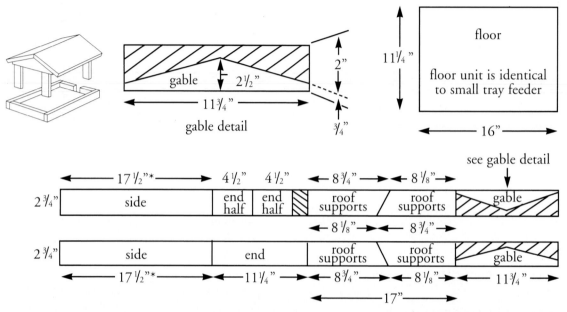

gable detail

floor

floor unit is identical to small tray feeder

11¼"

16"

see gable detail

17½"*   4½"   4½"   8¾"   8⅛"

2¾"   side   end half   end half   roof supports   roof supports   gable

8⅛"   8¾"

2¾"   side   end   roof supports   roof supports   gable

17½"*   11¼"   8¾"   8⅛"   11¼"

17"

* These dimensions assume a board thickness of ¾." If it is ⅞" thick, sides should be 17¾."

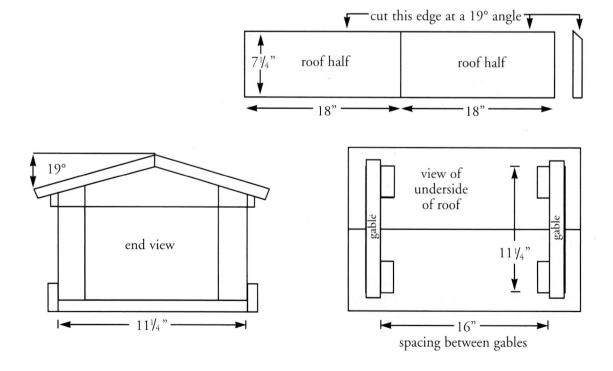

cut this edge at a 19° angle

7¼"   roof half   roof half

18"   18"

19°

end view

11¼"

view of underside of roof

gable   gable

11¼"

16"

spacing between gables

MATERIALS

One 1-inch x 12-inch x 12-inch sheet of plywood

One 1-inch x 4-inch x 51-inch board

One 1-inch x 8-inch x 56-inch board

One 2-inch x 2-inch x 11-inch board

One 4-inch piece of ⅜-inch quarter round

Two 9⅜-inch x 11⅛-inch or 9⅜-inch x 11⅜-inch single-pane glass

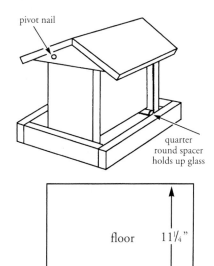

FIGURE 8-22. Small self-feeder.

DIRECTIONS

1. Cut boards, plywood sheet, and quarter round as shown. Cut the joined sides of the roof halves at a 23° angle.

2. Cut a kerf groove ⅜-inches deep in the upright sides of the feeder at ½ inch from each edge, as shown on diagram, to hold the glass panes.

3. Cut or rip the divider piece at a 45° angle, as shown.

4. Assemble floor and sides for feeder tray as shown in figure 8-20.

5. Attach the upright sides to sides of feeder tray with 2 screws or nails per side.

6. Place the divider piece at center of width of the upright sides of feeder. Attach piece to feeder tray with 2–3 screws or nails.

7. Glue the pieces of quarter round to the inside of the feeder sides. This will hold up the glass so seeds can flow underneath.

8. Assemble the roof and gables, making sure the gables are set 12 inches apart.

9. Place roof on feeder. Attach roof to upright sides of feeder with one pivot nail at each end so the roof can be opened for adding more seed.

10. Insert glass panes in kerf grooves. Plexiglas may be used instead of glass, but glass is recommended as squirrels can easily chew through Plexiglas to destroy the feeder.

* This dimension assumes wood is ¾" thick. If it is ⅞" thick, floor sides should be 13 ¾."

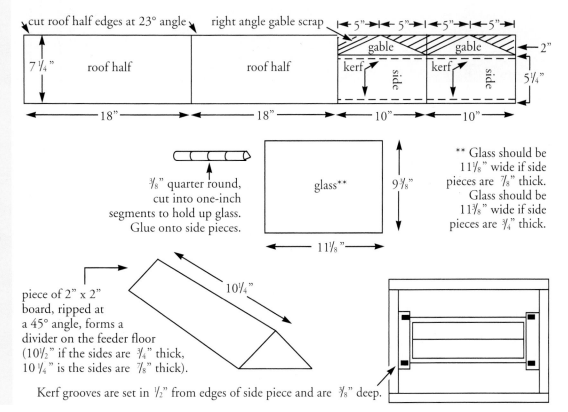

** Glass should be 11⅛" wide if side pieces are ⅞" thick. Glass should be 11⅜" wide if side pieces are ¾" thick.

⅜" quarter round, cut into one-inch segments to hold up glass. Glue onto side pieces.

piece of 2" x 2" board, ripped at a 45° angle, forms a divider on the feeder floor (10½" if the sides are ¾" thick, 10 ¼" is the sides are ⅞" thick).

Kerf grooves are set in ½" from edges of side piece and are ⅜" deep.

CHAPTER 9

Problem Guests or Pesky Pests?

If you're lucky and have created a balanced wildscape, a diverse group of animals and plants will inhabit it. However, you can't always control which insects, birds, and other animals will visit your property. On occasion, some animals behave more like pests than welcomed visitors, which means adapting your behavior to theirs—outsmarting or excluding them when they create a nuisance you can't live with.

You have several options for controlling unwanted or problem visitors. First, try excluding them from your yard with fences, screens, or nets. You can also lure them away from problem areas by offering them food or roosting sites in places where they will not be a nuisance. If these methods do not work, discourage them by removing food for one week. Then consider live trapping and relocating them; check local, county, and state regulations first, because you must have landowner permission to relocate wildlife on private and public land. Finally, contact your municipal animal control office for further suggestions.

Although relocation may seem to be an easy answer, it too has problems, as adult animals that are relocated often return or die trying to find their way back to where they once lived. When placed in an unfamiliar area, they are as lost as you would be if you were stranded in a new area. Relocated birds, however, will simply fly back to your wildscape, undoing all your work.

The following pages explore some of the most common problems people experience with wildlife. Several recommendations are given and should be tried before contacting the animal control office. Remember, you began developing a wildscape to attract wildlife closer to you; it makes sense to try to work out a solution that will be fair to you and to the wildlife now using the setting you have provided.

FIGURE 9-1. Secure trash containers with tight-fitting lids to exclude opossums and raccoons.

Competition for Food

When much of your wildscaping effort has been directed toward offering food sources for wildlife, it should be no surprise to find various species competing for the food. This kind of competition illustrates success! It's worth noting again that there are far fewer sharing problems with natural food sources such as berry bushes than with feeding stations. But there are several ways to minimize trouble at feeders too.

SQUIRRELS EATING ALL THE BIRD FOOD

Most backyard wildlife watchers enjoy the playful antics of squirrels, whether the animals are receiving a scolding from an irate blue jay or energetically chasing each other through the trees. However, squirrels can become a nuisance at bird feeding stations. In no time flat, a couple of squirrels can polish off a feeder full of expensive thistle or sunflower seeds. You can reduce squirrel feeding expenses and still enjoy their presence, though, by following these suggestions.

Avoid locating feeders near trees or buildings where squirrels can jump onto them. Try greasing bird feeder poles with vegetable oil or shortening, or invest in a commercially made baffle. Luring squirrels to other areas of your yard with less expensive food, like whole kernel corn, is an alternative option. Many catalogs for bird enthusiasts now offer feeders that are precisely counterweighted to shut feeder ports when a heavy bird or squirrel lands on the feeding platform.

It's a good idea to seal all entrances to attics and other buildings to prevent squirrels from nesting inside. Once these rodents find their way in, they can cause serious damage to wiring and insulation.

EUROPEAN STARLINGS AND HOUSE SPARROWS

Sometimes referred to as "flying rats," these introduced birds have been an unwanted part of the American landscape since the late 1800s. Starlings and house sparrows are very damaging in outcompeting our native birds for food and for nesting cavities.

To discourage house sparrows at backyard feeders, develop your feeding program around small hanging feeders that offer unstable footing. Avoid offering the house sparrow's favorite foods like cracked corn, wheat, and bread. Starlings can also be discouraged from using your backyard feeders. Unlike most birds, starlings like to feed late in the morning and early in the afternoon, so try feeding in early morning or late afternoon. Again, avoid bakery items and other scrap-type foods. Try using suet feeders that force birds to hang upside down; starlings cannot feed that way.

If your feeding operation is being overrun by starlings, you might consider building a funnel trap (fig. 9–2) to catch multiple individuals. This trap is simple to construct and is extremely effective, capturing a dozen or more birds in a day. Bait the trap with bread scraps and the curious starlings will soon enter through the funnel. Leave any captured birds in the trap for the whole day to attract others. Once the trap is full, release any native birds that might remain inside. You may then humanely dispose of the starlings.

All birds other than house sparrows, starlings, and rock doves are native species protected by federal laws and cannot be harmed. This includes the birds, their young, eggs, and nests.

BLACKBIRDS EATING ALL THE FOOD

Feeding a few grackles, starlings, or other blackbirds usually is not a problem, but wintering blackbirds can quickly overwhelm a feeding station. Because these blackbirds feed throughout the day, one solution is to put out just enough food out at about 6:00 P.M. to last until 9:00 A.M. the following morning.

If the blackbird problem persists, you might consider erecting a grackle log roller (fig. 9–3) developed by Dr. Bernie Daniel of Cincinnati, Ohio, on your hopper-style feeders. The log roller is a ½-inch-diameter wooden dowel rod placed 2 inches above the perching ledges of a hopper feeder. The ends of each dowel have screws threaded through cotter pins, allowing the rod to spin like a log in water whenever a large bird such as a grackle lands on it. After several moments of wild wing flapping, the grackle leaves, while smaller birds such as chickadees, finches, and tufted titmice can perch between the rod and feeder and still reach the food. Woodpeckers can also continue using the feeder by perching on the ledge and reaching under the rod for food.

EXOTIC RATS AND MICE AT THE FEEDER

Norway and black rats and the common house mouse are non-native pests that live in close association with humans, relying on us to provide food and shelter. Your first step in controlling them is to eliminate their food supply. Store food in sealed containers with tight-fitting lids and do not stock platform or ground feeders with more than one day's food supply.

Don't leave pet food out overnight, because this is a sure attraction for unwanted rats and mice

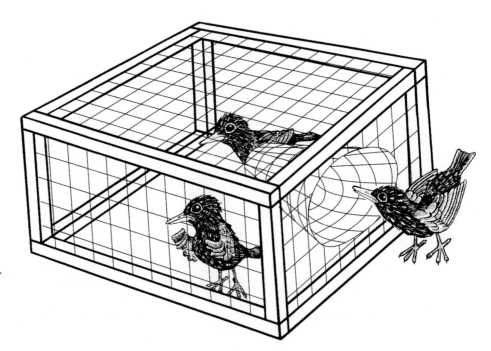

FIGURE 9-2. A funnel trap is highly effective for starlings.

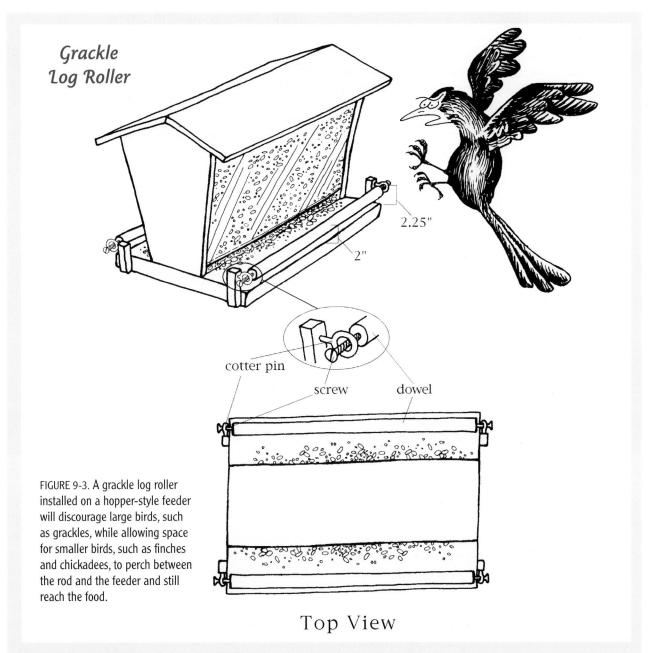

Grackle Log Roller

2.25"

2"

cotter pin

screw   dowel

FIGURE 9-3. A grackle log roller installed on a hopper-style feeder will discourage large birds, such as grackles, while allowing space for smaller birds, such as finches and chickadees, to perch between the rod and the feeder and still reach the food.

Top View

MATERIALS NEEDED

Two ½-inch-diameter dowel rods cut the length of the feeder

Wood preservative

Brush

Four 3¼-inch cotter pins

Electric drill

Tack hammer

Saw

Four 1-inch stainless steel screws

DIRECTIONS

1. Treat the dowel rods with wood preservative or they will rot rapidly.

2. Drill four ³⁄₃₂-inch-diameter holes a ½-inch deep at the corners of the feeder. Each hole should be located so that the eye of the cotter pin is 2¼ inches above the outer edge of the feeder tray.

3. Drive the cotter pins into the holes with a tack hammer.

4. Cut the dowel so that it fits loosely just inside the two cotter pins.

5. Drill a hole into the center of each end of the rods with a bit that is slightly smaller than the screws.

6. Insert each screw through the eye of the cotter pin and into the hole in the dowel. Ensure that the dowel spins freely and is 2 inches above the edge of the feeder where smaller birds will stand.

as well as for raccoons, oppossums, and skunks. Although brush piles are extremely beneficial wildlife attractions, they should not be established directly next to your house foundation. You may wish to place the brush pile above the ground by placing the foundation on concrete blocks.

Predators

Attracting wildlife effectively means you will also be attracting natural predators. As with drawing in unwanted competitors for food, the presence of predators should be viewed as a sign of success. Again, with a little planning, there are ways to keep losses to a minumum.

CATS PREYING ON SONGBIRDS AND OTHER WILDLIFE

Cats can pose a major threat to your backyard wildlife community. Although cats may be fed and sustained by their owners, their natural instincts cause them to attack and kill any small moving animals they encounter. Recent research indicates that a single house cat may kill as many as 100 animals a year, 60 percent being small mammals, lizards, and snakes and the remaining 40 percent being birds. Multiply that by the number of cats roaming the neighborhood, and you could have very high mortality rates in your wildscape.

The best thing that can be done is to keep your cat indoors and ensure that it is spayed or neutered. Not only does this keep the smaller wildlife safe, but it also ensures your pet's safety from other cats and dogs and from wildlife such as coyotes and bobcats. If a number of strays are loose in your neighborhood, contact your animal control office to see how they can be captured.

Other means of controlling cats simply aren't effective. Tying bells onto your cat's collar will have limited success; once the cats understand that the ringing warns the other animals, they will learn to walk without ringing the bell. Additionally, wild animals don't associate the ringing sound with a source of danger.

To protect any birds that you feed, don't provide mixed grain directly on the ground. Instead, use sunflower or thistle seeds in tube or platform feeders off the ground. Brush piles should be at least 10–15 feet from feeding stations, because they provide excellent cover for cats to use as they wait to ambush birds.

HAWKS PREYING ON SONGBIRDS

Hawks are an interesting and important component of the environment. Most hawks are opportunistic and eat a wide variety of animals including rodents, rabbits, amphibians, reptiles, insects, and some birds. Although a few hawk species rely on small birds for a majority of their diet—for example, the prairie falcon and sharp-shinned and Cooper's hawks—don't worry that these avian predators will deplete the songbirds in your yard. Many of the birds they take are slow, injured, or unwary.

To minimize songbird losses, avoid attracting and concentrating songbirds at feeding stations that lack quick access to shrub or brush pile cover. Additional feeders spread throughout the yard will decrease concentrations of birds, which are easy pickings. Remember that all birds of prey, including hawks, owls, and kites, are protected by federal law.

CONTROLLING NEST BOX PREDATORS

After placing nest boxes on poles, clear the vegetation from the pole base. If you're using wooden poles, wrap a 2-foot length of sheet metal just below the nest box to prevent access by climbing predators (see "Nest Box Designs," chapter 8). Place a 40-inch-wide baffle around poles to deter snakes from getting in the nest box. See figure 8–18 for instructions on constructing a predator guard. The baffle will deter raccoons and cats, also predators of nest boxes, unless the nest box is placed on a tree. To ensure protection from all climbing predators, mount the nest box on a metal or wooden pole with a baffle and at least 6 feet out from any trees and out from under any overhanging branches. This will discourage raccoons, cats, and snakes from dropping down to the nest box.

OUTWITTING STARLINGS AND SPARROWS

Sparrows and starlings also use natural or artificial nesting structures to raise their young, readily evicting and even killing native species that occupy the nest box. The house sparrow is notorious for attacking a female bluebird that is sitting on her brood, pecking in her skull with its sharp beak, and then building a new nest over the dead bluebird and her young.

Keeping starlings out of most nest boxes can be accomplished relatively easily. These large chunky birds need equally large entrances. If you keep entrance hole diameters less than 2½ inches, starlings will be restricted from most houses.

House sparrows have proven to be a more difficult matter. Since they are approximately the same size as or even smaller than many native songbirds, reducing entrance dimensions is not effective. Trapping and humanely dispatching house sparrows is the best method to help eliminate them from your area. This can be accomplished by using homemade or commercially available traps.

If your bluebird house is known to have problems with house sparrows, you might consider installing the Joe Huber Trap-in-the-box (fig. 9–4), which consists of two screws, a metal trap plate, and a trip rod located inside the nest box. These remain in the box permanently and will not affect nesting bluebirds or other desirable species. This trap should only be used to capture house sparrows; all other species that might nest in bluebird boxes are protected by state and federal law. When house sparrows begin building a nest, hang the trap plate on the top screw. Set the trap by placing the upper arm of the trip rod under the bottom of the trap plate. The next bird to enter will touch the lower arm of the trip rod and cause the plate to fall across the entrance hole.

Once you have set the trap, leave the area for a few minutes and allow the sparrows to return. If you catch the male house sparrow, humanely dispose of him and remove his nest and the trap plate so that native birds can begin using the bird house. However, if you capture the female house sparrow, it's a good idea to dispose of her and reset the box trap for the male. The male house sparrow does much of the nest building and considers the box as his territory. If you only trap the female, the male will return with another mate and continue to exclude native birds. Therefore, the male is the primary target for controlling bird house sparrow problems.

This trap should be used carefully and responsibly. To avoid catching a protected native bird, set the trap only when an active sparrow nest is present. Although you may release a bluebird or wren physically unharmed, the bird will probably abandon the nest box. Also, check active traps frequently to minimize risk to other birds that might enter the house. Once a full clutch of four to five house sparrow eggs is laid or young have hatched, house sparrows will enter the bird house frequently and may be captured within a few minutes after you have set the trap. Carefully open the nest box

FAMILY ACTIVITIES

Create a photo record of your wildscape

Having a photographic record of the changes in your wildscape is a fun way to record progress. As a family, choose three to five places on the property that would make good photo spots. Scatter these photo spots for complete coverage of the yard or landscaped area. Let the children decide on four photography dates each year (one per season), and mark the dates on a calendar. Have the photographer face in the same direction at each location each time so that changes are easier to recognize. Place photos in a scrapbook the children create. This will be especially handy when you certify your property as an Oklahoma Wildscape.

and remove the sparrow. To prevent escape, cover the box with a plastic bag or onion sack before opening the bird house.

After the offending male house sparrow is removed and humanely destroyed, the bird house is available for use by several native songbirds that nest in cavities. If the house is properly located, it is often quickly inhabited by these birds.

Remember, European starlings and house sparrows are not protected by law, so they may be humanely destroyed. Do not release these birds elsewhere! Studies have shown that unless you take birds hundreds of miles away, they will return to your area. Even if they don't return, you have only increased the problem for people and native birds in the release area.

Complications with Homes and Yards

Wild creatures are adaptable. If our homes and yards provide them with tempting opportunities, they may take advantage of these in unexpected ways.

FIGURE 9-4. The Joe Huber Trap-in-the-box is designed to prevent house sparrows from invading nest boxes.

BATS IN THE ATTIC

Bats occasionally crawl into the attics of buildings to live for the summer. Although they are helpful to have around because they eat insects, they should not be encouraged to live in your home because their guano will smell and will foul attic insulation. If you seal off the attic when you first notice the bats, you may trap any young that are inside and cause them to starve to death. Instead, wait until about late July, when the young are old enough to fly, to exclude the bats from your attic. Until then, cover and seal all holes but one for the bats to continue roosting and feeding their young.

After late July, staple a sheet of flexible mesh just above the main entrance hole and on either side. Leave the bottom side open so that the bats can crawl out and fly away for the evening. When they return in the morning, they will be unable to enter the attic and will have to seek out other shelter. If you wish to keep the bats around your residence, erect a bat house near the eaves of your home. Once the bats have left in the fall, repair the hole and clean out your attic.

BIRDS FLYING INTO WINDOWS

Birds collide with windows for a variety of reasons. The most common is that windows often appear as tunnels that birds can fly through, either due to reflections or because a second window can be seen on the opposite side of the building. Birds also col-

FIGURE 9-5. Female house sparrow excluding native bird.

lide with windows located near feeding stations, especially if a predator such as a house cat frightens them into flight. And sometimes, birds crash into windows because they see their own reflections and are territorial about any apparent competitor entering their space.

Many birds are injured or die by flying into windows, but in most cases these collisions only stun the bird. If you find such a bird, simply place it in a warm, dry, quiet location until it recovers and can be released, usually in around 90 minutes.

Prevent birds from flying into glass by putting a mobile or a silhouette of an owl or hawk in your window (fig. 9–6). You can also place vertical and horizontal lines on the glass to help frame it. Windows that are slanted to mirror the ground are best at preventing collisions. You can also place a stick-on window feeder in the center of the glass.

To prevent future window collisions, you can do several things:

1. Pull curtains to eliminate the tunnel appearance created by a second window.
2. Underscore that the window is a barrier by hanging strips of silver paper or colored ribbons or by placing decals or suncatchers on the window.
3. Place or hang netting across the window.

4. Place feeders only 1 to 3 feet away from the window so that if birds strike the glass, they won't have gained enough speed to hurt themselves.

WOODPECKERS DRUMMING ON HOUSES

Woodpeckers are adapted to finding food, as well as mates, by drumming on dead trees. However, since fewer snags exist in the urban environment, the birds now have few drumming sites to use. They have therefore begun drumming on the outsides of wooden homes, becoming quite a source of irritation. Because modern homes have air pockets for insulative value, the drumming woodpecker thinks the wood is hollow. In snags, these hollow areas are where the woodpecker normally finds its insect foods.

Try hanging a suet feeder where birds are causing a problem, which can distract them from damaging your property (fig. 9-7). If the woodpecker is drumming on one spot, cover it with a plastic coffee can lid to muffle the hollow echo the woodpecker hears. You also might cover the home's siding with a sheet of thick (8–10 mm) plastic, which the birds can't easily grip. If woodpeckers are roosting at night in the eaves, spray them with a water hose several nights in a row to drive them off. Noise makers also may be effective.

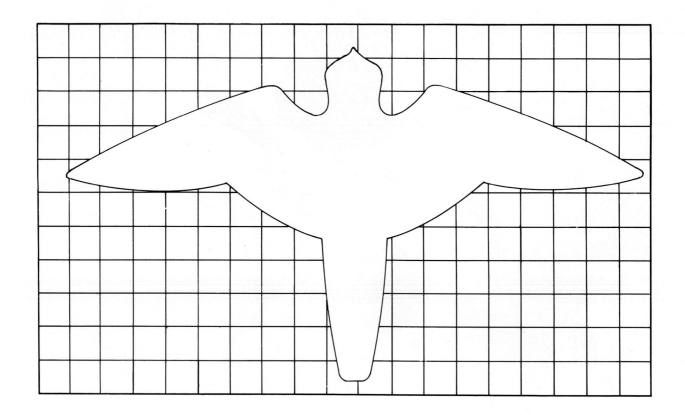

1″

FIGURE 9-6. Falcon silhouette pattern for use on window. Cut out silhouette to scale—each square on the pattern is equal to 1 inch. The actual size of the pattern's wingspan should be about 18 inches. Paint the pattern black and affix it to outside of window pane with head angled downward as if falcon is diving at prey.

SNAKES IN THE HOUSE

Snakes are beneficial in that they eat mice and insects, but they usually aren't welcome in basements. They often crawl into those areas during warm weather or high water. Keep them out by sealing all foundation cracks and put a cover or netting over basement window wells.

ARMADILLOS DIGGING UP THE YARD

Although armadillos seem harmless enough and are appealing to watch, they are great diggers. When foraging, they can leave a messy trail of excavations all over a neatly kept lawn. These mammals are searching for beetle grubs; therefore, to keep them from digging up your yard, you can treat the lawn for beetle grubs. The correct time to treat for grubs is during August, because the beetles have just laid their eggs and are near the ground surface. Bio-Safe is an environmentally friendly application that contains beneficial nematodes, but it may be difficult to find. Check with your local feed store for other safe alternatives.

If you don't wish to use any pesticides or insecticides, you might consider gradually phasing out your lawn area and converting it to more wildlife-friendly habitat, such as a butterfly garden, where any armadillo digging will be much less noticeable and bothersome. Also, once you are no longer watering your lawn, the ground will become hard and difficult for the grubs to dig into.

Another option is to install chain-link fencing

around your property, although it has a higher cost and will exclude other wildlife you might desire. Fencing should be buried at least 18–24 inches below ground to prevent armadillos from digging under it.

RABBITS AND RACCOONS EATING GARDEN VEGETABLES

Conflicts sometime arise between rabbits or raccoons and vegetable garden owners. Left unprotected, a cultivated garden may become a smorgasbord for these small mammals. The only truly effective deterrent is fencing. Electric, chicken-wire, or woven-wire fences perform well and are very cost effective.

To exclude rabbits, fencing should be buried at least 18 inches below ground and should extend at least 30 inches above ground. Raccoons can climb over such a low fence, so place a low-voltage electric wire at the top that will shock them without harming them.

SKUNKS IN THE YARD

Skunks can be a gardener's best friend by eating insects and rodents, but sometimes they become a nuisance, and caution must be used when dealing with these animals. Obviously, you want to avoid being sprayed, but equally important is to avoid being bitten. Skunks may carry the rabies virus but not exhibit any symptoms.

If you are concerned by high skunk activity in your yard, take a look around your wildscape. Skunks may be attracted to garbage or other food sources, so take sanitary precautions to reduce this. Skunks also eat mice in barns, crawl spaces, sheds, and garages, requiring a rodent-control program to eliminate this attraction. Finally, debris such as fence posts, lumber, brush piles, junk cars, etc., provide shelter for skunks and may need to be removed.

Trapping a skunk should be done in coordination with an animal control agent (look in the yellow pages of the local phone book under "animal control"). Skunks can not be relocated to another area due to the potential for spreading diseases, such as rabies. An animal control agent can humanely

FIGURE 9-7. Female downy woodpecker on suet feeder.

dispose of the skunk. Shooting skunks is an option only outside city limits and away from neighbors as you can expect a discharge of scent.

WILDLIFE EATING OFF FRUIT TREES

Many bird species, including mockingbirds, cedar waxwings, and robins, eat berries and soft fruit, occasionally visiting a landowner's cherry or peach trees. To discourage wildlife from eating all the fruit, cover fruit-producing plants with plastic bird netting, and then plant native berry producers such as choke cherry, blackberry, mulberry, or pokeweed. The native plants will still attract birds, but the netting will protect your cultivated fruit.

You also might consider letting wildlife have everything that drops from the tree, gathering it and placing it in a specific area away from your orchard. "Recycling" your bruised fruits will provide a food source and attract birds, small mammals, and even butterflies.

FINDING "LOST" WILDLIFE

People often find eggs or young birds in their yards during the spring and summer. If the nest is visible, place the eggs or young birds back in the nest. Contrary to popular belief, songbirds do not have a well-developed sense of smell and will not abandon their young if you touch them. If you have eggs but cannot find the nest, leave them alone— it is illegal to possess wild bird eggs. Generally, the parents will renest.

If a partially or completely unfeathered hatchling is found out of the nest, put it back in the nest. If the nest is too high or is not visible, construct an artificial nest by wiring a grocery store berry basket or other open-top container to the trunk of the same tree. Line the basket with grass clippings to form a cup. If you find a completely feathered young bird, you can assume that it has left the nest on its own and is still under parental care. Place the young bird on the top of a shrub away from predators.

Mammals are a different story, however. Most young mammals that are found alone, including deer, rabbit, squirrel and raccoon, are only hiding or have wandered away from their parents, which are nearby searching for food. If you touch the young mammal, your scent may either frighten the parent away or make it easier for predators to find the animal. The best thing to do is simply to leave it alone.

Most people are not equipped to care for wild animals adequately, and most "rescued" young will die. Although they may look cute at first, those that survive quickly turn into unmanageable adults that don't make good pets. Legality also is an issue. Possessing some native animals and all migratory birds without a permit is illegal and subject to a fine.

IF ALL ELSE FAILS . . .

If you have tried the listed recommendations and still have not been able to solve your nuisance wildlife problem, contact your state Wildlife Services (formerly Animal Damage Control) office. In Oklahoma, the telephone number is 405/521–4039. Ask for the local animal damage officer for your county.

Remember that all bird species except house sparrows, European starlings, and rock doves (pigeons) are protected by state and federal law. It is illegal to harass or kill any other native birds or their young. Also, many other species of wildlife are protected by various state laws. For example, it is illegal to "take" a Texas horned lizard in New Mexico, Oklahoma, and Texas. Consult your state wildlife agency if you need to know what species are protected by law.

Times have changed. Many people of our grandparents' era lived in more rural settings than most of us do today. They were often surrounded with wildlife, and some wild animals were a significant threat to their safety or to their homegrown fruit, vegetables, and poultry. In our parents' and our own generations, many people have moved into cities where we are distant from wildlife. The combination of large-scale agribusiness and burgeoning urban growth has produced widespread problems for populations of wild animals and birds.

The beginning of the wildscaping movement is partly a response to our growing awareness that we are the losers if we have too little interaction with the natural world, and it is partly an effort to compensate for losses where we can. Having your own wildscape right at home produces the immediate satisfaction of regular wildlife sightings to punctuate every day and week. And it also produces the long-term reward of knowing you are contributing to a wholesome future.

FIGURE 9-8. Mammal parents must often leave their young temporarily while they forage for food. It is best to leave baby wild animals alone. Usually the parents of these "orphaned" animals are hiding nearby.

Checklist to Design a Wildscape

GOALS AND INVENTORY

1. I intend to design my wildscape to attract the following wildlife species or groups of species:

   _____

   _____

   _____

2. My wildscaping goals for the next two years are:

   _____

   _____

   _____

3. My wildscaping goals for the next five years are:

   _____

   _____

   _____

4. Other uses of my property and special landscaping needs are:

   _____

   _____

   _____

5. I want to keep the following plantings and structures:

   _____

   _____

   _____

6. I want to replace the following plantings and structures:

   _____

   _____

   _____

7. I have identified wildlife viewing areas at the following locations:

   _____

   _____

   _____

8. I have discussed the following major changes with my neighbors:

   _____

   _____

   _____

BASIC WILDLIFE NEEDS

1. I have provided year-round water for the following wildlife species:

   _____

   _____

   _____

2. I have or am planning a butterfly and hummingbird nectar garden with the following plantings:

   _____

   _____

   _____

3. I have snags and other potential nesting sites or will build and maintain nest boxes or nesting structures for the following wildlife species:

   _____

   _____

   _____

4. My property has brush piles or rock piles used as escape and winter cover for the following wildlife species:

   _____

   _____

   _____

FIGURE APP-1. Determining what you have and what you want are the prelude to designing your wildscape.

5. The following wildlife species currently use my wildscape to raise their young:

_____

_____

6. The following wildlife species currently use my wildscape for roosting or for hibernation:

_____

_____

PLANTINGS

I plan to provide year-round food and cover by planting the following species (preferably native to my area), by incorporating vertical and horizontal layering, and by providing curving edges:

1. Trees:

_____

_____

_____

_____

2. Shrubs:

_____

_____

_____

_____

3. Vines:

_____

_____

_____

_____

_____

4. Native grasses:

_____

_____

_____

_____

_____

5. Flowers and ground covers:

_____

_____

_____

_____

_____

FEEDERS

I plan to supplement natural food sources with the following foods and feeders:

_____

_____

_____

_____

_____

_____

_____

_____

_____

Monthly Activities Checklist for Your Wildscape

JANUARY

Install heaters in your metal or cement birdbaths.

Continue feeding birds and make sure the feeders are clean.

Participate in the annual Winter Bird Feeder Survey and submit your results to the Oklahoma Wildlife Diversity Program.

Make plans for spring plantings and design your wildscape.

Monitor water level in ponds to ensure use by frogs and toads.

Some owls will begin nesting at this time.

FEBRUARY

Open purple martin house entrances and monitor to keep out house sparrows and starlings.

Clean and erect bluebird nest boxes.

Check for warping on bat houses; caulk if needed or replace if warping is significant.

Make plans for spring plantings and design your wildscape.

Frogs and toads will begin using ponds during late February.

Put out kestrel nest boxes.

MARCH

Plant trees, shrubs, wildflowers, and vines for wildlife after mid-March.

Monitor nest boxes; clean out house sparrow and starling nests.

Keep written reports of nesting activity for Oklahoma Wildlife Diversity Program's Bluebird Nest Box Summary Form.

Help out Oklahoma wildlife financially by "Searching for the Scissortail" on the state income tax form and sharing your refund with wildlife.

Begin checking your bat house for occupancy.

Frogs and toads will use ponds during this month.

APRIL

Erect hummingbird feeder and note the first day birds are seen for Oklahoma Wildlife Diversity Program's Hummingbird Survey.

Watch for migrating warblers.

Continue checking bat houses for occupancy.

Help out Oklahoma wildlife financially by "Searching for the Scissortail" on the state income tax form and sharing your refund with wildlife.

Continue planting trees, shrubs, and flowers for wildlife.

Frogs and toads will use ponds during this month.

Most birds begin nesting.

Summer birds begin returning: scissor-tailed flycatcher, indigo bunting, chimney swift, and Baltimore oriole.

MAY

Continue to monitor nest boxes; remove nests after each nesting is completed.

Begin watching for young birds that have fledged (left the nest). Although they are not good flyers, their parents are still taking care of them. If you find a chick on the ground, place it back in the nest or up in a tree or shrub; do not try to take care of it yourself.

Watch for migrating warblers.

Frogs and toads will use ponds during this month.

JUNE

Provide water for birds.

Continue checking your bat house for occupancy.

Continue monitoring your nest boxes.

Monitor water level in ponds to ensure use by frogs and toads.

Watch for reptiles.

JULY

Tree-dwelling female red bats may be found with their young on the ground after a storm. Wearing thick gloves, gently place the mother and young up in a tree as high as possible.

Clean your hummingbird feeder every three to four days.

Monitor water level in ponds to ensure use by frogs and toads.

Continue checking your bat house for occupancy.

Watch for reptiles.

AUGUST

Provide water for birds.

Continue cleaning hummingbird feeder.

Monitor water level in ponds to ensure use by frogs and toads.

Continue checking bat house for occupancy.

Clean out purple martin house and plug the entrance holes after they leave.

SEPTEMBER

Keep your hummingbird feeder up all month.

Clean out nest boxes for the next nesting season.

Monitor water level in ponds to ensure use by frogs and toads.

Submit your Bluebird Nest Box Summary Form to the Oklahoma Wildlife Diversity Program.

Submit Bat House Survey Form to the Oklahoma Wildlife Diversity Program.

Order plants for spring delivery and planting.

OCTOBER

Keep your hummingbird feeder up all month.

Clean your bird feeders for the winter season.

Continue monitoring bat house for occupancy.

Monitor water level in ponds to ensure use by frogs and toads.

Plant trees and shrubs for wildlife.

Sow wildflower seeds for butterfly and hummingbird gardens.

NOVEMBER

Submit Hummingbird Survey Form to the Oklahoma Wildlife Diversity Program.

Check birdbath heater to make sure it works.

Monitor water level in ponds.

Plant trees and shrubs for wildlife.

DECEMBER

Continue cleaning your bird feeders.

Participate in a local Christmas Bird Count.

Monitor water level in ponds to ensure use by frogs and toads.

Make plans for spring plantings and design your wildscape.

Install heaters in your metal or cement birdbaths.

Oklahoma Native Plant and Seed Sources

Many local nurseries are beginning to carry native plants in their stock. If yours does not, let them know that you wish them to carry more native plants. Following are current Oklahoma native plant and seed producers; inclusion on these lists carries no official endorsement.

When ordering wildflower seed, ask about the seed source. Seed grown out of state or out of the region is less likely to be adapted to the climate of the Great Plains. Also, when comparing prices, the purity and germination rate of the seed should be considered.

Clear Creek Farms
Kirk and Loretta Bowers
P.O. Box 89
Peggs, OK 74452-0089
918/598-3782
Ccreek@chouteautel.com
Trees, shrubs, flowers

Grasslander
Chuck Grimes
Rt. 1 Box 56
Hennessey, OK 73742
580/853-2607
Grass and wildflower seeds

Guy's Seed Company
Rodney Guy
2520 Main Street
Woodward, OK 73801
580/254-2926
Grass and wildflower seeds

Hortco
10901 NE 23rd
Choctaw, OK 73141
405/769-2678
Wholesale perennials

Johnston Seeds
Ed Shovanec
P.O. Box 1392
Enid, OK 73702
580/233-5800
www.johnstonseed.com
johnseed@johnstonseed.com
Grass and wildflower seeds

Lorenz OK Seeds
Fred Lorenz
101 N. Main
Okeene, OK 73763
800/826-3655
www.okeene.com/lorenzokseeds/
okseeds@okeene.com
Grass and wildflower seeds

Morning Star Farms
Steve and Alice Jo Dobbs
Rt. 2 Box 101-A
Vian, OK 74962
918/773-5389
www.mstarfarms.com
mstar@mstarfarms.com
Shrubs, flowers, herbs

Northcutt's Nursery
9501 Duffy Road
Lexington, OK 73501
800/682-6671
www.northcuttsonline.com
Trees, shrubs, wildflowers

Rose Rock Landscape
Wayne and Susan Chambers
238 E. Robin Road
Midwest City, OK 73130
405/769-7917
Trees, shrubs, perennials

Satterlee's Nursery
6922 N. May Ave.
Oklahoma City, OK 73116
405/848-6228
www.satterleenursery.com
jlsatt@satterleenursery.com
Trees, shrubs, wildflowers

Steve's Sod
1120 S. Broadway
Edmond, OK 73034
405/341-2552
Hybrid buffalo grass sod

Sunshine Nursery
Steve and Sherry Bierberich
Rt. 1 Box 4030
Clinton, OK 73601
580/323-6259
www.sunshinenursery.com
gardening@sunshinenursery.com
Trees, shrubs, wildflowers

Tulsa Grass and Sod
10717 S. Delaware
Tulsa, OK 74137
918/299-7737
Hybrid buffalo grass sod

Warren's Nursery
10901 NE 23rd
Oklahoma City, OK 73141
405/769-2678
Trees, shrubs, wildflowers

Martin Perennial Farm, Inc.
Lillian Martin
Rt. 2 Box 750
Fort Cobb, OK 73038
800/554-3139
Martinpf@carnegienet.net
Perennials

StoneBridge Garden Center
Martin Stone
700 E. Will Rogers Blvd.
Claremore, OK 74017
918/341-1228
stonbrdg@busprod.com
Trees, shrubs, wildflowers

APPENDIX D
Regional Plant and Seed Producers

Abbott-Epco
P.O. Box 551329
Dallas, TX 75355-1329
800/525-1379
Wholesale perennials

Applewood Seed Co.
5380 Vivian Street
Arvada, CO 80002
www.applewoodseed.com
info@applewoodseed.com
303/431-7333

Arborvillage Farm Nursery
P.O. Box 227
Holt, MO 64048
816/264-3911
arborvillage@aol.com

Arrow Seed Company, Inc.
P.O. Box 72
Broken Bow, NE 68822
800/622-4727

Bamert Seed Company
Rt. 3 Box 1120
Muleshoe, TX 79347
800/262-9892
www.bamertseed.com
natives@bamertseed.com

Casterline Seed
Box 1377
Dodge City, KS 67801
800/444-4137

Dean Swift Seed Company
P.O. Box B
Jaroso, CO 81138
719/672-3739

Dry Country Plants
5840 N. Main Street
Las Cruces, NM 88001
505/522-4434

Grassland West
P.O. Box 1604
Greeley, CO 80632
866/214-2947
www.grasslandwest.com

Hamilton Seeds
16786 Brown Road
Elk Creek, MO 65464
417/967-2190

High Country Garden
2902 Rufina Street
Santa Fe, NM 87505-2929
800/925-9387
www.highcountrygardens.com
plants@highcountrygardens.com

Holland Wildflower Farm
P.O. Box 328
Elkins, AR 72727
800/684-3734
www.hwildflower.com
info@hwildflower.com

Indian Creek Nursery
2222 Parker Road
Carrollton, TX 75010
214/394-9896

Ion Exchange
1878 Old Mission Drive
Harpers Ferry, IA 52146
800/291-2143
www.ionxchange.com

Izard Ozark Natives
P.O. Box 454
Mountain View, AR 72560

Missouri Wildflower Nursery
9814 Pleasant Hill Road
Jefferson City, MO 65109
573/496-3492
mowldflrs@sockets.net

Native American Seed
610 Main Street
Junction, TX 76849
800/728-4043
www.seedsource.com
info@seedsource.com

Pine Ridge Gardens
832 Sycamore Road
London, AR 72847
479/293-4359
www.pineridgegardens.com
office@pineridgegardens.com

Plants of the Southwest
1570 Pacheco Street
Santa Fe, NM 87501
www.plantsofthesouthwest.com
contact@plantsofthesouthwest.com

Prairie Basse Native Plants
Rt. 2 Box 491F
Carencro, LA 70520

Seed Savers Exchange
P.O. Box 70
Decorah, IA 52101
563/382-5990
www.seedsavers.org
catalog@seedsavers.org

Seeds of Change
P.O. Box 15700
Santa Fe, NM 87506-5700
888/762-7333
www.seedsofchange.com
gardener@seedsofchange.com

Sharp Bros. Seed Company
P.O. Box 140
Healey, KS 67850
800/759-1520
www.sharpseed.com
buffalo@sharpseed.com

Sharp Bros. Seed Company
396 SW Davis Street
Clinton, MO 64735
800/451-3779
www.sharpbro.com
sales@sharpbro.com

Southwestern Native Seeds
Box 50503
Tucson, AZ 85703

Stock Seed Farms, Inc.
28008 Mill Road
Murdock, NE 68407-2350
800/759-1520
www.stockseed.com
stockseed@alltel.net

Western Native Seed
P.O. Box 188
Coaldale, CO 81222
719/942-3935
www.westernnativeseed.com
info@westernnativeseed.com

Wildflower Nursery
1680 Hwy. 25-70
Marshall, NC 28753

Wildseed Farms
P.O. Box 3000
Fredericksburg, TX 78624
800/848-0078
www.wildseedfarms.com
sales@wildseedfarms.com

APPENDIX E
Mail-order Seeds and Plants

Albright Seed Company
487 Dawson Drive, Bay 5S
Camarillo, CA 93012
805/484-0551
www.albrightseed.com
Native plant seeds

Bitterroot Restoration
445 Quast Lane
Corvallis, MT 59828
406/961-4991
www.bitterrootrestoration.com
Trees, shrubs, wildflowers

Environmental Seeds
P.O. Box 2709
Lompoc, CA 93438
805/735-8888
Wildflowers, grasses, herbs

Ernst Conservation Seeds
9006 Mercer Pike
Meadville, PA 16335
800/873-3321
www.ernstseed.com
Flowers, grasses, shrubs

Forest Farm
990 Tetherow Road
Williams, OR 97544-9599
541/846-7269
www.forestfarm.com
Native shrubs, wildflowers

Garden Perennials
85261 Hwy. 15
Wayne, NE 68787
402/375–3615
www.gardenperennials.net
Perennials

H.G. Hastings Co.
1036 White Street SW
Atlanta, GA 30302
Perennials, shrubs

Kester's Nurseries
P.O. Box 516
Omro, WI 54963
800/558-8815
Native grasses, wildflowers

Lawyer Nursery Inc.
950 Hwy. 200 West
Plains, MT 59859
800/551-9875
www.lawyernursery.com
Trees, shrubs

Lofts Seed, Inc.
P.O. Box 26223
Winston-Salem, NC 27114
888/563-8726
www.turf.com
Native grasses, wildflowers

Native Plants, Inc.
1697 W. 2100 North
P.O. Box 177
Lehi, UT 84043
Native shrubs, wildflowers

Natural Habitats Unlimited
811 Matthies Dr.
Papillion, NE 68046
402/592-5652
Prairie grasses, flowers

Prairie Moon Nursery
Rt. 3 Box 1633
Winona, MN 55987
866/417-8156
www.prairiemoonnursery.com
Trees, shrubs, flowers

Prairie Nursery
P.O. Box 306
Westfield, WI 53964
800/476-9453
www.prairienursery.com
Grasses, perennials

Prairie Restorations, Inc.
P.O. Box 327
Princeton, MN 55371
763/389-4342
www.prairierest.com
Native wildflowers, grasses

Schumacher's Nursery
711 Chapman Avenue
Heron Lake, MN 56137
507/793-2288
Native tree seedlings

Springhill Nurseries
P.O. Box 330
Harrison, OH 45030-0330
513/354-1509
www.springhillnursery.com
Perennials

Taylor Creek Restoration
17921 Smith Road
P.O. Box 256
Brodhead, WI 53520
608/897-8641
www.appliedeco.com/tcrn
info@appliedeco.com
Flowers, grasses, sedges

Thompson and Morgan Seedsmen
P.O. Box 1308
Jackson, NJ 08527
800/274-7333
www.thompson-morgan.com
Native seeds

Wayside Gardens
1 Garden Lane
Hodges, SC 29695
800/213-0379
www.waysidegardens.com
Shrubs, vines, perennials

Wind River Seed
3075 Lane 51½
Manderson, WY 82432
307/568-3364
www.windriverseed.com
Flowers, grasses, shrubs

Aquatic/Wetland Seed Producers

Applied Ecological Services
P.O. Box 256
Brodhead, WI 53520
608/897-8641
www.appliedeco.com

Aquatic and Wetland Company
1830 17th St., Suite 100
Boulder, CO 80302
303/442-5770
www.aquaticandwetland.com

Burr Oak Nursery
Rt. 1 Box 310
Round Lake, IL 60073
773/546-4700

Environmental Concern, Inc.
P.O. Box P
St. Michaels, MD 21663
410/745-9620
www.wetland.org

Environmental Seeds
P.O. Box 2709
Lompoc, CA 93438
805/735-8888

Freshwater Farms
5851 Myrtle Ave.
Eureka, CA 95503
800/200-8969
www.freshwaterfarms.com

Gardens of the Blue Ridge
P.O. Box 10
Pineola, NC 28662
828/733-2417
www.gardensoftheblueridge.com

Genesis Nursery, Inc.
23200 Hurd Road
Tampico, IL 61283
815/438-2220

Hastings
1036 White Street NW
Atlanta, GA 30302

Hawkersmith & Sons Nursery
950 Hawkersmith Road
Tullahoma, TN 37388
931/455-5436

Hild & Associates
326 S. Glover Road
River Falls, WI 54022
715/426-5131
www.hildnatives.com

J & J Transplant Aquatics
W4980 County Road West
Wild Rose, WI 54984
414/622-3552

Kester's Nurseries
P.O. Box 516
Omro, WI 54963
800/558-8815

Mangrove Systems, Inc.
504 S. Brevard Avenue
Tampa, FL 33606

Savage Farms Nursery
6255 Beersheba Hwy.
McMinnville, TN 37110
913/668-8902

Seeds of Change
P.O. Box 15700
Santa Fe, NM 87506-5700
888/762-7333
www.seedsofchange.com

Sharp Brothers Seed Co.
P.O. Box 140
Healy, KS 67850
800/759-1520
www.sharpseed.com

Slocum Water Gardens
1101 Cypress Gardens Road
Winter Haven, FL 33880
863/293-7151
www.slocumwatergardens.com

Spence Restoration Nursery
P.O. Box 546
Muncie, IN 47308
765/286-7154
www.spencenursery.com

Van Ness Water Gardens
2460 N. Euclid Avenue
Upland, CA 91784-1199
800/205-2425
www.vnwg.com

Vick's Wildgardens, Inc.
Box 115
Gladwyne, PA 19035
972/525-6773

Wetland Restoration Nursery
311 Crooks Road
Apollo, PA 15613
724/334-3780
wetplants@aol.com

Wildlife Nurseries, Inc.
P.O. Box 2724
Oshkosh, WI 54903
920/231-3780

APPENDIX G
Field Guides and References

NATURAL LANDSCAPING

"Ecoregions of the Conterminous United States."
J. M. Omernick. *Annals of the Association of American Geographers* 77(1):118–25. 1987.

The Four Season Landscape. Susan Roth. Rodale Press, 1994.

How to Grow Native Plants of Texas and the Southwest. Jill Nokes. Texas Monthly Press, 1986.

Landscaping with Nature: Using Nature's Designs to Plan Your Yard. Jeff Cox. Rodale Press, 1991.

Landscaping with Wildflowers and Native Plants. William Wilson. Ortho Books, 1984.

The Natural Garden. Ken Druse. Crown Publishers, 1989.

The Natural Habitat Garden. Ken Druse and Margaret Roach. Clarkson Potter Publishing, 1994.

The Natural Shade Garden. Ken Druse. Clarkson Potter, 1992.

The Naturalist's Garden. Ruth Shaw Ernst. Rodale Press, 1987.

Nature's Design: A Practical Guide to Natural Landscaping. Carol A. Smyser. Rodale Press, 1982.

Oklahoma's Biodiversity Plan: A Shared Vision for Conserving Our Natural Heritage. Oklahoma Biodiversity Task Force. Norman L. Murray, ed. Oklahoma Department of Wildlife Conservation, 1996.

Shade Gardens. Oliver E. Allen. Time-Life Books, 1979.

Southern Herb Growing. Madelene Hill, Gwen Barclay and Jean Hardy. Shearer Publishing, 1987.

Southwestern Landscaping with Native Plants. Judith Phillips. Museum of New Mexico Press, 1987.

Taylor's Guide to Natural Gardening. Roger Holmes, ed. Houghton Mifflin, 1993.

Taylor's Guide to Perennials. Houghton Mifflin, 1986.

WATER GARDENS

Garden Pools, Fountains and Waterfalls. Elizabeth L. Hogan, editor. Sunset Publishing Corporation, 1993.

Managing Pond Fisheries in Oklahoma. Oklahoma Department of Wildlife Conservation, 1996.

Water Gardens. Peter Stadelmann. Barron's Educational Series, 1992.

Water in the Garden. James Allison. Bullfinch Press, 1991.

Waterscaping: Plants and Ideas for Natural and Created Water Gardens. Judy Glattstein. Garden Way Publishing, 1994.

TREES, SHRUBS, AND VINES

An Annotated List of the Ferns, Fern Allies, Gymnosperms, and Flowering Plants of Oklahoma. John R. Taylor and Constance E. S. Taylor. Southeastern Oklahoma State University, 1991.

Flora of Oklahoma. 1996. Order from: Flora of Oklahoma, Inc., 15100 Etowah Road, Noble, OK 73068, 405/872-8361.

Forest Trees of Oklahoma. Elbert L. Little, Jr. Oklahoma Department of Agriculture Forestry Division, 1996.

The Illustrated Book of Trees. William Carey Grimm. Stackpole Books, 1983.

Native Plant Selection Guide for Oklahoma Woody Plants. Darlene Michael. Oklahoma Native Plant Society, 1995.

Native Trees, Shrubs and Vines for Urban and Rural America. Gary L. Hightshoe. Van Nostrand Reinhold Company, 1988.

Oklahoma Gardener's Guide. Steve Dobbs. Cool Springs Press, 1999.

Peterson's Field Guide to Eastern Trees and Shrubs. George A. Petrides. Houghton Mifflin 1988.

Peterson's Field Guide to Trees and Shrubs. George A. Petrides. Houghton Mifflin, 1986.

Roadside Trees and Shrubs of Oklahoma. Doyle McCoy. University of Oklahoma Press, 1981.

Roadside Wild Fruits of Oklahoma. Doyle McCoy. University of Oklahoma Press, 1980.

The Shrub Identification Book. George W. D. Symonds. William Morrow and Company, 1963.

Trees, Shrubs and Woody Vines of the Southwest. Robert A. Vines. University of Texas Press, 1974.

NATIVE GRASSES

100 Native Forage Grasses in 11 Southern States. Agriculture Handbook no. 389. Horace L. Leithead, Lewis L. Yarlett, and Thomas N. Shiflet. United States Department of Agriculture, 1971.

Common Weeds of the United States. United States Department of Agriculture, Research Service. Dover Publications, 1971.

Manual of the Grasses of the United States, 2 vols. A. S. Hitchcock, revised by Agnes Chase. Dover Publications, 1971.

Range Plant Handbook. United States Department of Agriculture, Forest Service. Dover Publications, 1988.

Texas Range Plants. Stephan L. Hatch and Jennifer Pluhar. Texas A&M University Press, 1993.

WILDFLOWERS

The Audubon Society Field Guide to North American Wildflowers—Eastern Region. William A. Niering and Nancy C. Olmstead. Alfred A. Knopf, 1979.

The Audubon Society Field Guide to North American Wildflowers: Western Region. Richard Spellenberg. Alfred A. Knopf, 1979.

Gardening with Wild Flowers. Frances Tenebaum. Charles Scribner and Sons, 1973.

A Grower's Guide to Wildflowers. Wildseed, Inc. 1988.

Growing and Propagating Wildflowers. Harry R. Phillips. University of North Carolina Press, 1985.

A Guide to Field Identification of Wildflowers of North America. Frank D. Venning. Golden Press, 1984.

A Guide to Wildflowers of the Mid-South. Arlo Smith. Memphis State University Press, 1979.

Landscaping with Wildflowers and Native Plants. William H. W. Wilson. Ortho Books, 1984.

Landscaping with Wildflowers: An Environmental Approach to Gardening. Jim Wilson. Houghton Mifflin, 1992.

Oklahoma Wildflowers. Doyle McCoy. McCoy Publishing Company, 1987.

Peterson's Field Guide to Southwestern and Texas Wildflowers. Theodore F. Niehaus, et al. Illustrations by Charles L. Ripper and Virginia Savage. Houghton Mifflin, 1980.

Photographing Wildflowers. Craig and Nadine Blacklock. Voyageur Press, 1987.

Prairie Plants of the Midwest: Identification and Ecology. Russell R. Kirt. Stipes Publishing, 1995.

Roadside Flowers of Oklahoma, 2 vols. Doyle McCoy. McCoy Publishing Company, 1976–78.

Roadside Wildflowers of the Southern Great Plains. Craig C. Freeman and Eileen K. Schofield. University Press of Kansas, 1991.

Tallgrass Prairie Wildflowers. Doug Ladd and Frank Oberle. Falcon Press Publishing Company, 1995

Wild Flowers of the United States, vol. 2: *The Southeastern States.* H. W. Rickett. McGraw-Hill, 1967.

Wildflowers of the Southeastern United States. Wilbur Duncan and Leonard Foote. University of Georgia Press, 1975.

BACKYARD WILDLIFE

American Wildlife and Plants: A Guide to Wildlife Food Habits. Alexander C. Martin, Herbert S. Zim, and Arnold L. Nelson. Dover Publications, 1961.

Attracting Backyard Wildlife: A Guide for Nature-lovers. Bill Merilees. Voyageur Press, 1989.

Developing Backyard Wildlife Habitats in Mississippi. John DeFazio. Natural Resources Conservation Service, 1990.

Gardening with Wildlife. National Wildlife Federation, 1974.

Landscaping for Wildlife. Carrol L. Henderson. Minnesota Department of Natural Resources, 1987.

Planting a Refuge for Wildlife. Susan Cerulean. Florida Game and Fresh Water Fish Commission, 1992.

Planting an Oasis for Wildlife. National Wildlife Federation, 1986.

Sharing Your Space: A Homeowner's Guide to Attracting Backyard Wildlife. Eileen Dowd Stukel et al. South Dakota Department of Game, Fish and Parks, 1995.

Urban Wildlife Habitats: A Landscape Perspective. Lowell W. Adams. University of Minnesota Press, 1994.

Woodcrafting for Wildlife. Pennsylvania Wild Resource Fund and Pennsylvania Game Commission, 1998.

Woodworking for Wildlife: Homes for Birds and Mammals. Carrol L. Henderson. Minnesota's Bookstore, State of Minnesota, 1992.

BIRDS

Attracting Birds to Southern Gardens. Thomas Pope, Neil Odenwald, and Charles Fryling. Taylor Publishing Company, 1993.

Audubon Society Guide to Attracting Birds. Stephen Kress. Charles Scribner's Sons, 1985.

The Bluebird Book. Donald W. and Lillian Q. Stokes. Little, Brown and Company, 1991.

Birds of North America. C. S. Robbins, B. Bruun, and H. S. Zim. Golden Press, 1983.

Birds of the Great Plains: Breeding Species and Their Distribution. Paul A. Johnsgard. University of Nebraska Press, 1979.

Birdscaping Your Garden: A Practical Guide to Backyard Birds and the Plants that Attract Them. George Adams. Lansdowne Publishing, 1994.

Field Guide to the Birds of North America. National Geographic Society, 1983.

Fifty Common Birds of Oklahoma and the Southern Great Plains. George Miksch Sutton. University of Oklahoma Press, 1977.

A Guide to the Nests, Eggs, and Nestlings of North American Birds. Paul J. Baicich and Colin J. O. Harrison. Academic Press, 1997.

A Guide to Western Bird Feeding. John V. Dennis. Bird Watcher's Digest Press, 1991.

How to Attract Birds. Michael McKinley. Ortho Books, 1983.

The Hummingbird Book. Donald W. and Lillian Q. Stokes. Little, Brown and Company, 1989.

Hummingbirds of North America. Dan True. University of New Mexico Press, 1993.

National Audubon Society North American Birdfeeder Handbook. Robert Burton. Dorling Kindersley, 1992.

The New Handbook for Attracting Birds. T. P. McElroy. W. W. Norton and Company, 1985.

Oklahoma Bird Life. Frederick M. and A. Marguerite Baumgartner. University of Oklahoma Press, 1992.

Peterson's Field Guide to Birds. R. T. Peterson. Houghton Mifflin, 1980.

Wild about Birds: The DNR Bird Feeding Guide. Carrol L. Henderson. Minnesota Department of Natural Resources, 1995.

MAMMALS

Audubon Society Field Guide to North American Mammals. J. O. Whitaker. Alfred A. Knopf, 1980.

The Bat House Builder's Handbook. Merlin D. Tuttle and Donna L. Hensley. Bat Conservation International, 1993.

The Bats of Texas. David J. Schmidly. Texas A&M University Press, 1991.

Mammals of Oklahoma. William Caire, Jack Tyler, Bryan Glass, and Michael Mares. University of Oklahoma Press, 1989.

The Mammals of Texas. William B. Davis and David J. Schmidly. Texas Parks and Wildlife Department, 1994.

Peterson's Field Guide to the Mammals. W. H. Burt and R. P. Grossenheider. Houghton Mifflin, 1976.

REPTILES AND AMPHIBIANS

Amphibians and Reptiles in Kansas. Joseph T. Collins. University of Kansas Museum of Natural History, 1993.

Amphibians and Reptiles of Oklahoma. Gregory and Lynnette Sievert and Jeffrey H. Black. Oklahoma Department of Wildlife Conservation, 2003.

The Amphibians and Reptiles of Missouri. Tom R. Johnson. Missouri Department of Conservation, 1992.

Amphibians and Reptiles of New Mexico. William G. Degenhardt, Charles W. Painter, and Andrew H. Price. University of New Mexico Press, 1996.

Audubon Society Field Guide to North American Reptiles and Amphibians. J. L. Behler and F. W. King. Alfred A. Knopf, 1979.

A Field Guide to Reptiles and Amphibians of Texas. Judith M. Garrett and David G. Barker. Gulf Publishing Company, 1987.

A Guide to Amphibian and Reptile Conservation. Tom R. Johnson. Missouri Department of Conservation, 1979.

Peterson's Field Guide to the Reptiles and Amphibians of Eastern and Central North America. Roger Conant. Houghton Mifflin, 1975.

BUTTERFLIES

The Audubon Society Field Guide to North American Butterflies. Robert M. Pyle. Alfred A. Knopf, 1981.

Butterflies and Moths of Missouri. J. Richard and Joan E. Heitzman. Missouri Department of Conservation, 1987.

Butterflies of the Rocky Mountain States. Clifford D. Ferris and F. Martin Brown. University of Oklahoma Press, 1981.

Butterflies through Binoculars: The East. Jeffrey Glassberg. Oxford University Press, 1999.

The Butterfly Garden. Matthew Tekulsky. Harvard Common Press, 1985.

Butterfly Gardening for the South. Geyata Ajilvsgi. Taylor Publishing Company, 1990.

Butterfly Gardening. Xerces Society–Smithsonian Institution. Sierra Club Books, 1990.

A Field Guide to Butterflies of North America. Alexander Klots. Houghton Mifflin, 1951.

Handbook for Butterfly Watchers. Robert M. Pyle. Houghton Mifflin, 1984.

How to Attract Hummingbirds and Butterflies. Ortho Books, 1991.

Peterson's Field Guide to Eastern Butterflies. Paul A. Opler. Houghton Mifflin, 1992.

Peterson's Field Guide to Insects. Donald J. Borrer and Richard E. White. Houghton Mifflin, 1970.

Peterson's Field Guide to Western Butterflies. J. W. Tilden and Arthur C. Smith. Houghton Mifflin, 1986.

Photographing Nature: Insects. Heather Angel. Fountain Press, 1975.

Simon and Schuster's Guide to Butterflies and Moths. Mauro Daccordi, Paolo Triberti, and Adriano Zanetti. Simon and Schuster, 1987.

Simon and Schuster's Guide to Insects. Dr. Ross H. Arnett, Jr., and Dr. Richard L. Jacques, Jr. Simon and Schuster, 1981.

APPENDIX H

Wildscaping Internet Sites

Bat Conservation International,
www.batcon.org

Birder Home Page,
www.birder.com

Birdnet: The Ornithological Information Source,
www.nmnh.si.edu/BIRDNET

The Bluebird Box,
www.audubon-omaha.org/bbbox

Butterfly Zone,
www.butterflies.com

Find Nurseries.com,
www.findnurseries.com

Garden.com,
www.garden.com

Gardening,
www.gardening.com

GardenNet,
www.GardenNet.com

GardenWeb,
www.gardenweb.com

Herb Growing,
www.herbnet.com

Horticultural Web,
www.horticulture.com

Keeping Wildlife at a Safe Distance,
cc.usu.edu/~rschmidt/welcome.html

Lady Bird Johnson Wildflower Center,
www.wildflower.org

Monarch Watch,
www.MonarchWatch.org

National Audubon Society,
www.audubon.org

National Wildlife Federation,
www.nwf.org/backyardwildlifehabitat

Native Plant Societies,
www.acorn-online.com/hedge/h-socs.htm

The Nest Box,
www.nestbox.com

North American Bluebird Society,
www.nabluebirdsociety.org

Northern Prairie Science Center,
www.npwrc.usgs.gov

Plants by Mail—Rating Nurseries,
www.plantsbymail.com

Related Organizations and Agencies

Bat Conservation International
P.O. Box 162603
Austin, TX 78716
512/327-9721
www.batcon.org

Bat Conservation Society of Oklahoma
P.O. Box 18303
Oklahoma City, OK 73154
405/341-9539
OKBATS@aol.com

Butterfly Club of America
736 Main Avenue, Suite 200
Box 2257
Durango, CO 81302

Central Oklahoma Water Garden Society
418 South Lewis Lane
Mustang, OK 73064

Cooperative Extension Services
See "County Government" in local phone book

George M. Sutton Avian Research Center
P.O. Box 2007
Bartlesville, OK 74005
918/336-7778
www.suttoncenter.org

Green Country Water Garden Society
15907 East 110th Street North
Owasso, OK 74055

Horned Lizard Conservation Society
P.O. Box 122
Austin, TX 78767
www.hornedlizards.org

Hummingbird Society
P.O. Box 394
Newark, DE 19715
800/529-3699
info@hummingbird.org
www.hummingbird.org

Kerr Center for Sustainable Agriculture
P.O. Box 588
Poteau, OK 74953
918/647-9123
mailbox@kerrcenter.com
www.kerrcenter.com

Make Every Home a Wildlife Habitat
7412 West 38th Street
Tulsa, OK 74107

Martin Park Nature Center
5000 West Memorial
Oklahoma City, OK 73142
405/672-6500
martinpkok@aol.com

National Audubon Society
700 Broadway
New York, NY 10003
212/979-3000
www.audubon.org (See "States & Centers" link for local chapters)

NATIONAL WILDLIFE FEDERATION, STATE CHAPTERS
www.nwf.org

Arkansas Wildlife Federation
9700 Rodney Parham Road, Suite I- 2
Little Rock, AR 72205
501/224-9200

Colorado Wildlife Federation
P.O. Box 280967
Lakewood, CO 80228
303/987-0400
www.coloradowildlife.org

Kansas Wildlife Federation
4840 W. 15th Street
Lawrence, KS 66049
785/843-7786
KWF@kswildlife.org

Louisiana Wildlife Federation
P.O. Box 65239
Baton Rouge, LA 70896-5239
225/344-6762
lawildfed@aol.com

Conservation Federation of Missouri
728 W. Main
Jefferson City, MO 65101
800/575-2322
www.confedmo.com

Nebraska Wildlife Federation
P.O. Box 81437
Lincoln, NE 68501-1437
402/994-2001
dh43048@navix.net

New Mexico Wildlife Federation
3240-A Juan Tabo NE, Suite 204
Albuquerque, NM 87111
505/299-5404

Oklahoma Wildlife Federation
P.O. Box 60126
Oklahoma City, OK 73146-0126
405/524-7009
www.okwildlife.org

Texas Committee on Natural Resources
1301 S. I-35, Suite 301
Austin, TX 78741
512/441-1122
tconr.home.texas.net

THE NATURE CONSERVANCY, STATE CHAPTERS
www.tnc.org

Arkansas
601 N. University Ave.
Little Rock, AR 72205
501/663-6699

Colorado
1881 Ninth Street, Suite 200
Boulder, CO 80302
303/444-2985

Kansas
700 SW Jackson, Suite 804
Topeka, KS 66603
785-233-4400

Louisiana
P.O. Box 4125
Baton Rouge, LA 70821
225/338-1040

Missouri
2800 S. Brentwood Blvd.
St. Louis, MO 63144
314/968-1105

Nebraska
1722 St. Mary's Ave., Suite 403
Omaha, NE 68102
402/342-0282

New Mexico
212 E. Marcy Street
Santa Fe, NM 87501
505/988-3867

Oklahoma
23 West 4th Street, Suite 200
Tulsa, OK 74103
918/585-1117

Texas
P.O. Box 1440
San Antonio, TX 78295
210/224-8774

North American Bluebird Society
P.O. Box 74
Arlington, WI 53530-0074
www.nabluebirdsociety.org

Oklahoma Bluebird Society
656 South 161st West Avenue
Sand Springs, OK 74063-3635
sialia@worldnet.att.net

Oklahoma City Beautiful
2325 Classen Boulevard
Oklahoma City, OK 73106
405/525-8822

Oklahoma City Tree Bank
405/842-3320

Oklahoma City Zoo
2101 NE 50th
Oklahoma City, OK 73111-7188
405/424-3344
www.okczoo.com

Oklahoma Conservation Commission
2800 North Lincoln
Oklahoma City, OK 73105
405/521-2384
www.okcc.state.ok.us

Oklahoma Department of Agriculture
2800 North Lincoln
Oklahoma City, OK 73105
405/521-3864
www.oda.state.ok.us

Oklahoma Garden Clubs
400 North Portland
Oklahoma City, OK 73107
405/945-3359

Oklahoma Gardening
www.oklahomagardening.ok.state.edu

Oklahoma Herpetological Society
Tulsa Zoo
5701 East 36th Street North
Tulsa, OK 74115

Oklahoma Horticultural Society
P.O. Box 770092
Oklahoma City, OK 73177
www.okhort.org

Oklahoma Master Gardeners
360 Agriculture Hall
Oklahome State University
Stillwater, OK 74078

Oklahoma Native Plant Society
2435 South Peoria
Tulsa, OK 74114

Oklahoma Nurseryman's Association
400 North Portland
Oklahoma City, OK 73107

Oklahoma Ornithological Society
Rt. 1 Box 1
Welling, OK 74471

Oxley Nature Center
5701 East 36th Street North
Tulsa, OK 74115
918/669-6644

Purple Martin Conservation Association
Edinboro University of Pennsylvania
Edinboro, PA 16444
814/734-4420

SIERRA CLUB, STATE CHAPTERS
www.sierraclub.org

Arkansas
P.O. Box 22446
Little Rock, AR 72221
arkansas.sierraclub.org

Colorado (Rocky Mountain)
1410 Grant Street, Suite B-303
Denver, CO 80203-1846
303/861-8819
www.rmc.sierraclub.org

Kansas
9844 Georgia Street
Kansas City, KS 66109-4326
913/299-4443
www.kssierra.org

Louisiana (Delta)
Box 19469
New Orleans, LA 70179-0469
504/836-3062
louisiana.sierraclub.org

Missouri (Ozark)
1007 N. College, Suite One
Columbia, MO 65201
800/628-5333
ozark.chapter@sierraclub.org
missouri.sierraclub.org

New Mexico (Rio Grande)
207 Ricardo Road
Santa Fe, NM 87501
505/988-5760
riogrande.sierraclub.org

Oklahoma
P.O. Box 60644
Oklahoma City, OK 73146-0644
oklahoma.sierraclub.org

Texas (Lone Star)
P.O. Box 1931
Austin, TX 78767
512/477-1729
texas.sierraclub.org

Tulsa Zoo and Living Museum
5701 East 36th Street North
Tulsa, OK 74115
918/669-6223
website: www.tulsazoo.com

The Wildlife Society
5410 Grosvenor Lane
Bethesda, MD 20814
301/897-9770
email: tws@wildlife.org
website: www.wildlife.org

WILDLIFE AGENCIES, STATE

Arkansas Game and Fish Commission
Rt. 1 Box 188-A
Humphrey, AR 72073
870/873-4651
www.agfc.state.ar.us

Colorado Division of Wildlife
6060 Broadway
Denver, CO 80216
303/291-7272
wildlife.state.co.us

Kansas Department of Wildlife and Parks
512 SE 25th Avenue
Pratt, KS 67124
316/672-5911
www.kdwp.state.ks.us

Louisiana Department of Wildlife
and Fisheries
P.O. Box 98000
Baton Rouge, LA 70898
504/765-2823
www.wlf.state.la.us

Missouri Department of Conservation
P.O. Box 180
Jefferson City, MO 65102
573/751-4115 ex.195
www.conservation.state.mo.us

Nebraska Game and Parks Commission
2200 North 33rd Street
Lincoln, NE 68503
402/471-5438
www.ngpc.state.ne.us

New Mexico Game and Fish Department
P.O. Box 25112
Santa Fe, NM 87504
505/827-6681
www.gmfsh.state.nm.us

Oklahoma Department of Wildlife
Conservation
1801 North Lincoln
Oklahoma City, OK 73105
405/521-4616
www.wildlifedepartment.com

Texas Department of Parks and Wildlife
4200 Smith School Road
Austin, TX 78744
512/389-4800
www.tpwd.state.tx.us

Certifying Your Wildscaping Efforts

The Oklahoma Wildlife Diversity Program coordinates a certification program to recognize Oklahomans who have made a commitment to create and maintain habitat for wildlife. Approved properties are issued an official number that is entered into the Oklahoma Wildscapes Registry maintained by the program. The property owner receives an official number on a framable certificate and a sign that can be placed in the habitat to let everyone know that the area is part of a statewide network of Oklahoma Wildscapes.

The process of applying for Wildscape certification is simple. Purchasers of this book are automatically eligible to apply for certification without any additional fees. Send in the voucher at the back of this book to the Oklahoma Wildlife Diversity Program and an application form will be returned to you. When you are ready, complete and return the application. You do not have to achieve a mature habitat before seeking certification.

Your application is reviewed by program biologists to determine that your habitat plan is meeting the needs of the wildlife you wish to attract. Following the certification guidelines will ensure a positive evaluation, upon which you will receive a numbered certificate and sign. Certified Oklahoma Wildscapes are recognized in *Watchable Wildlife News,* the newsletter of the Oklahoma Wildlife Diversity Program.

Certified Oklahoma Wildscapes must provide habitat, which contains elements of food, water, and shelter or cover. Applicants can strive for one of two different types of certification based upon the percentage of property dedicated to wildlife habitat:

- *Wildlife Garden Certification* (less than 50 percent of your property), or
- *Wildlife Habitat Certification* (more than 50 percent of your property).

People just beginning their wildscaping efforts are encouraged to apply for Wildlife Garden Certification, because initial efforts are valuable to many types of wildlife and deserve recognition. Later on, if you decide to increase the area dedicated to wildlife on your property, you can apply for Wildlife Habitat Certification.

To receive your free Oklahoma Wildscapes application form, photocopy and fill out the following voucher (one per household), then send it to:

Oklahoma Wildlife Diversity Program
Wildscapes Application
P.O. Box 53465
Oklahoma City, OK 73152

If you have additional questions, call 405/521-4616 You can also view wildscaping tips at www.wildlifedepartment.com/landscape.htm. Good luck and thanks for providing a home for wildlife!

Acknowledgments

This guide has been a labor of love several years in the making. It would have been impossible without my friends and family, who have encouraged my efforts as a writer and as an observer of the natural world. In particular, I would like to thank my wife Colleen for her unfailing love and friendship; my daughter Maya for providing me with a whole new perspective on the awesomeness of life; and my parents—Karen and Dave Bringham, and Jerry and Delinda Garrett--for their constant encouragement throughout my life.

I also would like to thank the Oklahoma Wildlife Diversity Program staff—Melynda Hickman, Julianne Hoagland, Mark Howery, and Ron Suttles—for their direction, persistence, and editing assistance. Norman Murray provided early editing input as well.

This book was funded in part by the Wildlife Diversity Program of the Oklahoma Department of Wildlife Conservation. The Wildlife Diversity Program is funded primarily through tax-deductible donations from the Wildlife Tax Check-off on the state tax form, purchases of Wildlife Conservation License Plates, and direct contributions. Thanks to contributions from many concerned Oklahomans, this program has assisted in a variety of worthy projects including bald eagle and river otter restoration, endangered species work, statewide Watchable Wildlife opportunities, habitat restoration, and publication of informational items on bats, bluebirds, purple martins, and other subjects. To make your tax-deductible contribution to the Wildlife Diversity Program:

- "Search for the Scissortail" on Oklahoma tax forms and contribute all or part of your refund to state wildlife efforts.
- Purchase a Wildlife Conservation License Plate in one of four designs: scissor-tailed flycatcher, white-tailed deer, bobwhite quail, or largemouth bass. The colorful wildlife plates cost an additional $25, with $20 going to the Wildlife Diversity Program, and function as the regular plate. They are valid for one year from the date of issue, can be personalized, and are available at tag agencies statewide.
- Send a donation directly to the Wildlife Diversity Program. By sending a contribution of $10 or more, you will receive a special wildlife-related thank-you gift. Make your check or money order out to Wildlife Diversity Program, 1801 N. Lincoln, Oklahoma City, OK 73105.

To learn more about the Wildlife Diversity Program and the many backyard products and informational items it offers, call 405/521–4616; write to Wildlife Diversity Program, 1801 N. Lincoln, Oklahoma City, OK 73105; or visit us at www.wildlifedepartment.com. You'll be placed on the mailing list for the free newsletter *Watchable Wildlife News*, which includes information about current projects, wildscaping hints, animal natural history, and other items.

(clockwise from upper right)
Wildlife Conservation License Plates in four designs: scissor-tailed flycatcher, white-tailed deer, bobwhite quail, and largemouth bass.

Additional Partners

The Wildlife Diversity Program is extremely appreciative of the following, who provided financial assistance toward production of this guide:

American Association of Zoo Keepers,
    Oklahoma City Chapter
Bat Conservation Society of Oklahoma
Dan and Debbie Towns
Darlene Michael, Landscape Architect
Donald E. Horne
Kerr Center for Sustainable Agriculture
Oklahoma Native Plant Society
Payne County Audubon Society
The Samuel Roberts Noble Foundation, Inc.
Tulsa Audubon Society
Tulsa Zoo Friends, Inc.
University of Oklahoma Press

Additional technical assistance was provided by Susan Cerulean, Florida Game and Fresh Water Fish Commission; John DeFazio, Natural Resources Conservation Service (Mississippi); Frank Felbaum, Pennsylvania Wild Resources Conservation Fund; Carrol L. Henderson, Minnesota Department of Natural Resources; Tom R. Johnson, Missouri Department of Conservation; Paul D. and Georgean Z. Kyle, Driftwood Wildlife Association; Coral McCallister; Claire Puchy, Oregon Department of Fish and Wildlife; and Eileen Dowd Stukel, South Dakota Department of Game, Fish and Parks.

Credits

All line drawings are by Coral McCallister unless otherwise noted.

INTRODUCTION: Epigraph from *The Blue Lion and Other Essays,* Robert Lynd (1923), reprint Freeport, N.Y.: Books for Libraries Press, 1988. Figures I-1, I-4, I-5, I-6, I-7, I-8, and I-11: Oklahoma Department of Wildlife Conservation. Figure I-2: Jeremy Garrett. Figure I-9: Gregory Sievert.

CHAPTER 1: "Providing Wildlife Necessities" and "Creating a Wildscape Plan" and relevant illustrations adapted courtesy of *Planting a Refuge for Wildlife,* Susan Cerulean, Florida Game and Fresh Water Fish Commission, 1992. Figure 1–1: Donald S. and Pricilla F. Karo, Tulsa, OK. Figure 1–2: Laurie Stillings, Harrah, OK. Figures 1–3, 1–4, and 1–7: Oklahoma Department of Wildlife Conservation. Figure 1–5: Darlene Michael, Oklahoma City. Figure 1–8: Jeremy Garrett.

CHAPTER 2: "Trees, Shrubs and Vines" adapted courtesy of both *Planting a Refuge for Wildlife,* Susan Cerulean, Florida Game and Fresh Water Fish Commission, 1992, and from *Developing Backyard Wildlife Habitats in Mississippi,* John DeFazio, Natural Resources Conservation Service, 1990. "Wildflowers for Wildlife" adapted courtesy of *Developing Backyard Wildlife Habitats in Mississippi,* John DeFazio, Natural Resources Conservation Service, 1990. Figures 2–1, 2–8, 2–10, and 2–12: Colleen Garrett. Figure 2–3: Gregory Gray. Figures 2–4, 2–6, and 2–13: Jeremy Garrett. Figure 2–5: Darlene Michael. Figure 2–7: Richard Heitz. Figure 2–9: Ann Giffert. Figure 2–11: Laurie Stillings.

CHAPTER 3: "Building a Patio Pond," "Building a Wading Pool Pond," "Building a Large Pond," and "Building a Recirculating Stream" text and artwork adapted courtesy of *Naturescaping a Place for Wildlife,* Oregon Department of Fish and Wildlife, 1993. Figure 3–1: Colleen Garrett. Figure 3–4: Jeremy Garrett. Figure 3–6: Gregory Gray.

CHAPTER 4: "Bird Species List" adapted courtesy of *Planting a Refuge for Wildlife,* Susan Cerulean, Florida Game and Fresh Water Fish Commission, 1992. Figures 4–1, 4–5, and 4–8: Oklahoma Department of Wildlife Conservation. Figure 4–2: Hugh and Susan Edgmon. Figure 4–6: Philip and Esta Hansen. Figure 4–7: Laurie Stillings.

CHAPTER 5: Figures 5–1 and 5–2: Oklahoma Department of Wildlife Conservation. Figure 5–4: Anna Miller, Newcastle.

CHAPTER 6: "Managing Ponds for Amphibians and Reptiles," "Managing Woodlands for Amphibians and Reptiles," and "Managing Prairies for Amphibians and Reptiles" adapted courtesy of *A Guide to Amphibian and Reptile Conservation,* Tom R. Johnson, Missouri Department of Conservation, 1979. Figure 6–1: Oklahoma Department of Wildlife Conservation. Figure 6–2: Don and Bobbie McFall.

CHAPTER 7: Figures 7–1, 7–2, and 7–3: Oklahoma Department of Wildlife Conservation. Figure 7–4: Colleen Garrett.

CHAPTER 8: Figures 8–1 and 8–19: Oklahoma Department of Wildlife Conservation. Figure 8–5: Anna Miller. Figure 8–17: Laurie Stillings. Figures 8–2, 8–3, 8–4, 8–6, 8–7, 8–10, 8–13, 8–15, 8–16, and 8–18: Courtesy of *Woodcrafting for Wildlife,* Pennsylvania Wild Resources Conservation Fund and Pennsylvania Game Commission, 1998. Figures 8–11 and 8–14: Courtesy of *Woodworking for Wildlife,* Carrol L. Henderson, Minnesota Department of Natural Resources, 1992. Figure 8–12: Courtesy of Paul D. and Georgean Z. Kyle (Driftwood Wildlife Association), Texas Partners in Flight and Texas Parks and Wildlife. Figures 8–20, 8–21, and 8–22: Courtesy of *Wild about Birds,* Carrol L. Henderson, Minnesota Department of Natural Resources, 1995.

CHAPTER 9: Figures 9–1, 9–7 and 9–8: Oklahoma Department of Wildlife Conservation. Figure 9–6: Courtesy of *Landscaping for Wildlife,* Carrol L. Henderson, Minnesota Department of Natural Resources, 1987.

FAMILY ACTIVITIES: Adapted courtesy of *Sharing Your Space: A Homeowner's Guide to Attracting Backyard Wildlife,* Eileen Dowd Stukel et al., South Dakota Department of Game, Fish and Parks, 1995.

Index

All references to illustrations are in italic type.